Dutch graphic design

Jan Ros, Blooker's Cacao, poster, 1895.
Ros was a painter who taught at the
Academy of Fine Arts, The Hague.

ALSTON W. PURVIS · CEES W. DE JONG

Dutch

graphic

design

A CENTURY OF INNOVATION

Thames & Hudson

Piet Zwart, page from advertising booklet for the printer Nijgh en Van Ditmar, 1931.

CONTENTS

6

pasgeboren kunst
onopgevoed en veeleisend
spreekt niet maar schreeuwt

willem sandberg

een uitgave van D E B A L I E , centrum voor theater, politiek en literatuur - Amsterdam 1984

Wild Plakken, poster, *Newborn Art*,
Amsterdam, 1984.

A CENTURY OF INNOVATION

Graphic design in the Netherlands is internationally known and widely acclaimed for its remarkable innovation and considerable influence. Bolstered by a strong and singular artistic tradition, it is the result of many outstanding individual talents supported by an unusually enlightened clientele and public.

Spanning the period from the nineteenth century to the present day, this book is the first to encompass the total spectrum of Dutch graphic design. Alston W. Purvis has written an in-depth history covering topics such as Art Nouveau, De Stijl, the *Wendingen* style, Dutch Constructivism, the traditional vanguard, post-war rationalism and expressionism, and contemporary graphic design. Richly illustrated with more than 500 color reproductions, this feast of visual imagery will delight and inspire graphic designers, students, artists, and art and design historians.

I would like to thank Alston W. Purvis, with whom I have produced many books on design and typography. Alston is a professor at Boston University College of Fine Arts in the US, and I work as a designer and publisher in Laren, the Netherlands. We both have a strong interest in Dutch graphic design, and it was a treat to work with him once again.

Cees W. de Jong, Laren

DE STIJL

MAANDBLAD VOOR DE MO-
DERNE BEELDENDE VAKKEN
REDACTIE THEO VAN DOES-
BURG MET MEDEWERKING
VAN VOORNAME BINNEN- EN
BUITENLANDSCHE KUNSTE-
NAARS. UITGAVE X. HARMS
TIEPEN TE DELFT IN 1917.

Theo van Doesburg and Vilmos Huszár, cover of *De Stijl*, year 1, no. 2, Leiden, 1917.

PROLOGUE

The graphic design achievements in the Netherlands dating roughly from 1890 until the present day constitute an intensely rich and diverse part of graphic design history. This development originated from numerous sources with historical, social, economic, cultural, religious, geographical, and technological factors all playing a role. In addition, the evolution of Dutch graphic design was tied to events and artistic movements in other parts of Europe including Dadaism, Futurism, and Constructivism.

The Netherlands has always wielded a cultural, political, and commercial dominance far surpassing its size. By the sixteenth century it had become one of the most significant artistic, financial, and trading nations in the West, and during the seventeenth century it helped to foster a cultural renaissance in Northern Europe. Its central location made the Netherlands ideally situated for maritime commerce. Dutch shipping had easy access to the British Isles, Russia, Scandinavia, and Africa, and its colonial possessions in the Dutch East Indies offered additional trading opportunities. The Rhine river also provided a natural approach to Central European markets.

To a large extent the Dutch vision has been influenced by the nation's geography. One can clearly see the bond between the landscape of the Netherlands and modern Dutch graphic design. The Netherlands' unique physical landscape has always had an indirect effect upon Dutch intellectual and artistic attitudes, a view supported by the painter Piet Mondrian (1872–1944) in a 1937 article:

All that the non-figurative artist receives from the outside is not only useful, but indispensable, because it arouses in him the desire to create that which he only vaguely feels and which he could never represent in a true manner without contact with visible reality and with the life that surrounds him. It is precisely from this visible reality that he draws the objectivity that he needs in opposition to his personal subjectivity. It is precisely from this visible reality that he draws his means of expression and, as regards the life that surrounds him, it is precisely this which has made his art non-figurative.[1]

The Netherlands has the densest population in Europe, with more than 16 million people living in 41,526 square kilometers, an area less half the size of Ireland. There are few places in the Netherlands that are not man-made, and one of their favorite adages is that 'God made the world, but the Dutch made the Netherlands.' Land, a hard-wrought commodity, is put to use as much as possible. Seen from above, the Dutch landscape brings to mind a quilted blanket. Highways, canals, and train tracks appear to partition the countryside like the lines in a Mondrian painting. The Dutch landscape is often described as the most organized of all Europe, and the silhouettes of steeples, windmills, and trees sporadically interrupt the level rural horizon. Professor Hans L. C. Jaffé discerningly addressed this topic in the book *De Stijl, 1917–1931:*

Following the – abstract – laws of nature and the precepts of economy, the Dutch engineers and dike-builders had already imparted a rigidly mathematical character to their countryside. They had, in common with the town planners of the modern metropolis, straightened the curves of the incidental streams and rivers into rectilinear canals, they had connected the cities by straight roads, often running parallel with the canals and, in the nineteenth century, the railroads had added another mathematical element to this accomplished construction.[2]

The Dutch do not seem to have a great craving for space, as this feature is clearly fulfilled by the expanse of the sky, and there is a shared tranquility between it and the flat acreage below. The sky's color is constantly altering from blues and grays to the violet crimson as portrayed in Jan Vermeer's painting *View of Delft*. Water is pervasive, and canals and dikes are bordered by rows of trees regularly bent by North Sea winds. Yet, opulent green tableaus and flower fields wondrously relieve the flat horizons and the grating climate.

To a large extent, the survival of the Dutch has rested upon their control of nature, and as a consequence, precision, calculation, organization, and preparing for the future have become an intrinsic part of their temperament. This character has also manifested itself at times in an uncompromising and occasionally vexatious defiance. Their achievement in withstanding aggressive neighboring countries, volatile weather, and the unpredictable North Sea has only enhanced the Dutch belief that effort, industry, and perseverance will eventually triumph. This accomplishment has also engendered a singular awareness of national consciousness, self-reliance, and confidence.

Throughout the centuries the Dutch have not only contended with their larger and often belligerent neighbors but also the variable and severe weather combined with the uncertain temperament of the North Sea. With twenty-seven percent of the Netherlands lying below sea level and roughly another thirty-three percent vulnerable to flooding, water is an integral part of Dutch life. From as early as the twelfth century, this created the need to maintain a complex system of dikes, storm barriers, sea walls, bridges, dams, canals, and pumping stations (a task previously handled by windmills). Today there are now 2,174 miles of mainline barriers and 8,699 miles of secondary defenses such as canal dikes, basin dikes, and holding ponds. During the Roman period, inhabitants of this corner of Europe first dug drainage ditches to make swamps into arable land. Although there have been recent plans to reverse this policy, the Dutch have always been skillful in reclaiming ponds and lakes to produce new polders.

In addition, the moist weather helped, early on, to create a fondness for home life. This is expressed by the word *gezellig* that is sometimes interpreted as 'cozy,' although 'contented' and 'intimate' better reflect its true meaning. Perhaps this attraction for domesticity has contributed to their fondness for the diminutive.

As the Dutch openly acknowledge, their nation is both disparate and complex. The Duke de Baena, Spanish ambassador to the Netherlands in the 1950s and 60s, was so intrigued by this complexity that he published a book in 1966 appropriately titled *The Dutch Puzzle*. The Dutch people's courage and probity in times of misfortune are aptly embodied by the national slogan, 'Je Maintiendrai' (I shall maintain). The singular nature of their language has made them accomplished linguists while at the same time contributing to their national awareness. While being amenable to new ideas, they remain resolute to their own convictions. As demonstrated by the large number of active political parties (there were twenty-seven in a recent count, a fact which occasions a consistent need for coalition governments), the Dutch can be critical both of themselves and their adversaries. The Dutch enjoy lively debates and will often defend their opinions with resolve and insight. Also, they are not unwilling to subject adversaries to harsh and often instructive upbraidings.

Religion is yet another factor that has helped to form the Dutch identity. In earlier times, Bible study was an important part of domestic life and helped to foster a singular and reflective interpretation of Calvinism. Many significant contributors to twentieth-century Dutch art grew up in religious households. Mondrian's father was director of a Protestant school, and Bart van der Leck (1876–1958) remained a devout Calvinist until his late twenties. Vincent van Gogh (1853–1890) and Willem Sandberg (1897–1984) were also raised in such milieus. It would not be an exaggeration to imply that their Calvinist backgrounds led them to avoid hypocrisy, extravagance, and triviality and instead helped them strive for spirituality and purity in the arts. Self-discipline is intrinsic to the Dutch character and cleanliness so much a part of their temperament that the word *schoon* means both 'clean' and 'beautiful.'

A search for perfection also helps to shape the Dutch identity. They reject that which they consider to be capricious and have a proclivity for sound reasoning. This in turn has engendered a constant search for an explicit and simple visual language. Of course, many of these traits are also evident in other nationalities, but the Dutch embody them to a high degree. Throughout the twentieth century and beyond we will encounter designers who display many of these features, yet there will be countless others, such as the maverick H. N. Werkman, who fit into no category and will passionately forge their own paths. However, these qualities at least begin to encapsulate what the Dutch historian Johan Huizinga characterized as the *Nederlands geestesmerk* – the Dutch spiritual imprint.

Prologue Notes

1 H.L.C. Jaffé, *De Stijl 1917-1931*, Amsterdam: Meulenhoff/Landshoff, 1956, p81.

2 H.L.C. Jaffé, *De Stijl 1917-1931*, Amsterdam: Meulenhoff/Landshoff, 1956, p80.

CHAPTER

Jan Toorop, *Delftsche Slaolie*
(Delft Salad Oil), NOF, poster, 1895

AT THE TURN OF THE NINETEENTH CENTURY

European typography had experienced a dramatic decline by the latter half of the nineteenth century. New innovations had introduced radical changes in printing that had seen only slight modifications since the fifteenth century. Craftsmanship was steadily supplanted by machinery, and the increasing demand for printing required more and improved equipment. Workmanship became less important, as supervisors and assistants could now perform tasks that in the past had required hundreds of skilled workers. Papers made from cotton and linen were superseded by cheaper varieties manufactured from wood pulp, straw, and grass.

A primary reason for the typographic decline was a general degeneration in the appreciation of design or quality in printed material. Printers took delight in adorning pages with numerous sizes and combinations of any typefaces available in the shop. Except for an occasional superficial imitation of traditional typography, there was little indication of any concern for page organization or well-designed typefaces, and bindings were either dull or garish. Legibility reached such a low ebb that some medical authorities even felt the need to present a written complaint to the Dutch government in 1866.

In 1951, M. R. Radermacher Schorer in his *Bijdrage tot de Geschiedenis van de Renaissance der Nederlandse Boekdrukkunst* (Contribution to the History of the Dutch Printing Arts) gave a dismal summary of the period:

When we compare the 19th-century book to the incunabula, the type is pallid and without character, often damaged and badly printed, the arrangement is confusing, the color faded, the paper is of bad quality, the spine is covered with gold stamping without beautiful ornaments.... And thicker paper is used to make the book look larger than it actually is.[1]

However, as Jan Middendorp recently noted in his recent book *Dutch Type*, the nineteenth century was perhaps not so bleak as generally painted by some design historians, myself included: 'In the history of type design, the nineteenth century is often described as a Dark Age in which the great Renaissance and Baroque traditions presented by Griffo, Garamond and Van Dijck all but dissipated; a period in which the virtuosity and speed of new reproduction techniques, as well as the advent of mass advertising, spawned excesses of ornament, affectation, kitsch and nonchalance. It is true that the nineteenth century experiments were not always tasteful – as shown by the staggering output of typefaces that were shaded, back-slanted, condensed and extended to the extreme, turned inside-out or otherwise deformed – but the taste for novelty also enriched the language of typography immensely. Sans serif ("grotesque") and slab serif ("egyptian") were invented during this period; more generally, the nineteenth century may be seen as the period which gave birth to the display or headline typeface. The abundance of title pages looking like circus posters and spiky, dazzling text faces has fed the common notion that by 1890 typography "had digressed into vapid clutter" and quality was non-existent; yet in the Netherlands the 1870s and 1880s also yielded industrially produced books that were well bound and well printed on paper that still looks good today.'[2]

During the latter half of the nineteenth century there were indeed attempts in the Netherlands to forge new directions. One such endeavor began at the studio of Dr. Petrus Josephus Hubertus Cuypers (1827–1921), architect of the Rijksmuseum and Central Station in Amsterdam. Cuypers stressed a restoration of traditional handwork, proven standards, and fundamental principles. His students and assistants were encouraged to learn calligraphy using examples from the Renaissance and Middle Ages. Although Cuypers shared some of the views of William Morris (1834–1896), he did not exclude new industrial innovations and advocated the use of mechanical reproduction. Both Morris and Cuypers and others like them at least established links between a period of generally low standards and a new dawn, and in this way they helped forge a path for modern typography. Two of Cuypers's students, the architects Karel Petrus Cornelis de Bazel (1869–1923) and Johannes Ludovicus Marthieu Lauweriks (1864–1932), continued his objective by establishing similar studio environments.

At the turn of the century, major changes in the printing industry were already in place. Although new cylinder steam-driven presses required expensive initial investments, it was soon obvious that they would be sound long-term investments. Offset printing was in its infancy, bookbinding machines were already in use, and photographic illustrations would soon provide new possibilities after Stephen H. Horgan's invention of the halftone screen technique in 1880. Type was set increasingly by machine after Ottmar Mergenthaler, a German immigrant working in a Baltimore, Maryland machine shop, introduced the Blower Linotype in 1886, the first line-casting keyboard typesetter. This was followed by the Monotype machine in 1887 invented by another American, Tolbert Lanston.

However, the persisting apathy of both publishers and their readers still influenced the caliber of printing material, and expedience continued to be a driving factor. Efforts to revive the typographic arts in the Netherlands were perceptible during the last few years of the nineteenth century and the beginning of the twentieth, but for the most part this incentive came from painters, sculptors, and architects instead of publishers and printers.

Early Dutch Poster Design

The art of poster design had a late start in the Netherlands, and most were the ordinary aggregation of assorted typefaces and sizes. Also, at the turn of the century the importance of posters in the Netherlands was not as significant as in most other European countries. Dutch cities did not have the broad avenues of Vienna, Berlin, and Paris so befitting the display of large posters. The Dutch public seemed to prefer to examine products in shop windows, and posters were designed to be perused in detail. Customers favored sound rationale over visual appeal and wanted to be convinced by reasoning instead of allurement.

One of the first contributors to modern poster design in the Netherlands was the Dutch architect and city planner, Hendrik Petrus Berlage (1856–1934). As demonstrated by his 1903 Exchange Building in Amsterdam, Berlage soon became an ardent champion of artistic harmony. After visiting the United States in 1911 Berlage was introduced to the work of Frank Lloyd Wright (1869–1959). Fascinated by Wright's architectural innovations, he soon became a prominent European supporter of Wright in Europe. Wright's influence on Berlage is evident in Berlage's design for the Gemeentemuseum (Municipal Museum) in The Hague.

In addition to his work in architecture, Berlage made a notable contribution to the development of Dutch graphic design. In 1893, he designed a poster promoting a 'new short route' between the Hook of Holland near Rotterdam and the port of Harwich on the English East Coast. The design is filled with a variety of themes, and the text is almost submerged in ornaments, still displaying the Victorian tendency to crowd as much information into a space as possible. However, his more restrained *Noord Hollandsche Tramwegmij* (North Holland Tram Company) poster for the opening of the Amsterdam–Purmerend Alkmaar line in 1895 is a step toward clarity in design. Also, in his article *Gedanken iiber Stil in der Baukunst* (Thoughts over Style in Architecture) published in Leipzig in 1905, it is evident that Berlage was conscious of a new direction when he stressed that decoration must always be secondary to structure.

Berend Modderman, initially foreman at the Amsterdam printing firm Ipenbuur en Van Seldam, founded in 1806, bought the company in 1895. He often commissioned artists to design posters, and his association with the brothers Antonius (Antoon) H. J. (1872–1960) and Theodorus (Theo) M. A. A. Molkenboer (1871–1920) was particularly beneficial. Theo's 1897 poster for the Amsterdam bookbinder Elias P. van Bommel was initially created as a woodcut. Its plain design and absence of superfluous detail differs from the Berlage posters made only few years earlier and displays a Calvinistic austerity that has frequently appeared in Dutch graphic design.

At this time designers began to feel a need for more distinct rules, and in 1898 the author Jan Kalf presented a significant talk called 'The Book' at the Architectura en Amicitia in Amsterdam. This was later published in their journal *Architectura*, and in this lecture he stated his opinions on good and bad typography and mere decoration and offered explicit

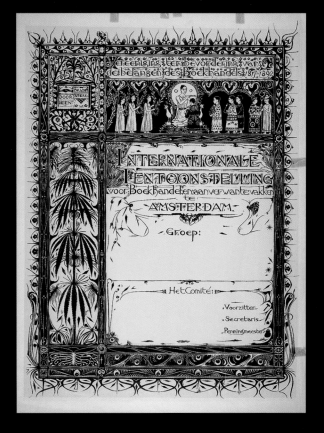

Opposite, above: G. W. Dijsselhof, diploma for the International Exhibition of the Book Trade and Related Subjects, 1892. An association to promote the book trade asked Dijsselhof, Cachet and Nieuwenhuis to submit designs.

Opposite, below: C. A. Lion Cachet, diploma for the International Exhibition of the Book Trade and Related Subjects, 1892

Right: R. N. Roland Holst, cover of *Het boek van de liefde* (The book of love) by Johannes Viator, Amsterdam: Veen, 1892

Below: G. W. Dijsselhof, cover of *Een pic-nic in proza* (A Picnic in Prose), Amsterdam: Van Looy & Gerling, 1893

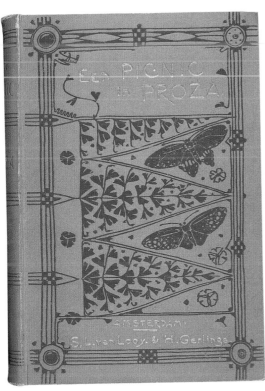

guidelines for designers. He emphasized the importance of typographic traditions, the unanimity of form and content, an open mind regarding new technology, a rejection of needless adornment, the use of quality materials, carefully considered proportions, good legibility, the employment of single, well-designed typefaces, proper letter and word spacing, and skillful printing and binding.

18 *Nieuwe Kunst*

Art Nouveau was a new artistic movement that represented a bridge between the nineteenth and twentieth centuries. It was called Nieuwe Kunst in the Netherlands, Art Nouveau in France, Belgium, and Great Britain, and Jugendstil in Germany, Austria, and the rest of Europe, the latter name being derived from the Munich-based magazine, *Jugend*, which first appeared in 1896. Art Nouveau was not only an art movement; it also reflected the society of a prosperous and liberal European bourgeoisie that was predominant around the turn of the century. Its roots can be found in diverse sources such as stained glass, Celtic manuscripts, and natural forms In addition, it was influenced by the crafts of India, Egypt, Persia, Japan, and in the Netherlands, the Dutch East Indies (now Indonesia). A typical characteristic of the Art Nouveau style is a recurring series of contours based on stalks and vines that serve to hold the composition together.

When any period in art history begins and ends is often equivocal, but it is generally agreed that Nieuwe Kunst in the Netherlands flourished from around 1892 until 1906. This was a significant period for both architecture and the applied arts, and helped to build a span between Victorian design and modernism. The Victorians relied upon established historical approaches prevalent in the nineteenth century, while the Art Nouveau artists adapted a new ornamental style based on elegant motifs derived from nature and often characterized by flowing graceful lines. Although manifestations of Art Nouveau displayed national characteristics, the work produced in various countries was all related stylistically. Through Nieuwe Kunst, many of the younger Dutch artists caused an artistic revival that was a basis for future movements including De Stijl, Art Deco and the *Wendingen* style. Nieuwe Kunst brought forth one of several creative catalysts that rejected the excesses of the Victorian era.

The source of the term Art Nouveau was Samuel Bing's Paris art gallery, the Salon de L'Art Nouveau, which opened in 1895. Although mainly dealing in Japanese art, 'new art' was displayed and sold as well. The Salon de L'Art Nouveau soon became an international rendezvous spot where the work of many new artists was exhibited, including the American glass designer Louis Comfort Tiffany. Art Nouveau eventually included all art sectors such as architecture, painting, arts and crafts, posters, vases, furniture, ornaments, and books.

Nikolaus Pevsner's 1936 book *Pioneers of Modern Design* was one of the first to allot Art Nouveau an important role in twentieth-century modern art and architecture. He described the movement's main attributes as 'the long sensitive curve, reminiscent of the lily's stem, an insect's feeler, the filament of a blossom or occasionally a slender flame, the curve undulating, flowing and interplaying with others, sprouting from corners and covering asymmetrically all available surfaces.'[3] Although these were indeed characteristics of Art Nouveau, the Dutch Nieuwe Kunst contribution, notably in book design, was far richer than Pevsner's perfunctory description.

Nieuwe Kunst book design influenced other art forms and was utilized by various individuals connected with this movement. Some of its unique aspects are an exceptional originality and an affinity for primitive forms. Compared to Art Nouveau book design in other parts of Europe, Nieuwe Kunst had a more playful and provocative tone. Especially in the beginning, floral decorative configurations were frequently used. Although there was no actual relationship between the plant and flower forms and the picture background, many Nieuwe Kunst artists followed a naturalistic approach in their illustrations. These included Theodoor (Theo) van Hoytema (1863–1917) and Ludwig Willem Reijmert (L.W.R.) Wenckebach (1860–1937). Others such as Gerrit Willem Dijsselhof (1866–1934) tended to simplify the forms into ornamental designs. Ultimately an abstract approach emerged using surging lines combined into complex patterns, with color and line taking on independent roles. After 1895, mathematics became a source for designers who began to employ both symmetry and rationalism in their work. This can be seen in the book-binding designs of Theodorus Johannes Josephus (Theo) Neuhuys (1878–1921), Joris Johannes Christiaan (Chris) Lebeau (1878–1945), the early work of Sjoerd Hendrik (S.H.) de Roos (1877–1962) and the later work of Berlage.

Art motifs from the Dutch East Indies were especially important in Nieuwe Kunst design. The Netherlands had unique ties with these colonies that were quite different from those of the other colonial powers. Dutch artists enthusiastically absorbed East Indian design themes and methods, which engendered a singular aesthetic approach that became an important Dutch contribution to international Art Nouveau. Assimilating the East Indian artistic traditions, artists turned them into a modern design form. In 1863, the founding of the Colonial Museum in Haarlem and in 1878 the Museum voor Land- en Volkenkunde (Museum for Geography and Ethnography) in Rotterdam reflected an increasing interest in East Indian culture and was an added impetus for utilizing Javanese motifs as a basis for the new decorative arts.

Basically, there were two approaches to Nieuwe Kunst book design. The first consisted of designers who continued to work more in a decorative fashion. The others sought a rational use for the materials with which the books were made. Technical matters were of major concern to the latter group, and they strove to use the materials as a basis for the decorative elements. Unlike some of the Art Nouveau produced in other countries, their work was not dictated by fleeting vogues, but rather they attempted to establish solid foundations for subsequent creative growth.

Writing, giving talks, and participating in debates were important activities for Nieuwe Kunst designers. They warned against what they deemed reactionary views, defined and justified their work, and deliberated over its place in the spectrum of modern art. They enthusiastically embraced various crafts simultaneously, and many were active in fields such as architecture, painting and ceramics in addition to book design.

The popular use of natural elements in Nieuwe Kunst designs gave rise to several instruction books on producing decorative designs based on nature. One was *Driehoeken bij ontwerpen van ornament* (Triangles in the Design of Ornament) by J. H. de Groot, professor at the Quellinus arts and crafts school in Amsterdam, and his sister Jacoba M. de Groot. Published in 1896, it gave exercises on the design of abstract images from nature based on 30- and 45-degree triangles. This was inspired by the book *The Claims of Decorative Art* published by the English illustrator and writer Walter Crane (1845–1915) in 1892.

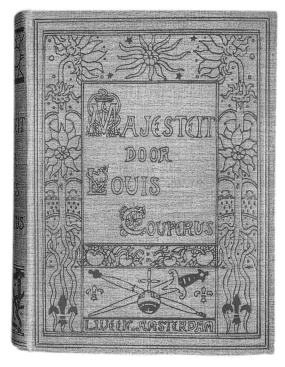

Above: R. N. Roland Holst, cover of a catalog for an Exhibition of Contemporary Dutch Art, Genootschap Arti et Amicitiae (Artists' society), Amsterdam, June–July 1892.

Left: R. N. Roland Holst, cover of *Majesteit* by Louis Couperus, Amsterdam: Veen, 1893. This is one of the first examples of Art Nouveau in Dutch book design.

Opposite: G. W. Dijsselhof, book decoration for the deluxe edition of *Kunst en samenleving* (Art and Society), after Walter Crane's *The Claims of Decorative Art*, 1892. The Dutch version is by Jan Veth. Amsterdam: Scheltema and Holkema's Boekhandel, 1894.

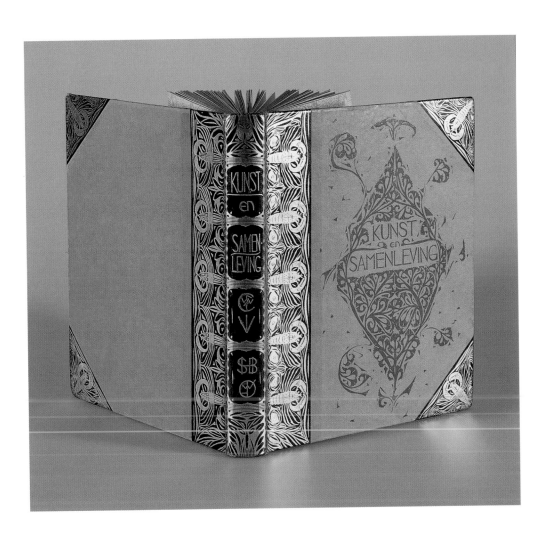

A similar book, *Motieven voor het teekenonderwijs ontleend aan het ambacht* (Motifs for Drawing Instruction Derived from the Trade) by P. Herman and H. J. van Dijk, had been published in 1895. In 1905 more Dutch books on this subject including *Ornament ontwerpen voor iedereen* (Ornament Design for Everyone) by Herman Hana and *Het Ontwerpen van vlakornament* (The Design of Flat Ornament) by Jan D. Ros, instructor at The Hague Academy of Fine Arts. *Het ontwerpen van ornamenten op systeem en naar natuurvormen* (The Design of Ornaments According to a System and after Nature Forms) by W. Bogtmans was also published that year.

The most important leaders of the Nieuwe Kunst avant-garde included Johan Thorn Prikker (1868–1932), Dijsselhof, Theodoor Willem Nieuwenhuis (1866–1951), W. A. van Konijnenburg (1868–1943), Carol Adolph Lion Cachet (1864–1945), Van Hoytema, Lauweriks, De Bazel, Roland Holst, Jan Theodoor Toorop (1858–1928), and Wenckebach. Thorn Prikker, born in The Hague in 1868, studied at The Hague Art Academy, now the Koninklijke Academie van Beeldende Kunsten (Royal Academy of Fine Arts). He taught art in Germany for much of his life and died in Cologne in 1932. His work underwent a number of transitions, and pieces such as the harsh 1896 poster for the *Revue Bimestrielle pour L'Art Appliqué* in Haarlem is still linked to the Victoria era in spite of a torrent of Nieuwe Kunst devices.

His 1903 poster *Hollandische Kunstausstelling in Krefeld* (Dutch Art Exhibition in Krefeld) is a symmetrical composition within an austere framework and art nouveau decorative devices composted of flora and fruit. As with many Dutch posters of this period, Thorn Prikker's designs bore only a tangential connection to the matter at hand.

Lion Cachet's earlier designs such as the woodcut illustration for the *Internationale Tentoonstelling voor Boekhandel en aanverwante vakken* (International Exhibition for the Book Trade and Related Subjects) diploma were influenced by design motifs from the Dutch East Indies. Later, though, as with his 1917 poster for *Delftsche Slaolie*, they are more in the Nieuwe Kunst tradition.

Wenckebach and Van Hoytema share many similarities. Both were born in The Hague around the same year, both studied at the Hague Art Academy and neither ever moved from the city of their birth. Wenckebach's linear illustrations are the most lyrically dazzling of the Nieuwe Kunst designers. He produced a staggering amount of work, primarily illustrations for children's books, novels, and print books. His 1894 design for *In de muizen wereld: Een nieuwe vertelling aan 't klavier* (In the World of Mice: A New Tale on the Piano) by Agatha Snellen & Catharina van Rennes shows familiar characteristics of Art Nouveau as the vines intertwine into a symmetrical pattern.

Van Hoytema's 1893 illustrations for *The Ugly Duckling*, the 1895 designs for *The Happy Owls* and *De Kroniek* (The Chronicle), and the 1898 designs for *Twee Hanen* (Two Roosters) display a clear break with the Victorian tendency toward packed and complicated illustrations. Many of his books feature animals that he treated as characters. In contrast to earlier picture books he exercised a greater decorative freedom using whimsical contours. His drawing style had not yet attained the elegant line work of Crane, and the book would not have been possible without the English influence, but the appearance of these simple children's books was of great importance to the Dutch decorative arts.

Van Hoytema never departed from an accurate observation of nature, but his illustrations became gradually more stylized in the Art Nouveau manner. By 1896, his work became more playful and no longer restrained by the edges of the page. The illustration is not bound by the rectangle borders and implies an uninterrupted Art Nouveau-inspired rhythm.

In 1899 the spirited cover for *De Tuin, Geïllustreerd maandschrift. Kunst, letterkunde, tooneel, muziek, politiek, sociologische wetenschappen en maatschappelijk werk* (The Garden, Illustrated Monthly Magazine. Art, Literature, Theater, Music, Politics, Social Sciences, and Social Work) the flower fragrances seem visually implied by the exuberance of his line. This displays the influence of Japanese prints, and although he retains a reference to naturalistic space the illustration is not tied to illusion. Van Hoytema's drawings never become silhouettes or two-dimensional such as those of Dijsselhof. His use of asymmetry and natural forms depicted through graceful and refined line rhythms in his poster and calendar designs show Van Hoytema's strong adherence to Art Nouveau characteristics.

Although Dijsselhof was mainly known as a painter of aquarium scenes, he was asked in 1893 by Klaas Groesbeek, manager of the Amsterdam bookstore Scheltema en Holkema's Boekhandel, to design *Kunst en samenleving* (Art and Society). A translation by the artist and critic Jan Pieter Veth of Crane's 1892 book, *The Claims of Decorative Art*, this would be one of the masterworks of Nieuwe Kunst book design. It was Dijsselhof's principal work in the Nieuwe Kunst tradition, and after 1900 he went back to painting. Dijsselhof approached *Kunst en samenleving* as a totality and the result was a model for other Nieuwe Kunst designers. Using his own woodcuts for the binding, dustjacket and vignettes, he was the first Dutch book designer to successfully integrate typography with fine-line woodcuts. Flora and fauna images are simplified into ornaments.

Dijsselhof won a competition in 1892 to design a diploma for the Vereeniging ter Bevordering van de Belangen des Boekhandels (Society for the Promotion of the Interests of Booksellers). It was produced as a woodcut, and because of this and *Kunst en samenleving*, there was a moderate resurgence of interest in the woodcut in the Netherlands. Dijsselhof's decorative designs were mainly derived from nature. Trees, flowers, dragonflies, beetles, spiders, frogs, fish, crustaceans, and peacock feathers appear as motifs. Although *Kunst en samenleving* concerned Western art it clearly displayed a fascination with design motifs from the Dutch East Indies. The material used for *Kunst en samenleving* was painstakingly selected. Only the highest quality paper and leather was used, and the binding was stamped with real gold.

Dijsselhof had begun working on the design of *Kunst en samenleving* in 1892, and it took a year for him to complete the designs for the binding and jacket. Unfortunately, Crane was disappointed with Dijsselhof's elaborate interpretation of his book, but Groesbeek obviously did not share these sentiments. He issued a second edition in 1903 and afterwards used the vignettes in some of his other publications.

In 1892 and 1893 the design of Nieuwe Kunst bindings often began to suggest the contents of books. For the next eight years the book began to be treated more as an object, and sometimes the design implied the way the binding was made. Dijsselhof later said that the brown color of the binding for *Kunst en samenleving* suggested wood and the white lines the linen string used for sewing the book. On the spine, five batches of lines designate binding strands and become lobster tails as they cross over the fold. While the lobsters are realistically drawn on the book's front, on the back and spine they become abstractions.

Opposite: Theo van Hoytema, advertising flyer for the journal *De Kroniek, Een Algemeen Weekblad* (The Chronicle, a General Weekly), Amsterdam: C. M. van Gogh, 1895.

Right and below: Theo van Hoytema, *The Happy Owls*, cover and page, London: H. Henry & Co, 1896. The book was an English translation of Uilengeluk by Theo van Hoytema, Amsterdam: C. M. van Gogh, 1895.

pages 28–29: R. N. Roland Holst, Henriëtte van der Schalk, double-page spread from *Sonnetten en verzen in terzinen geschreven* (Sonnets and Verses Written in Terza Rima), Amsterdam: Scheltema & Holkema's Boekhandel, 1895. The guidelines are a reference to medieval calligraphy.

AFTER A GOOD WASH, HE SETS OUT, LOOKING VERY STATELY.

Using batik in design was one of the significant Dutch contributions to international Art Nouveau, and the technique quickly spread throughout Europe. Batik was a traditional women's craft in the Dutch East Indies, and Javanese batik designs intrigued artists such as Lebeau and Toorop. This soon became immensely popular, and in 1883 a batik display was one of the main attractions at the Internationale Koloniale en Uitvoer Tentoonstelling (International Colonial and Export Exhibition) held in Amsterdam.

Batik is made by first drawing on fabric with a wash and then tracing the forms by dripping wax through a pointed metal instrument. The cloth is then immersed in a paint medium, and the places where the wax has been applied protect the fabric from the paint. When the wax is melted, an image remains in the original fabric color. The process can be repeated, and an elaborate layered pattern can be created using unlimited colors.

The 1897 design by T. W. Nieuwenhuis of the illustrations and batik binding for the second edition of *Gedichten* (Poems) by Jacques Perk, took two years to finish. The binding has a restrained look because of the dark gray background and brown lines. His calendar designs are far more energetic, colorful, and playful.

As publisher of the prolific and immensely popular writer from The Hague, Louis Couperus, Lambertus Jacobus Veen was an influential figure in the early years of modern Dutch graphic design. His unwavering objective was to publish books of the highest caliber using the best designers, printers, binders, and materials. The batik process captivated him in 1899, after he saw a batik binding by another publisher for Couperus's book *Psyche*. This had been produced by Loeber and Smits in Leiden, a firm that helped to advance the level of bookbinding in the last decade of the nineteenth century. Veen's encounter with the *Psyche* binding provided the inspiration for one of the foremost Nieuwe Kunst bookbindings, *De stille kracht* (The Quiet Power), designed by Lebeau. As this was the most East Indian-based of all Couperus's novels, batik was an appropriate choice for the binding material.

Lebeau created some of his best designs using batik and was able to make traditional East Indian patterns a part of his own work. Most of his batik fabrics were made in Haarlem and then distributed in Amsterdam through the progressive interior and industrial design concern, 't Binnenhuis. The first and most influential batik center in the Netherlands was the Arts and Crafts workshop in The Hague where thirty women workers were supervised by Agathe Wegerif-Gravestein. She learned the technique in Java, and largely because of her efforts and those of the workshop's owner John Uiterwijk, the center soon became the largest in the Netherlands. Because of his close connection with the Arts and Crafts workshop, Lebeau began working as a designer at their Apeldoorn studio in June 1900 where he produced the binding design for *De stille kracht*.

There were several versions, and an unused design is part of the Drents Museum collection in Assen. In October 1900, the final batik design for *De stille kracht* was produced and stamped with gold before being used for the binding. In addition to the standard edition, there was a limited edition with the binding printed on velvet. Both the binder and the batik studio are cited on the back of the binding, a rare formality for this time. The vertical spine divides the symmetrical design, and the pattern on the front is continued on the back. Although the design suggests flowers, it was actually made according to a mathematical system based on diamond shapes. *De stille kracht* had a large print-run that reached thousands of readers, and as a result Lebeau and Veen were largely responsible for the popularity of batik in The Netherlands. Especially in his theater posters, Lebeau's designs would soon evolve into a singular style independent of Nieuwe Kunst.

Toorop was born on the island of Java and went to the Netherlands at the age of thirteen. He received his artistic training at the Polytechnic school in Delft, the Amsterdam Academy and finally the Ecole des Arts Décoratifs in Brussels. As he spent his early childhood there, the Dutch East Indies was a special source of inspiration for Toorop. The source of his linear approach, use of silhouettes, and even the hair styles of people in his designs can be traced back to in Javanese *wajan* shadow puppets. This influence is evident in his 1895 poster for *Delftsche Slaolie* (Delft Salad Oil), which shows two elegantly clad female figures preparing some kind of magical salad. The product being promoted is almost lost in a deluge of sensual, intricate and interwoven lines – while twenty-four floating peanuts framed by a vine in the upper left are turned into a kind of formal garden. The standing figure gazes at them and the NOF company emblem with veneration. The *Delftsche Slaolie* poster is an excellent example of early Nieuwe Kunst graphic design and shows a superb union of lettering and images.

As with the *Delftsche Slaolie* poster, Toorop's 1896 design for *In den nevel, Delftsche studenten tijdschrift* (In the Mist, Delft Student Magazine) is dominated by two willowy figures prancing through a bed of tulips and cloud shapes. The magazine's introductory poem shows that students were surely lost in a fog:

In jonge levens hangt een dikke mist
Dicht bij en tot de verren horizont
Omhullend scherpe vorm. Wat jeugd ook wist
Rees op uit neveling, maar zoekend vond
Het oog van leven duiding onbetwist,
Door flauwe schijn, van wat in ziel al stond.

(In young lives there hangs a thick mist
Nearby and on the far horizon's
Surrounding sharp form. Whatever youth knew
Arose out of mist, but seeking found
Without doubt the eye of life's meaning
Through weak light, from what was already in the soul.)

Veen was Toorop's friend and commissioned him to design numerous book-bindings. Toorop's distinctive approach was ideal for illustrating the lyrical and metaphorical tales of Couperus, and the artist was especially adept at symbolically suggesting a book's message through his drawings. His 1898 binding for Couperus's *Psyche* reveals his ability to integrate text with images. This is an erotic and symbolic tale of Princess Psyche, Prince Eros, and a winged stallion named Chimera. Psyche, who came from the Land of Today and yearned for the Land of Tomorrow, dreamt of flying to other regions with her two little ineffectual wings. One day while she was ruminating in a tower in her father's castle, a knight on Chimera appeared in the clouds and swooped down to take Psyche to the lands of her fantasies. The design is typical of Toorop's 'whiplash' linear style, and the lettering and illustration are in total harmony. Human figures are often used on Toorop's bindings, and this is unusual in Nieuwe Kunst book design. In many of his designs for Couperus the figures are engulfed in a linear vortex, and the text is so much a part of the decoration that it becomes barely legible.

Hoe door het inzicht der onvolkomenheid van ons zintuigelijk weten, de Geest geleid wordt tot de beginselen der Goede Mystiek

OVER DE ONMACHT ONZER ZINNEN EENIG DING NAAR
WAARHEID TE KENNEN✳✳✳✳✳✳✳✳✳✳✳✳✳✳✳✳✳✳✳✳✳✳✳✳✳✳✳✳✳ 115

Wij kennen alleen geestelijke dingen.
  Al wat gestalte is leeft de oogen gesloten
  en gaat zwijgend voorbij zooals een groote
stoet van altijd zwijgende kloosterlingen.
De praatzieke en verstrooide wereldlingen
  starend naar hun tot in den dood besloten
  werend gelaat, sturen vergeefs de vloten
van hun gedachte uit om binnen-te-dringen

in de wat'ren dier geloovige kracht.
  Zóó gaan de zinnen naar lijflijke rijken
en keeren weer, arm aan de goede vracht
  van 't weten dat zij niet kunnen bereiken
  want in alle landen waar zij neerstrijken
maakt hunner vleug'len schaduw diepe nacht.

Veen also used Wenckebach's illustrations for a number of his publications. Wenckebach's binding for the second edition of Couperus' *Orchideeën* (Orchids) published in 1895 consists of distinctively elegant orchid forms. The image on the front is repeated as a mirror image on the back of the binding with vertical plant forms on the spine.

Gustaaf (Gust) Frederik van de Wall Perné, was an individualist captivated by the art forms of the East Indies. In many of his designs, lettering is the only connection with the the West. His designs have an expressive and uninhibited exuberance as can be seen in his lively 1902 binding for *Het Eeuwige Licht* (The Eternal Light) by Peter Rosegger. Van de Wall Perné is highly underrated, partially because he appeared toward the end of the Nieuwe Kunst movement and died at the age of 37.

Inspired by books such as *Driehoeken bij ontwerpen van ornament* there were also Nieuwe Kunst designers who worked principally from a mathematical and geometrical basis. An outstanding example is *Het leven een zegen* (In Tune with the Infinite) by Ralph Waldo Trine. This was a 1902 design by S. H. de Roos, a book and type designer who would later be a key figure in the renewal of typography in the Netherlands.

Usually one person did not design an entire book. Customarily only the binding was commissioned, and the printer handled the rest. A binding design was frequently reused for numerous unrelated titles, and there could be disparate binding designs and colors for the same publication. In the initial edition of Toorop's design for *Metamorfoze* there are black and white versions as well as brown on white. His bindings for *God en goden* (God and Gods) are also in varied color combinations. At times this was due to the availability of paper colors. Also, the publisher often disregarded the designer's advice, and designers were kept at a distance from the printing process. If there was a sudden upsurge in sales, any available bindings were used, and if the original stock was used up another binding that required only the insertion of a new title was quickly substituted.'

By 1903, the rich experimental period of Nieuwe Kunst had begun to reach an end, and the movement assumed an established form. With a few exceptions, Nieuwe Kunst had digressed into predominantly vapid commercial imitations by 1910. What some consider its last extension, Art Deco, finally brought it to a close.

Johann Georg van Caspel (1870–1928) started as a portrait artist and eventually painted murals for houses and public buildings. One mural was for an artists' pub in Amsterdam. This was seen by C. J. Schuver, director of the Koninklijke Stoomsteendrukkerij Amand (later Senefelder), who then asked Van Caspel to produce designs for his company. He always worked from models and worked in oil, and for seven years, until 1903, Van Caspel designed posters, book jackets, catalog covers, and a calendar for Schuver. At that time he moved to what was then the painters' village of Laren where he worked as an architect and painted portraits and still lives.

The illustration showing a woman reading on the 1900 poster for *Boon's geillustreerd magazijn* (Boon's Illustrated Magazine) is repeated on the cover of the magazine in her hands. This in turn is repeated in a still smaller size, like a Russian doll which contains a series of smaller duplicates of itself. Van Caspel's design moved a step further toward simplification in his 1899 poster for Ivens & Co. Foto-Artikelen, a photographic equipment company. In this poster, the combination of type and illustration is very structured with the colors reduced to flat areas. The hair of the female figure is in the typical Art Nouveau style, and the text is contained in rectangular shapes that frame the image on the top and the bottom of the composition.

The colorful 1895 poster for *Blooker's Cacao* by Jan Ros was one of his few attempts at poster design. In the scene, a gracefully dressed lady is being served from a steaming pot of cocoa by what appears to be a waitress. On the left, a column is created from cocoa leaves and beans and is crowned by the Amsterdam crest. The patterns created by the plant forms and the steam from the pot have clear Art Nouveau characteristics.

After 1905 there were fewer Dutch commercial posters than in the past. Posters produced for the theater and for art exhibitions became the most popular and had the greatest interest among viewers. The theater posters by Roland Holst were designed according to his socialist principles and were drawn directly on lithographic stones. Since his main subjects were socialism and theater, his posters and other designs were directed toward a very selective audience which gave him the opportunity to develop his personal vision and singular symbolic style. Roland Holst was educated at the Amsterdam Academy and in the earlier stages of his career painted landscapes in an impressionist style. Later, influenced by Van Gogh and Toorop his work became far more expressive. He then learned the lithographic technique and began to concentrate more on drawing. His interest in literature placed him in contact with many writers and poets for whom he was able to design books. In 1892 an early binding designs was *Johannes Viator* in the manner of Wenckebach. Four years later his design for *Sonnetten en Verzen in Terzinen Geschreven* (Sonnets and Verses Written in Terzarima, 1896) by his future wife Henriëtte van der Schalk (1869–1952) (after her marriage Henriëtte Roland Holst van der Schalk). Was more in the Nieuwe Kunst style. In the winter months of 1894–95 Roland Holst traveled to London where he met many of those associated with the 'Private Press Movement' including Walter Crane, William Morris (1834–96), T. J. Cobden-Sanderson (1840–1922), Charles Ricketts, and Charles Shannon (1863–1931). Not only did he share their artistic ideas but was in sympathy with some of their socialist views. Later as director of the Rijksacademie in Amsterdam, Roland Holst was able to influence a generation of young designers.

The graphic designer and painter Jacob (Jac.) Jongert (1883–1942) studied with Roland Holst at the Rijksacademie in Amsterdam and later became his assistant. Roland Holst's influence on his student's work can be seen in Jongert's 1920 lithographic poster for Apricot Brandy. As his later designs grew more functional, Jongert's principal client became the Van Nelle company.

The political sector was another venue for post-1905 poster design. Notable examples are those of Albert Hahn (1877–1918), a political cartoonist who designed for the theater as well as the Social Democratic Workers Party and related labor unions. His posters are simple and direct with definitive lines and bold colors.

The painter Jan Sluijters (1881–1957), although an excellent poster designer, was far out of the Dutch mainstream and more in the French tradition. With its vibrant colors, bold gestures, and exuberant drawing style, his vigorous 1919 poster for the *Artisten Winterfeest* (Artists Winter Festival) displays many of the qualities of Fauvism. The Belgian painter Raoul Hynckes immigrated to the neutral Netherlands during the First World War. He was essentially a painter of 'magic realist' landscapes, but the Amsterdam lithographic printer Kotting commissioned him to design a number of posters at the end of the war

and afterwards. These are characterized by a sensuous linear approach and flat areas of color. During the 1930s his work would move more in the direction of Art Deco.

The work of the political cartoonist, painter, and book illustrator Piet van der Hem (1885–1961) was more refined than that of Sluyters with a simple balance of illustration and text. Although undated, his graceful poster for Spyker Autos must have been printed before 1914, the year the company closed, because of the first World War Most of his posters were for the theater, and many incorporated portraits of leading actors. J. W. (Willy) Sluiter (1873–1949) was another painter who worked in a mode similar to that of Van der Hem. Sluiter was also a political cartoonist and used caricature in his drawing. Strong contours and an energetic use of color distinguish his posters. Sluiter created some of the liveliest posters of his day. His 1914 poster *Naar Keulen via Kesteren Nijmegen* (To Cologne via Kesteren and Nijmegen) is typical of his tendency to depict the carefree side of life. His 1916 poster for the Laren Tentoonstelling (Laren Exhibition) is equally light-hearted. Lion Cachet's 1917 poster for the Utrecht Jaarbeurs (Utrecht Trade Fair) still retains some Art Nouveau features as seen in the silhouetted figure. Many of the poster designers such as Leo Gestel remained outside other movements and continued in their own particular directions well into the next two decades.

The Netherlands remained neutral during World War I, and life there remained relatively economically and culturally stable compared with the rest of Europe. Around this time there was much discussion about advertising's place in society. In 1917, the Stedelijk Museum in Amsterdam displayed an exhibition of advertising art, prompting a vigorous debate between Roland Holst and the political cartoonist Hahn. Roland Holst was against artists who, according to him, sold themselves for commerce. He contended that advertising could be either accurate information or a 'shout,' the latter being comparable to visual histrionics. His approach is to some extent implied in an essay by the typographic historian Beatrice Warde (wife of the American typographer and type designer Fredric Warde and writing under the pseudonym Paul Beaujon). She contended that 'Printing Should Be Invisible' and subordinate to the writer; content is supreme, and clarity and legibility are the preeminent objectives. On the other hand Hahn found advertising a necessary 'street' art that reached those who never went to museums or galleries. For him the 'shout' was quite relevant, and he stressed the expressive and plastic possibilities of typography. This dichotomy is clear when one sees two of their designs from the same period. Roland Holst's 1919 ANDB program with its classical symmetrical style almost gently delivers the message. On the other hand, Hahn's 1918 poster *Stem Rood* (Vote Red) has the force of a visual steam drill. The argument between 'shouting' and information would prove to be an issue never totally resolved, but the emergence of De Stijl at the end of 1917 and the first publication of the magazine *Wendingen* in January 1918 were clear signs of a new beginning for Dutch graphic design.

1 M. R. Radermacher Schorer, *Bijdrage tot de Geschiedenis van de Renaissance der Nederlandse Boekdrukkunst*, Utrecht: School voor de Grafische vakken, 1951, p. 4.

2 Jan Middendorp, *Dutch Type*, Rotterdam: 010 Publishers, 2004, p. 30.

3 Nikolaus Pevsner, *Pioneers of Modern Design: From William Morris to Walter Gropius*, London: Penguin, 1984. p. 68.

REVUE BIMESTRIELLE POUR L'ART APPLIQUÉ

EDITEUR IMPRIMEUR

H. KLEINMANN ET Cⁱᵉ KENAUPARK 9. HARLEM, HOLLANDE.

PRIX 45 FRANCS PAR AN. 15 ESTAMPES LA LIVRAISON.

J THORN PRIKKER.

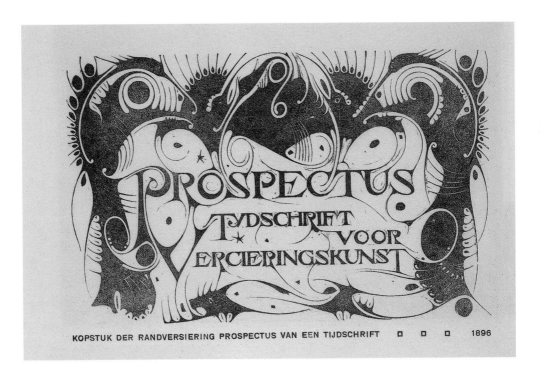

KOPSTUK DER RANDVERSIERING PROSPECTUS VAN EEN TIJDSCHRIFT □ □ □ 1896

Opposite: J. Thorn Prikker, poster for the magazine *Revue bimestrielle pour l'art appliqué*, Haarlem: Kleinmann, 1896.

Above: K. P. C. de Bazel, woodcut heading in a prospectus for the *Tijdschrift voor Vercieringskunst* (Magazine for Decorative Art), Haarlem: Kleinmann, July 1896.

Right: C. A. Lion Cachet, advertising flyer for the March issue of the magazine *Revue bimestrielle pour l'art appliqué*, Haarlem: Kleinmann, 1896.

Above: Jan Toorop, *Work for Women*
Amsterdam, 1898. This poster was
designed for a national exhibition
to provide 'an overview of the
female workforce'.

Opposite: T. Nieuwenhuis, calendar
page for April 1896, printed using color
lithography, Scheltema & Holkema's
Boekhandel (booksellers), Amsterdam.

Left and below: T. Nieuwenhuis, binding and title page for *Gedichten* (Poems) by Jacques Perk, reprinted with foreword by William Kloos, Amsterdam: S. L. van Looy, 1897.

Opposite: Theodorus M. A. A. Molkenboer, poster for Elias P. van Bommel, bookbinder, 1897.

42

Left and below left: Theo van Hoytema, cover and page from *Twee Hanen* (Two Roosters) by Hans Christian Andersen, Amsterdam: C. M. van Gogh, 1898.

Opposite: G. W. Dijsselhof, woodcut text for *Van Reynaerde* (an old Dutch fable), 1898. This was an attempt by Dijsselhof to design his own faces, with the names Klei-type, Hei-type, and Wei-type. This piece was never published.

VANDEN VOS REINAERDE

Willem, die den Madoc maecte,
Daer hi dicke omme waecte,
Hem vernoyede so haerde,
Dat davonturen van Reinaerde
In Dietsce onghemaket bleven,
Die hi hier hevet vulscreven
Dat hi die vite dede soeken,
Ende hise naden walscen boeken
In Dietsce dus hevet begonnen.
Atant i vint la reine Bramimunde:
Jo vus-aim mult, Sire, dist ele a l'cunte,
Kar mult vus preiset mis sire e tuit sihum
A vostre femme enveierai dous nusches:
Bien i ad or, matistes e jacunces,
E valent mielz que tut l'aveir de Rume;
Vostre emperere si bones n'en vit unkes.
Jamais n'iert jur que de l'mien ne vus dunge
Guenes respunt: E nus vus servirument.
Il les ad prises, en sa hoese les butet.

Above: Jan Toorop, *Het Hooge Land, Beekbergen*, poster for a charitable institution, 1896. Shown are the tools used by the residents. Toorop's sister Janet Hall posed for the female figure.

Opposite: Jan Toorop, cover for *Psyche* by Louis Couperus, Amsterdam: Veen, 1898. The repetitive swirls are typical of Toorop's designs from around the turn of the century.

Left: C. A. Lion Cachet, scroll for the Municipality of Apeldoorn, celebrating the coronation of Queen Wilhelmina, 1898.

Below left: Jan Toorop, cover design for *Egidius en de vreemdeling* (Egidius and the Stranger) by W. G. van Nouhuys, Haarlem: De Erven F. Bohn, 1899. The design was inspired by the work of William Morris, which Toorop had seen in Oxford in 1899.

Opposite, above: J. L. M. Lauweriks, cover of *De Architect* (The Architect), Haarlem: Kleinmann, 1899. The magazine was edited by the architectural association Architectura et Amicitia and distributed to other architectural groups in The Hague, Rotterdam, and Groningen.

Opposite, below: Theo van Hoytema, cover of *De Tuin* (The Garden), Haarlem: Kleinmann, 1899. An illustrated monthly on art, literature, music, polities, social sciences, and social work, it was edited by Albert Plasschaert, and published six times in 1899.

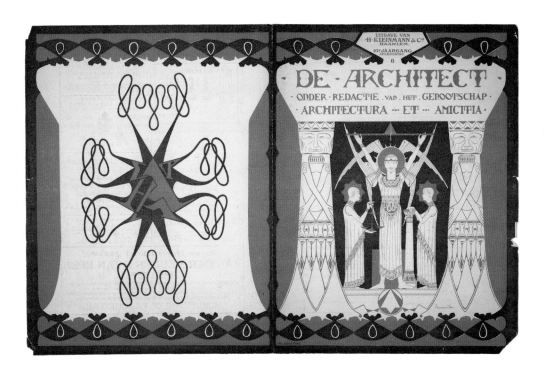

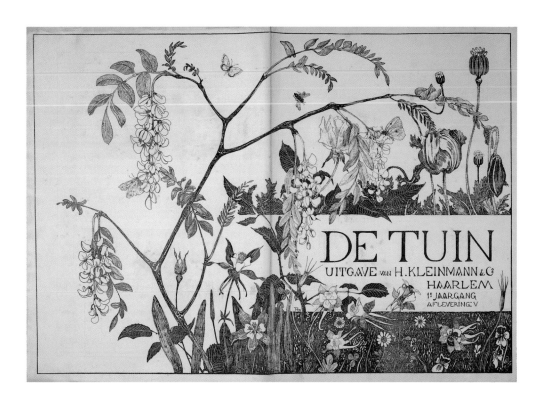

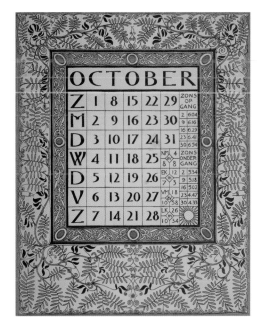

Above left: T. Nieuwenhuis, calendar page for June 1899.

Above: C. A. Lion Cachet, calendar page for August 1899.

Left: G. W. Dijsselhof, calendar page for October 1899.

Nieuwenhuis, Lion Cachet, and Dijsselhof each produced four months for this 1899 calendar.

Opposite: J. G. van Caspel, poster for Ivens & Co. Photographic Supplies, Nijmegen and Amsterdam, 1899.

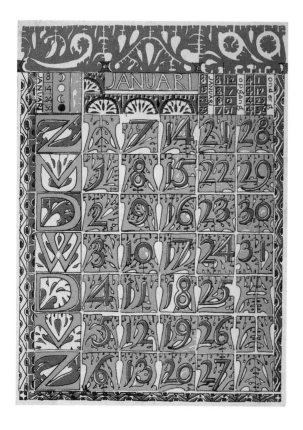

Left: C. A. Lion Cachet, calendar page for January 1900.

Below left: T. Nieuwenhuis, calendar page for February 1900.

Each designer produced six months for this 1900 calendar. Lion Cachet inventively combined letterforms and decoration, and Nieuwenhuis put aside his more severe design approach to be more consistent with Lion Cachet.

Opposite: J. G. van Caspel, poster for *Boon's Illustrated Magazine*, 1900, first published in 1899 by Boon, Amsterdam.

Opposite, above left: Theo Neuhuys, cover for *De boeken der kleine zielen* (The Books of Small Souls), a novel in four parts by Louis Couperus, Amsterdam: Veen, 1901–3.

Opposite, above right: Chris Lebeau, cover of *De stille kracht* (The Quiet Strength) by Louis Couperus, Amsterdam: Veen, 1903. The Javanese batik technique was extremely popular in the Netherlands and used in the applied arts in many forms.

Opposite, below: Jan Toorop, binding for *Babel* by Louis Couperus, Amsterdam: Veen, 1901. Toorop often used female figures to suggest spiritual themes in art and literature.

Above: C. A. Lion Cachet, advertising flyer for *Delftsche Slaolie Extra*, Dutch Oil Factory, Calvé, Delft, *c.* 1917. Here he uses a subdued, almost naturalistic approach.

Right: Willem van Konijnenberg, *Fop Smit & Co., Watertochtjes* (Boat trips), poster, Rotterdam, 1901.

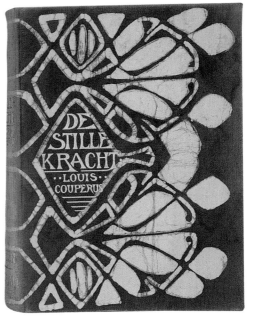

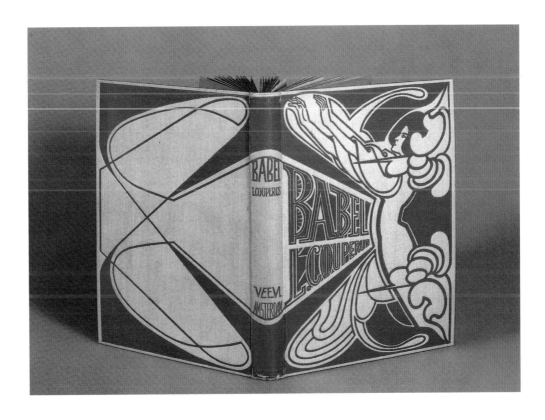

Above: Theo van Hoytema, calendar pages for June 1902 and August 1903, published privately by Van Hoytema.

Opposite: J. Thorn Prikker, poster for the Holländische Kunstausstellung (Dutch Art Exhibition), Krefeld, Germany, 1903. The expressive abstract decoration is reminiscent of Thorn Prikker's batik fabric designs.

HET DOEL EN STREVEN DER
HEDENDAAGSCHE ENGELSCHE
✠   SOCIALISTEN   ✠
LEZING GEHOUDEN VOOR HET
ANTI-KLERIKAAL GENOOTSCHAP TE
✠   LEICESTER, 23 JANUARI 1883   ✠

ijne vrienden, ik verzoek u een blik te
werpen op de verhouding tusschen de
Kunst en den Handel, waarbij ik dit laatste woord bezig in zijn meest gebruike-
lijken zin, nl. dien van het concurrentie-
stelsel, in waarheid den eenigen vorm,
waaronder men zich tegenwoordig den Handel denkt.
Terwijl er tijdperken zijn geweest in de wereldgeschie-
denis, toen de Kunst den schepter zwaaide over den
Handel, toen Kunst een zaak van gewicht was en Handel, zooals wij het woord opvatten, weinig beteekende,
zal men nu integendeel algemeen erkennen, dat de
Handel van zeer groot en de Kunst van zeer weinig
belang is. Ik zeg, dat men dit algemeen zal erkennen,

105

Left: S. H. de Roos, page design
for *Kunst en maatschappij* (Art
and Society) by William Morris.
Amsterdam: A. B. Soep, 1903.
De Roos used the French typeface
Grasset (1898) for the text
and added his own ornaments
and initials.

Opposite, above: K. P. C. de Bazel,
cover of the bi-monthly magazine
Bouw- en Sierkunst (Architecture
and Decorative Art), jointly edited
until 1904 by De Bazel and
J. L. M. Lauweriks, Haarlem:
Kleinmann, July 1898.

Opposite, below: *Het ontwerpen
van Vlak Ornament* (Designing Flat
Ornament) by Jan Ros, Rotterdam:
W.L. & J. Brusse, c. 1903

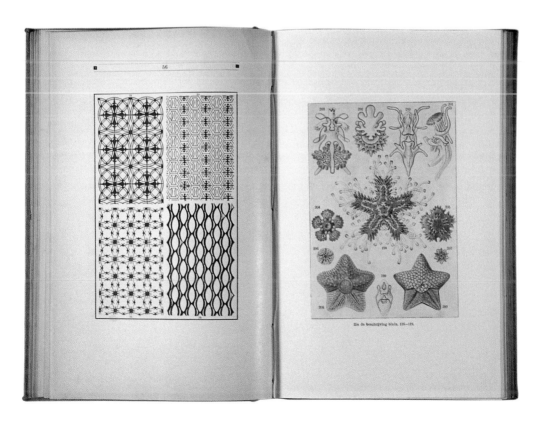

58

Left: H. P. Berlage, cover for *Onze Kunst* (Our Art), vols. 4 and 5, 1905. This magazine was devoted to the Flemish School and appeared between 1902 and 1929.
It was published in Antwerp and Amsterdam by I. J. Veen.

Below: Chris Lebeau, cover of *Van oude menschen de dingen die voorbijgaan* (The Things That Pass Old People By) by Louis Couperus, Amsterdam: Veen, 1906. The spare structure of this design resembles the patterns on the damask table linen that Lebeau designed in 1905.

Opposite: Theo van Hoytema, poster for an exhibition at The Hague Zoo, Dutch Natural History Society and the Royal Zoological and Botanical Association, 1910.

Below: R. N. Roland Holst, cover of
De Architect, vol. 18, no. 2, Haarlem:
Kleinmann, 1911.

Opposite: Chris Lebeau, poster for
Shakespeare's *Hamlet*, 1914. This is one of
several posters Lebeau designed for Eduard
Verkade for the 1914–16 theater season.

Overleaf, left: Chris Lebeau, poster for *De
Magiër* (The Magician) by G. K. Chesterton,
1915, for Eduard Verkade's theater group.

Overleaf, right: Chris Lebeau, poster for
Shakespeare's *Hamlet*, 1915, for Eduard
Verkade's theater group.

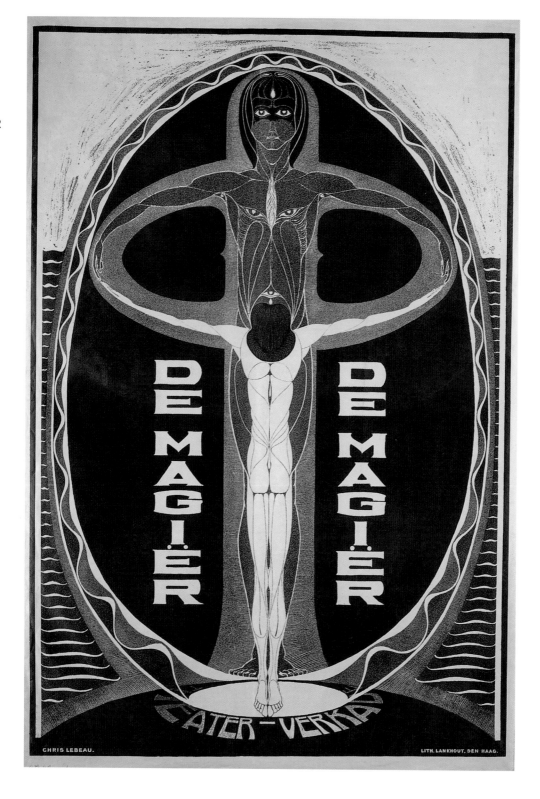

Opposite: Jacob (Jac.) Jongert, *Apricot Brandy*, poster, Pumerend: Wed. G. Oud, 1920.

Below: Willy Sluijters, poster for an exhibition at the Hotel Hamdorff, Laren, 1916. The hotel was famous for its exhibitions and parties for artists.

Above: C. A. Lion Cachet, poster for the
Utrecht Trade Fair, 1917. The swirling,
semi-abstract shapes are a late vestige
of Art Nouveau.

Opposite: Jacob (Jac.) Jongert, poster for
De Paradijsvloek (The Curse of Paradise)
by Alphonse Laudy, Schouwtoneel, 1919.
The decorative approach shows the
influence of his mentor, R. N. Roland Holst.

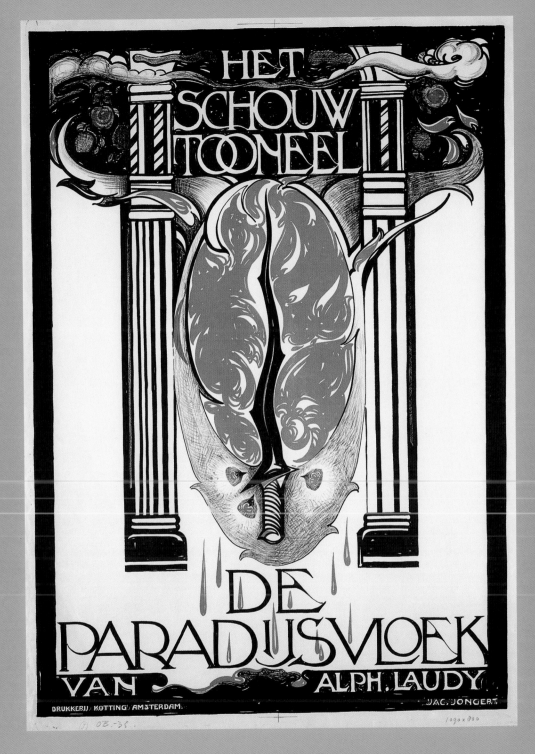

HET
SCHOUW
TOONEEL

DE
PARADIJSVLOEK
VAN   ALPH. LAUDY

DRUKKERIJ KOTTING AMSTERDAM.

JAC. JONGERT.

Left: Jaap Gidding, poster for
an interior design exhibition,
D'Audretsch Art Rooms,
The Hague, 1921.

Below: R. N. Roland Holst, program
celebrating the Dutch Diamond
Cutters' Federation achieving
an eight-hour working day,
Amsterdam, 1911.

Opposite: Piet van der Hem,
Spyker Autos, poster, before 1914.

Left: Chris Lebeau, poster for the William Brok Fine Art Gallery, Hilversum, 1919. A visitor is shown looking through his hands at a painting.

Below: Raoul Hynckes, Poster for *Regata, reclame en grafische arbeid tentoonstelling*. (Regata, Advertising and Graphic Work Exhibition), 1919.

Opposite: Albert Pieter Hahn, *Stem Rood! Kiest de Kandidaten der Soc. Dem. Arb. Partij* (Vote Red! Choose the Candidates of the Socialist Democratic Workers' Party), poster, 1918. A laborer is shown slaying a creature made up of anarchy, capitalism, hunger, profiteering, and the affliction of war.

Opposite: Leo Gestel, poster for the
annual Utrecht Industrial Fair, 1922.
Mercury, the god of commerce,
is depicted in a Cubist style.

Above: M. W. de Klerk, S. H. de Roos
and N. J. van der Vecht, three
postage stamps for the PTT,
The Hague, 1923. The designs were
the winners of a competition.

THEO VAN DOESBURG

KLASSIEK

BAROK

MODERN

DE SIKKEL - ANTWERPEN

02

THE IMPACT OF DE STIJL

Theo van Doesburg, cover for
Klassiek Barok Modern(Classic,
Baroque, Modern), Antwerp:
De Sikkel, 1920.

The armistice ending World War I was signed on November 11, 1918, concluding the most devastating armed conflict in history and the loss of almost an entire generation. An abiding pessimism and a longing for a new beginning took hold among intellectuals who saw the war as a result of serious flaws in the makeup of modern European society. Many of those who lived through the war wrote about their feelings of alienation. *Goodbye to All That*, the 1928 autobiography of the English poet Robert Graves, was an unsentimental chronicle of lost dreams and a look back at a way of life that no longer existed. Graves joined the army in 1914 and was part of the Battle of the Somme. He was wounded in July 1916, and survived, even though his family had been sent news of his death. In *Goodbye to All That*, Graves explained how members of his generation said 'goodbye' to previous beliefs and social standards and how they questioned accepted patterns of privilege and culture, and rejected all forms of patriotism and religion.

Even before the war, new political, social, and artistic movements were profuse throughout Europe. On February 20, 1909 the Italian poet Filippo Marinetti published his Futurist manifesto and became the group's spokesman. In 1910, only fourteen months later, a group of painters and poets in Russia, led by David and Vladimir Burliek, published *Sadok Sudei* (A Trap for Judges), which is considered to be the first publication by a similar movement in Russia. In 1914 the French poet Stéphane Mallarmé published the poem *Un Coup de Dés Jamais n'Abolira le Hasard* (One Roll of the Dice Will Never Abolish Chance); begun as early as 1897, it was an early instance of text augmented by typography. During the war in 1916, Dada was conceived in Zurich by Tristan Tzara, Hans Arp, Hugo Ball, Hans Richter, and others. The French poet Guillaume Apollinaire's 1918 series of poems *Calligrammes: Poèmes de la paix et de la guerre, 1913–1916* (Calligrammes: Poems of Peace and War, 1913–1916) is another example of evocative typography. On March 20, 1919, the Staatliches Bauhaus was opened in Weimar by Walter Gropius, a sequel to the Grand Ducal School of Applied Arts.

Together with the architect Jacobus Johannes Pieter (Ko) Oud; the writer, poet, and music critic Anthony Kok; and the painters Vilmos Huszár, and Piet Mondrian, Theo van Doesburg began the De Stijl movement in 1917. The name De Stijl can be traced to Van Doesburg's 1916 lecture 'The Aesthetic Principle of Modern Art' when he mentioned a new style that would arise through an alliance of architecture and painting. Although probably unrelated, in Dutch the word 'stijl' can also mean the vertical section of a cross-connection in carpentry. Volume 1, number 1 of their journal *De Stijl* ('The Straight Line' was another name that was considered) was published in October 1917, and one year later the first De Stijl manifesto was issued. By then the founding group had been joined by the architects Jan Wils and Robert van 't Hoff, the sculptor Georges Vantongerloo and the painter Bart van der Leck. Later the group would include the furniture designer and architect Gerrit Rietveld, the painters and graphic designers Vordemberge-Gildewart and Cesar Domela Nieuwenhuis, the interior designer Truus Schröder-Schräder, and the film-maker Hans Richter.

De Stijl was one of many critical intellectual responses to the calamity of World War I. The movement disavowed all emotion which was associated with nationalism and militarism, and was considered part of a tarnished past. In addition to being an artistic movement, De Stijl was an endeavor to help prevent a similar tragedy to the one just suffered throughout Europe. This aim was implicit in De Stijl's first manifesto, published in 1918:

There is an old and a new awareness of time. The old is based on the individual. The new is based on the universal. The struggle of the individual against the universal is manifesting itself in the World War as well as in contemporary art…. The war is destroying the old world with its contents; the dominance of the individual in every sector.[1]

In 1921 a similar sentiment followed in the fourth volume of *De Stijl*:

For Europe there is no longer any way out. Centralization and property, spiritual and material individualism was the foundation of the old Europe. In that it has caged itself. It is falling to pieces. We observe this calmly. We would not want to help even if we could. We do not want to extend the life of this old prostitute.[2]

De Stijl advocated an idealistic goal to liberate art from nonessential and outdated qualities such as subject matter, naturalism, subjectivity, and decoration. Its diverse advocates rejected outright what they saw as the sentimentalism and degeneration of the nineteenth century. They expressed a desire for a new rational art that better suited the modern world, a 'collective impersonal style.... destined, they felt, for adoption by architects and designers of the machine age.'[3] They were not, however, a 'lost generation'; instead they enthusiastically espoused a new industry-based culture. In order to meet the needs of a new epoch, the members of De Stijl advocated a revision of old understandings of beauty which had been based solely on craft. They realized that twentieth-century technology could be utilized to create a union of art and industry. In October 1917 Van Doesburg wrote in the first issue of *De Stijl*:

It is the endeavor of this small magazine to make a contribution toward the development of a new consciousness of beauty. It desires to make modern man receptive to what is new in the plastic arts. It desires, as opposed to anarchy and confusion, the 'modern baroque,' to establish a mature style based on pure relationship of the spirit of the age and expressive means. It desires to combine in itself contemporary ideas on the new plasticity, which, although fundamentally the same, developed independently from one another.[4]

Van Doesburg was born in Utrecht in 1883, his original name being Christiaan Emil Marie Küpper. His father was Wilhelm Küpper, a Bonn photographer who went back to Germany when Van Doesburg was still an infant. His mother remarried when he was eleven, and he took his stepfather's name, Doesburg, later adding the 'Van', an early indication of his attraction for using pseudonyms. In the beginning, Van Doesburg seemed headed for a stage career, but it soon became clear that painting was his true interest. He was working in a semi-impressionist manner in 1908 when he had his first exhibition in The Hague, but within two years, this approach would change radically as his paintings moved toward abstraction. In 1912 he produced art criticism for an avant-garde newspaper, which was an early sign of his interest in writing.

Van Doesburg was an ingenious, eclectic, volatile, and inflexible artist, who was able to approach various media with equal fervor; concurrently active as a lecturer, writer, painter, architect, poet, sculptor, furniture and industrial designer, and typographer, his own versatility reflected De Stijl's multidimensional character. In 1917, Van Doesburg began designing posters, books, and other printed matter, and in addition to serving as *De Stijl*'s editor, he experimented with typography by helping to create the layout.

The first three volumes of *De Stijl* have a Spartan appearance, as only the design on the front and some of the advertisements give an indication as to how the magazine would develop. When Van Doesburg and Mondrian redesigned *De Stijl* in its fourth volume at the end of 1920, the publication reflected the influence of the Russian Constructivist El Lissitsky and the Hanover Dadaist Kurt Schwitters This influence was especially evident in the new Constructivist-based cover design which replaced the original logo. Thereafter *De Stijl*'s pages wavered between fairly conventional designs and expressive compositions that actively engaged the reader.

The logo for the first three volumes of *De Stijl* was designed by Huszár, and the style of the lettering is reminiscent of his paintings from the same period. Huszár was influenced by both Van Doesburg and Van der Leck, the latter of whom contributed an article entitled 'The Place of Modern Painting in Architecture' for *De Stijl*'s first issue. The basis for the fragmented letters on the cover of *De Stijl* is also evident in earlier Van der Leck designs.

ZEVENDE JAARGANG 1926-1927

DE STIJL

NB

WARSCHAU

LE STYLE . N°
DER STIL . . N°
THE STYLE N°
IL STYLE . . N°

75/76

LEIDEN HANNOVER PARIJS BRNO WEENEN

INTERNATIONAAL MAANDBLAD
VOOR NIEUWE KUNST WETEN-
SCHAP EN KULTUUR REDACTIE
THEO VAN DOESBURG

Above: Theo van Doesburg, mailing wrapper for *De Stijl*, 1921.

Opposite: Theo van Doesburg, cover for *De Stijl*, 1926–27, vol. 7, nos. 75/76. During its fourth year, *De Stijl* was given a dynamic new look with the *De Stijl NB* (new images) logo on the cover.

DE STIJL - LE STYLE - DER STIL - THE STILE -

LE SEUL ORGANE D'UNE NOUVELLE CONSCIENCE PLASTIQUE ET POÉTIQUE FONDÉ EN 1917 EN HOLLANDE

PÉRIODIQUE
DRUKWERKEN

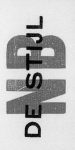

MAANDBLAD VOOR NIEUWE KUNST, WETENSCHAP
EN KULTUUR. REDACTIE : THEO VAN DOESBURG.
ABONNEMENT BINNENLAND f6.. BUITENLAND f7.50
PER JAARGANG. ADRES VAN REDACTIE EN ADMIN.
UTRECHTSCH JAAGPAD 17 LEIDEN (HOLLAND).
À L'ÉTRANGER : AV. SCHNEIDER, 84, CLAMART.

A stained glass artisan, Van der Leck designed a window for Wm. Müller & Company in The Hague in 1914–15. This design led Van der Leck to receive other assignments for the firm, notably his *Batavier Line* poster of 1916. This work showed another step toward visual organization, and the rectangular division of space can be seen as a precursor to De Stijl. The composition is segmented by black bars that reflect Van der Leck's earlier work in stained glass. The figures recall Egyptian paintings, with bodies depicted frontally and heads in profile. The passengers appear to be in watertight compartments, assuring customers that the trip would be a safe one. Shipping between Rotterdam and London was of vital importance for Dutch trade. During World War I the shipping lanes were cut and many ships from the Batavier Line were either confiscated in Belgium or sunk by the German navy. For this reason the poster could not be used until the passages were cleared by minesweepers in 1919. As shown in this version, the company sometimes changed the color of the poster during the 1920s and in doing so angered Van der Leck immensely. The poster for his 1919 Utrecht exhibition and the advertising material for the Amsterdam furniture store and manufacturer Metz & Company are further examples of how Van der Leck's typography reflected his painting themes. His De Stijl-inspired alphabet appeared again in a 1941 collector's edition of one of Hans Christian Andersen's fairytales.

From their letters, it was clear that Mondrian and Van Doesburg had doubts about Van der Leck's suitability for De Stijl, and evidently Van der Leck had similar reservations. Fiercely independent, Van der Leck never signed the De Stijl manifesto and left the group in March 1918, only a few months after its inception. His work was always pictorially based, and he always insisted that total abstraction was never part of his artistic agenda.

Reflecting Van Doesburg's own philosophy, De Stijl was polemical, multifarious, and dedicated to bringing about a universal alliance between art and society. Van Doesburg not only wanted to produce a revolution in the visual arts, but he also wanted to change the very fabric of society itself. One origin of its objective spiritual purity and discipline was Dutch Calvinism.

De Stijl was based on both rational and theosophical ideology. As aptly noted by Professor Jaffé: 'It therefore attempts to render visible and subject to contemplation something very close to the platonic idea. In its striving after abstraction, after the liberation of the arts from all accidentals, De Stijl constantly aims at the visible expression of the universal principle which its members consider the rendering of exact and equilibrated relations.'[5] Mondrian believed that since natural forms are always independently determined, they could not be called universal. Thus, the new art form had to be completely abstract. Although De Stijl could to some extent be seen as an extension of Cubism, the original Cubists never sought pure abstraction and always retained a tie with nature.

Although the original goals were sometimes ignored, De Stijl was in theory based on function, asymmetry, and elementary rectangular elements limited to black and white, gray, and primary colors. Much to Mondrian's annoyance, in 1924 Van Doesburg began to also use diagonals in his paintings, justifying this shift by saying it permitted a more dynamic approach. New artistic terms were profuse in this period, and Van Doesburg's transformation resulted in one called 'Elementarism.'

De Stijl had increasingly become a forum for artists of different convictions to publish their doctrines. Dada was discussed by Raoul Hausmann and Arp; Merz by Schwitters; abstract filmmaking by Richter and Vicking Eggeling; Constructivism by Lissitsky and Laszlo

Moholy-Nagy; and Futurism by Gino Severini and Marinetti. This wide range of viewpoints heightened the rift between Van Doesburg and orthodox De Stijl advocates such as Mondrian. Van Doesburg was interested in exploring new expressive frontiers, while Mondrian saw painting was an end in itself. In 1924, Mondrian abruptly severed his connections with De Stijl, mainly because of his disapproval of 'Elementarism' and what he saw as Van Doesburg's unbearable discrepancies. Another possible reason for the break was Mondrian's apparent empathy for the expressive style of H. T. Wijdeveld and the magazine *Wendingen* which Van Doesburg openly detested. Except for helping to redesign *De Stijl*, Mondrian was never concerned with typography, and his influence in graphic design was felt primarily in the overall structure of the printed page.

Van Doesburg's upper-case alphabet was constructed from vertical and horizontal slabs of the same thickness and could be stretched vertically or horizontally to force texts to fit any format. Neither aesthetics nor legibility were major considerations, and the assumption that conveying information is a primary objective of typography was of marginal concern. Perhaps Moholy-Nagy was referring to Van Doesburg when he wrote that 'clarity is the first prerequisite of all typography. For the sake of legibility the message must never suffer from a priori aesthetics. The letter types must never be forced into a pre-planned form, for instance into a square.'[6] Yet, as demonstrated by the cover for his published 1920 Antwerp lecture *Klassiek Barok Modern*, Van Doesburg could use his alphabet quite effectively.

Two prominent De Stijl architects were Rietveld and Oud. Rietveld's father was a Utrecht furniture-maker, and initially Rietveld pursued the same craft. Although the model for his celebrated Lean Chair was finished in 1918, he did not begin producing his De Stijl-based furniture until 1919. Originally built out of natural wood, four years later he painted the Lean Chair in primary colors. Rietveld is primarily known for the 1924 Rietveld-Schröder house, a design disdained by Berlage who felt that it was the antithesis of the vernacular architecture he himself promoted. Oud was a social reformer and considered by many to be Rotterdam's principal architect. Concentrating on public housing, he exploited the modular device in urban architecture. His 1925 Café De Unie in Rotterdam has an asymmetrical facade that reflects De Stijl principles and was placed between two traditional houses to alleviate the 'serious character' of the street. The original building burned down in May 1940 during the bombing of Rotterdam and was rebuilt in 1985, not far from the original location.

Although he first approached it with reserve and somewhat belatedly, it was obvious in *De Stijl* that Van Doesburg had an affinity for Dadaism. The Dadaists were fundamentally nihilists who rejected all previous artistic doctrines, and they were not interested in replacing these with new dogma. They used any means at hand to promote their principles, and found the immediate quality of collage and montage to be especially suitable. The term Dada was first mentioned by Van Doesburg in a short article titled 'Rondblik' (Look Around) in volume 3, number 4 of *De Stijl* published in February 1920. Van Doesburg's first piece on Dada appeared on May 8, 1920, in *De Nieuwe Amsterdammer*, a weekly for which he periodically wrote articles. He stressed that that it would be missing the point to try to find rational definitions in Dada writing. 'Dada doesn't want that. Then what does Dada want? It wants nothing. But "nothing" in a positive sense.'[7] Or as the American scholar Roger Shattuck wrote in his 1968 book *The Banquet Years*, the 'absence of any value becomes in itself a value.'[8]

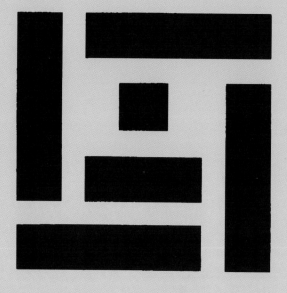

Above: Jan Wils, trademark, *c.* 1917.
Zwart used this for Wils's letterhead,
his first typographic assignment.

Opposite: Theo van Doesburg, alphabet
design, 1919. Van Doesburg designed a
set of capitals based on a 5 x 5 grid.

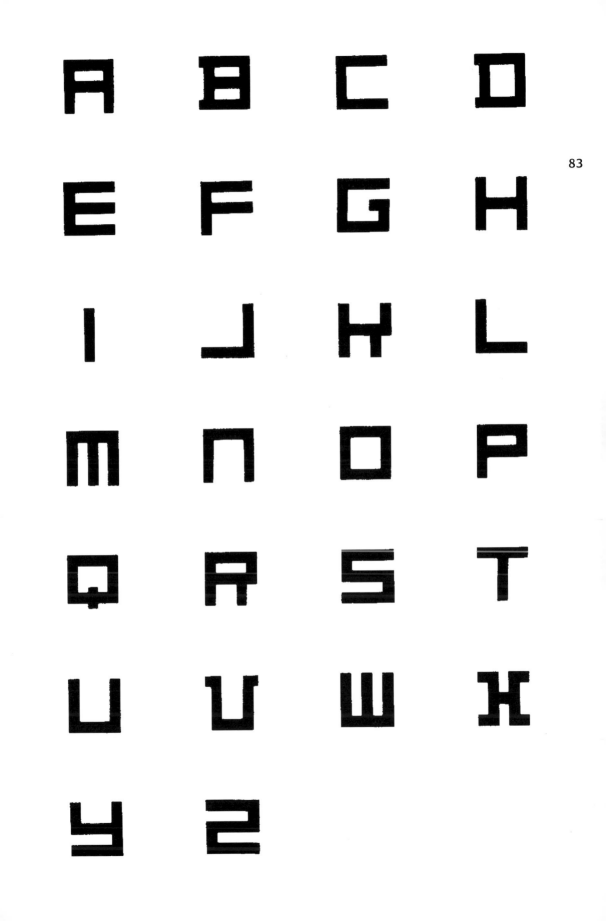

Together with Mondrian and Kok, Van Doesburg published an article on literature in Dutch, French, and German titled *Manifest II van 'De Stijl' 1920 – De Literatuur* (Manifesto II of 'De Stijl' 1920 – Literature) in volume 3, number 6 of *De Stijl*. This affirmed that they intended to confer 'a new meaning and new power of expression to words.' In the next issue, there appeared a series of poems titled *X Beelden, Letter klank beelden* (X Beelden, Letter Sound Images) by the mysterious writer I. K. Bonset, later discovered to be one of

Van Doesburg's pseudonyms. A footnote stated that the *X Beelden* were part of a series of *Kubistische Verzen* (Cubist Verses) produced between 1913 and 1919. In these poems it was Van Doesburg's objective to express sound typographically: the meanings of words were denoted through different type sizes and arrangements, recalling Apollinaire's *Calligrammes*. The *X Beelden* display many attributes of Dada typography such as assorted typefaces in numerous sizes and contrasting directions.

The first of four issues of Van Doesburg's journal *Mécano* was published in 1922 under the Bonset pseudonym, this time listing him as the *gérant littéraire* (literary editor). Van Doesburg was credited as the *mécanicien plastique* (plastic engineer). *Mécano* had a Dada appearance and according to Van Doesburg it was intended to 'poke fun at the solemnities of the Bauhaus.' It contained work by Schwitters, Max Ernst, Hausmann, Tzara, Arp, and the Paris Dada artists Georges Ribemont-Dessaignes, Francis Picabia, and Paul Eluard, and it even went so far as to satirize *De Stijl*. Each issue was distinguished by a primary color (the four numbers are labeled yellow, blue, red, and white). Numbers 1, 2, and 3 are folded out of a single sheet into sixteen sections with eight on each side. The texts in each section are often set in divergent directions, and the pages work as individual units within a loose typographic association when unfolded. The fourth issue is in four sections and bound into an eight-page booklet.

Van Doesburg met Schwitters during the summer of 1921 and at once saw him as a confidant. He published three poems by Schwitters's in *De Stijl*, and a 'Sonata' in *Mécano* 4/5. Schwitters came to the Netherlands in January 1923 where he met Van der Leck, Mondrian, Oud, Berlage, Rietveld, and the constructivist graphic designers Piet Zwart and Paul Schuitema. Schwitters published the initial issue of *Merz* in that same month and included Van Doesburg's 'Letter Sound Images.' Devoted to 'Holland Dada,' the formal structure of this first *Merz* number with text segments divided by bars and lines can be traced to *De Stijl* and *Mécano*. The typographic children's book *Die Scheuche* (The Scarecrow) was a 1925 Merz publication. Although this was a collective undertaking involving Schwitters and Käte Steinitz, the typography was mainly by Van Doesburg.

In a 1918 letter to Tristan Tzara, Van Doesburg first referred to I. K. Bonset as a 'Dutch Dadaist,' and Bonset soon became one of Van Doesburg's Dada alter egos. Returning from Milan in 1922, Van Doesburg announced that he had discovered an important manuscript by a lately deceased painter, Aldo Camini. This consisted of satires, scientific and philosophical theories, art criticisms, and poetry, most of which appeared in *De Stijl*. It was not until Van Doesburg died that it was discovered that Bonset, Camini, and Van Doesburg were all the same person. Even some of Van Doesburg's closest friends and associates were oblivious to the charade. Mondrian even went so far as to caution Van Doesburg about Bonset, whom he thought might be stealing their ideas. Taking the hoax even further, Van Doesburg published a photograph of his wife Nelly with a mustache and said it was Bonset. Nelly later remarked that her husband delighted in being able to place himself into any part. Had he not initially contemplated a stage career?

Inconsistency was always part of Van Doesburg's nature, and it is curious why he never revealed his Dada tendencies using his own name. Partially the assumed names were simply used in jest, but mainly they were a means to express beliefs that were outside of the realm of De Stijl. In this way Van Doesburg had additional critical weapons with which he could attack anything and everyone, even himself and De Stijl. An alias also provided him with anonymity. Adamant De Stijl proponents could abhor Bonset's views but nevertheless tolerate them, since a stranger was presenting them.

Van Doesburg exemplifies F. Scott Fitzgerald's hypothesis that an artist has the ability to sustain two antithetical doctrines: 'The test of a first-rate intelligence is the ability to hold two opposed ideas in the mind at the same time, and still retain the ability to function.'[9] Nevertheless, holding two opposing viewpoints will always remain a paradox. Van Doesburg was fully aware that Dada was in essence an anarchistic movement quite removed from De Stijl's rigorous dictums. Yet he was also aware that Dada, like De Stijl, was contesting accepted ideologies both in art and society, and for this reason he saw an affinity between them.

Van Doesburg and the Bauhaus
After the Staatliches Bauhaus was launched in Weimar in April 1921, Walter Gropius invited Van Doesburg to come for a week as an unofficial observer. Never reticent about offering his criticisms, Van Doesburg openly announced that the school was still bound to pre-war romanticism. He particularly disliked the teaching approach in Johann Itten's 'Vorkurs' (Foundation course), compulsory for all students. This stressed artistic expression, the opposite standpoint of Van Doesburg. Eventually, though, Van Doesburg was partially vindicated, for the Vorkurs changed radically when Moholy-Nagy later took it over and replaced the expressionist approach with a constructivist philosophy. Van Doesburg decided to stay on for a while longer and help to improve what he saw as an anachronistic situation. The Bauhaus historian Bruno Adler later remarked that Van Doesburg arrived in Weimar with 'his gospel of redemption through the right angle,' and the association of De Stijl and the Bauhaus was at best an 'unholy alliance.' Van Doesburg clearly wanted to be a Bauhaus colleague, but he was not accepted as an equal. He never got over it and, as a retaliation, began holding his own De Stijl courses in the studio of a Bauhaus student, Peter Röhl, which was also frequented by several dissident Bauhaus faculty members. Ultimately, Van Doesburg's brazenness aroused so much animosity from the Bauhaus faculty and students that windows of Röhl's studio were shattered by bullets and stones.

Among other objections, Gropius found Van Doesburg's philosophy too inflexible. His fundamental criticism, however, was Van Doesburg's unqualified renunciation of individualism, which was in strong contrast to the subjective philosophy of the Bauhaus. Van Doesburg's expulsion was also a result of his often inflexible, patronizing, and belligerent manner. Van Doesburg's fervor was apparent in a letter to Kok in January 1921 which discusses the Bauhaus episode:

In Weimar, I have radically turned everything upside down. This is the acclaimed academy with the most modern teachers! Each evening I have talked to the students and have spread the toxin of the new spirit. De Stijl will soon re materialize in an even more radical shape. I have mountains of strength and now know that our ideas will prevail over everything and everybody.[10]

BOND VAN
REVOLUTIONNAIR-
SOCIALISTISCHE
INTELLECTUEELEN

Opposite: Theo van Doesburg, letterhead for the Union of Revolutionary Socialist Intellectuals, 1919.

Above: I. K. Bonset (pseudonym of Van Doesburg), *Letter klank beelden* (Letter Sound Images), poem, *De Stijl*, vol. 4, no. 7, 1921. Varying type sizes and weights imply the poem's pronunciation.

At the end of 1923 Van Doesburg triumphantly left Weimar permanently and continued to deliver the De Stijl doctrine throughout Germany. Hanover was then a cultural hub, and encounters there between Van Doesburg, Lissitsky, and Schwitters led to ideas that had a momentous effect on Dutch graphic design. They all predicted a new era when advertising would erase subjectivity in graphic design, with the client's needs being the only issue.

At the Düsseldorf Congress of Progressive Artists in May 1922, Van Doesburg, Lissitsky, and Richter introduced a manifesto for international Constructivists. In October of that year, the Constructivists held a conference in Weimar with Van Doesburg officiating. Not only did Constructivists attend, but Dadaists were also there in droves. The latter included Schwitters, Richter, Lissitsky, Max Burchartz, Tzara, Arp, and Moholy-Nagy, and an uproar resulted when the Constructivists discovered that Dadaists had been invited without their knowledge. The Constructivists regarded Dada as negative, deleterious, and obsolete, and finding themselves in a spot where they would have to work with Dadaists was hard to accept. Although the Constructivists initially openly rebelled, Van Doesburg managed to calm them down, but to the further dismay of the Constructivists, the gathering ended up being a Dada occasion. Typically, Van Doesburg was amused at the commotion, and no one present had any notion that he had for some time been espousing both convictions, through his Dada writings under the pseudonym Bonset.

Lissitzky's Constructivist fairytale, which had earlier been published in Germany, was the theme of the October/November 1922 issue of *De Stijl* (vol. 5, no. 10/11). The Dutch translation was *El Lissitsky suprematisch worden van twee kwadraten in 6 konstrukties* (El Lissitsky becomes supremacist from two squares in 6 constructions). Although a shortened interpretation of the original Russian publication, it further demonstrated that words and abstract images could be used to convey messages effectively. In 1923 Lissitsky came to the Netherlands where avid proponents were ready to absorb his new typographic ideas. He gave talks on recent artistic developments in Russia, and met with Huszár, Zwart, and Oud, the latter of whom was a member of the Comité voor Economische Opbouw van Rusland (Committee for the Economic Development of Russia). The inspiration of Lissitsky would eventually be very evident in the Netherlands, notably in the early typography of Zwart.

Huszár was one of the more obscure figures of De Stijl and continued to be associated with the movement until 1922. He was born in Budapest as Vilmos Herz in 1884, and in 1904 the family took on the name Huszár, wanting one that sounded properly Hungarian. Huszár left Hungary in the same year, and by 1909 he was in the Netherlands where he settled for the rest of his life.

Not only did he design the woodcut logo for *De Stijl* in 1917, but he was instrumental in determining its initial typographic direction. Huszár was known for his contentious nature, and from 1918 until 1921 he and the equally impulsive Van Doesburg had heated arguments, during which time his work was banned from *De Stijl*. The actual breaking point came after Huszár abruptly ended his *De Stijl* subscription after learning that Mondrian and Van Doesburg had replaced his earlier design with one of their own.

Huszár worked in many fields, including painting and interior, furniture, fabric, and industrial design, and in 1915 and 1916 Van der Leck introduced him to stained glass. Later he worked with Zwart at the interior architectural firm Bruynzeel and also for the architect Wils. Although Huszár had dabbled in typography as early as 1906, it became a major part of his work when he helped design *De Stijl* in 1917.

His early typography, such as the 1919 cover for 'Volkswoningbouw, Haagsche Kunstkring' (Public Housing, The Hague Art Circle) and the 1922 bookplate design for Lena de Roos, with letter forms geometrically constructed from rectangles, is closely related to the De Stijl logo and his paintings from around the same time. In 1926 he began to work more in advertising design, which was to some extent a result of his contact with Lissitsky, Schwitters, and Zwart. His own typography, however, was quite different and not based on printing elements such as letters and rules. Instead, he worked with what he referred to as 'visual advertising compositions,' or flat pictorial designs that symbolically implied the nature of the products.

Huszár created new logos for the various cigarette brands of the Vittoria Egyptian Cigarette Company. His design for Miss Blanche Virginia Cigarettes was a new version of an earlier illustration showing a smoking woman wearing a hat. The designs were used in color and black and white on stationery, cards, billboards, and advertising wagons.

One of Huszár's goals was for his graphic design to have artistic as well as functional values. He attempted to express his ideas in various magazine articles, including one in 1927 for the international review *i10*, volume 1, number 5. In this essay, *De Reclame als Beeldende Kunst* (Advertising as Fine Art), he was unspecific as to when advertising could be considered art, but he was more precise in a 1929 article for *De Reclame, 8* (Advertising, 8) and *Bouwkundig Weekblad* (Architectural Weekly). Here he rejected contemporary Constructivist advertising as being 'anti-art.'

For example, it is the opponents of the so-called De Stijl group of 1917, those who at the time were still working in a romantic mode, the 'Vienna Seccession Style,' who were the first ones to brazenly imitate us and now surpass us with 'hyperrationalism.'[11]

Huszár was obviously aiming at Zwart, and his article did not help their friendship. In the same article, Huszár excluded typographic advertisements from the fine arts entirely, particularly targeting those which used printing elements exclusively, such as the NKF ads that Zwart began to produce in 1923. It is noteworthy that Huszár's cover for *Ruimte*, the 1929 VANK annual, reflected his own interest in Constructivism, even though he had dismissed it in his articles. Although Huszár had broken with De Stijl by the end of 1922, he completely severed his connection in 1930. After 1931 he ceased working in typography altogether.

De Stijl's Conclusion
In a 1929 article for the German magazine *Die Form*, Van Doesburg appeared to question some of his earlier beliefs, stating that the era of 'dynamic,' disorderly typography, infected by the advertising plague, had raped and muzzled the book. He now advocated a careful division of text and white space on pages with a pleasing 'dynamic balance' and added that 'Das Buch ist kein Bild' (The book is not a picture).[12]

Van Doesburg went to Davos in Switzerland for asthma treatment and died there of heart failure at the age of 47 on March 7, 1931. Except for an edition dedicated to Van Doesburg in 1932, the unnumbered *Dernier numéro* issue, De Stijl no longer appeared after 1928 (vol. 8, no. 87/89). Bonset and Camini were never heard of again, and with Van Doesburg's death, De Stijl lost its driving force.

TENTOONSTELLING

v.d. LECK. 12 JAN: 9 FEB:

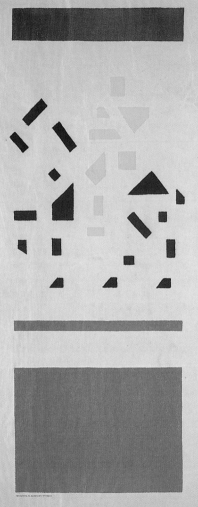

FOTOGRAVURE M. ACHENBACH UTRECHT

VOOR DE KUNST

NOBELSTR: UTRECHT

Opposite: Bart van der Leck, poster for the exhibition *Voor de Kunst* (For Art), Utrecht, 1919. In 1916 Van der Leck began to use fragmented shapes in his paintings that are reflected in the lettering.

Above: Bart van der Leck, *Batavier Line*, poster, Wm. H. Müller & Co., 1916. Through his contacts with Mrs. Kröller-Müller, Van der Leck was given commissions by the Müller & Co. steamship line.

An indigenous Dutch modern art movement, De Stijl is considered by many to be the most important Dutch development in twentieth-century architecture, painting, and design. For Van Doesburg, typography was yet another way to express De Stijl's objectives, and De Stijl's principal hallmark in modern graphic design was the application of vertical and horizontal rectangles for placement of text and images. Essentially a painter, Van Doesburg was concerned with color and form, unlike a typographer for whom pragmatic matters are essential and details are as significant as the total design. Yet the intensity of Van Doesburg's vision and the purifying nature of De Stijl were of major importance to graphic design and especially to the Dutch Constructivists.

1 Theo van Doesburg, *De Stijl*, vol. II, 1918, p. 2.

2 Theo van Doesburg, *De Stijl*, vol. IV, 1918, p. 2.

3 H. L. C. Jaffé, *De Stijl 1917–1931*, Amsterdam: Meulenhoff/Landshoff, 1956, p. 4.

4 Theo van Doesburg, *De Stijl*, vol. I, 1918, p. 1.

5 H. L. C. Jaffé, *De Stijl 1917–1931*, Amsterdam: Meulenhoff/ Landshoff, 1956, p. 5

6 Eckhard Neumann, *Functional Graphic Design in the 20s*, New York: Reinhold,

1967, p. 39.

7 K. Schippers, *Holland Dada*, Amsterdam: Em. Querido's Uitgeverij BV, 1974, p. 30.

8 Roger Shattuck, *The Banquet Years*, New York: Vintage, 1968, p. 33.

9 F. Scott Fitzgerald, *The Crack-Up*, New York: New Directions, 1945, p. 69.

10 Theo van Doesburg, letter to Antonie Kok, 1921.

11 Sjarel Ex and Els Hoek, Vilmos Huszár, *Schilder en Ontwerper 1884–1960*,

Utrecht: Reflex, 1985, p. 113.

12 Dick Dooijes, *Wegbereiders van de Moderne Boektypografie in Nederland*,

Amsterdam: De Buitenkant, 1988, p. 62.

MISS BLANCHE
VIRGINIA
CIGARETTES
☐ YELLOW LABEL ☐

125   VH

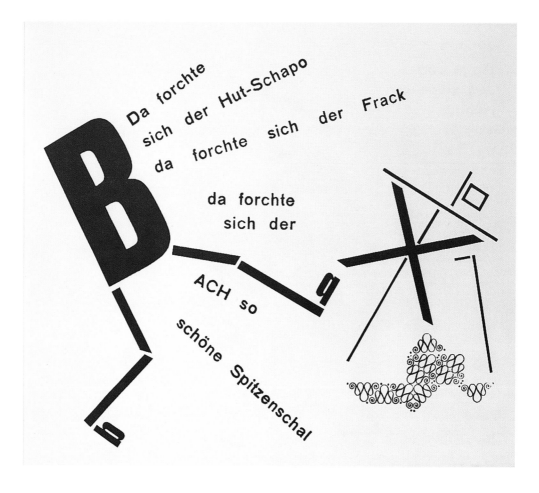

Above: Theo van Doesburg,
Kurt Schwitters, Käte Steinitz,
Die Scheuche (The Scarecrow), *Merz*
14/15, Hanover: Aposs Verlag, 1925.

Opposite: Theo van Doesburg, cover for
the booklet *Wat is Dada?* (What is Dada),
The Hague: De 8, 1923.

PRIJS 25 CENTS.

théo van doesburg

WAT

is

DADA?

? ? ? ? ? ? ?

Below and opposite: Kurt Schwitters and
Theo van Doesburg, cover and page from
Merz 1, Holland Dada, Hanover
Kurt Schwitters, 1923.

Inhalt: DADA IN HOLLAND. KOK: GEDICHT. BONSET: GEDICHT; AAN ANNA BLOEME.

PICABIA: ZEICHNUNG. HANNAH HÖCH: ZEICHNUNG; WEISSLACKIERTE TÜTE

MERZ

1

DA
DA DA
DA

HOLLAND

DADA

JANUAR 1923
HERAUSGEBER: KURT SCHWITTERS
HANNOVER · WALDHAUSENSTRASSE 5ᴵᴵ

DADA ISMUS IN HOLLAND

DADA

in Holland ist ein Novum. Nur ein Holländer, I. K. BON-
SET, ist Dadaist. (Er wohnt in Wien.) Und eine Holländerin,
PETRO VAN DOESBURG, ist Dadaistin. (Sie wohnt in
Weimar.) Ich kenne dann noch einen holländischen Pseudo-
dadaisten, er ist aber kein Dadaist. Holland aber,

HOLLAND IST DADA

Unser Erscheinen in Holland glich einem gewaltigen Sieges-
zug. Ganz Holland ist jetzt dada, weil es immer schon dada
war.

Unser Publikum fühlt, daß es DADA ist und glaubt, dada
kreischen, dada schreien, dada lispeln, dada singen, dada
heulen, dada schelten zu müssen. Kaum hat jemand von uns,
die wir in Holland Träger der dadaistischen Bewegung sind,
das Podium betreten, so erwachen im Publikum die ver-
schlafenen dadaistischen Instinkte, und es empfängt uns ein
dadaistisches Heulen und Zähneklappen. Aber wir sind die
dadaistische Hauskapelle, wir werden Ihnen eins blasen.

EERE
TENTOONSTELLING

C.TH.
COLENBRANDER

AARDEWERK
EN TAPIJTEN

STEDELIJK MUSEUM
AMSTERDAM 1923

31 OCT NOV 30

10.4 UUR ENTR: 0.25

CHAPTER

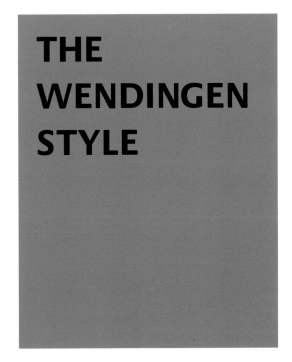

THE WENDINGEN STYLE

H. Th. Wijdeveld, poster for an exhibition of ceramics and carpets by the decorative artist T. A. C. Colenbrander, Stedelijk Museum, Amsterdam, 1923.

As World War I was drawing to a close, there was an increasing interest among designers in geometrically based letters. One such proponent was the Amsterdam architect Hendricus Theodorus Wijdeveld. In 1918, Wijdeveld founded the magazine *Wendingen*, a monthly publication produced for the Amsterdam society Architectura et Amicitia. Published in Dutch, German, and French editions, for fourteen years *Wendingen* addressed contemporary issues in the arts. *Wendingen*'s strict vertical and horizontal asymmetrical structure was eventually referred to as the Amsterdam School, the Linear School, the New School, Amsterdam Expressionism, and the *Wendingen* and Wijdeveld styles.

Born in The Hague in 1885, Wijdeveld died in February 1987, having become the oldest living artist in the Netherlands. Largely self-educated, his first training at the age of fourteen was working as an apprentice draftsman for Cuypers. However, his own work evolved in another direction, largely due to the influence and inspiration of two earlier Cuypers associates, the architects Lauweriks and De Bazel, who had left the firm in May 1895 to open their own studio. In addition to disagreements over design philosophy, Lauweriks and De Bazel were involved with the Theosophy movement, which was incompatible with the Catholicism of Cuypers. Both Lauweriks and De Bazel were members of Architectura et Amicitia and major players in the Nieuwe Kunst movement.

The interest of architects in typography is to some extent a result of similarities between the two disciplines. The architect builds with stone, wood, and steel, while the graphic designer uses typographic material and other visual elements. The architect establishes appropriate spaces for windows, doors, and other parts of buildings, just as the graphic designer determines the arrangement of letters, words, paragraphs, decorative elements, and images. In the Netherlands, it was not only Cuypers, De Bazel, Lauweriks, and Berlage who were involved with both architecture and typography but later Van Doesburg and Piet Zwart as well. Also, it is noteworthy that one of the finest French Art Nouveau book designs was *Histoire des quatre fils Aymon*, designed by the Swiss-born architect Eugène Grasset in 1883.

Lauweriks moved to Germany in 1904 where he published the magazine *Ring* in Düsseldorf and Hagen from 1908 to 1909. After returning to the Netherlands in 1916, he and Wijdeveld often met at Architectura et Amicitia. Founded in 1855, Architectura et Amicitia played an important cultural role in Dutch art and architecture. Members included architects, engineers, artists, artisans, technicians, and public servants, and its agenda included the organization of lectures and exhibitions, establishing pricing standards, and publishing pamphlets and magazines. Besides *Wendingen*, the group's other major publication was the magazine *Architectura*, which first appeared in 1893. A prelude to *Wendingen*, the 'Driebond' (union of three) issue of *Architectura* was published on October 6, 1917, its theme being to encourage an affiliation between industry, business, and art. Wijdeveld designed the cover, which showed the symbolist influence of Nieuwe Kunst and an awareness of a need to integrate text and decorative elements.

Wendingen was often the subject of discussion at Architectura et Amicitia in 1916 and 1917, and concrete proposals for its publication were presented at a meeting on October 24, 1917. Wijdeveld attended the meeting armed with an actual design model for the magazine. Most members agreed on a need for a magazine where contemporary Dutch architecture and other art forms could be reproduced and discussed. Even though Wijdeveld was the most enthusiastic advocate, Lauweriks, at that time an editor for *Architectura*, actively participated in the planning as well. It was agreed that contributions could also come from other organizations and that the magazine should embrace all of the arts. Lauweriks recommended that the visual aspects should be stressed more than the text, that only the best possible printing quality be used, and that the decorative arts be given a prominent place along with other art forms. Wijdeveld attempted to get Lauweriks more involved with the actual publishing and editing process of *Wendingen*, but Lauweriks declined, feeling that he had already satisfied most of his publishing ambitions. His imprint, though, is evident throughout, and he and Wijdeveld had many discussions about suitable design ideas. Although it was revived in 1921, *Architectura* ceased publication in December 1917. This event was followed by the publication of the first issue of *Wendingen* in January 1918, and from then until the end of 1932, 116 issues would be produced. Wijdeveld served as *Wendingen*'s designer and editor-secretary until his resignation over procedural issues at the end of 1925. He was so closely involved in the publication's production that the official address of the magazine was his own residence.

The name *Wendingen* was Wijdeveld's suggestion. Its arcane origin was inspired by a hike in Northern Italy a few years earlier when Wijdeveld encountered a road worker who casually turned a stone slab on its head while referring to it as 'the whole world.' Later, while reading Nietzsche's *Umwälzung aller Werte* (Upheaval of All Values), Wijdeveld remembered his encounter with the road worker and called Nietzsche a 'repairer of the roads of life.' He then translated 'Umwälzung' as 'Omwentelen' (rotating), which ultimately became *Wendingen* (translated as turnings, changes in direction, or upheavals). Wijdeveld saw *Umwälzung aller Werte* as symbolizing the critical attitude in Europe both during and after the First World War as well as the intellectual and artistic disruption that would follow in its wake. It was his dream that artists and architects would find new and mutual objectives though *Wendingen*.

In the initial publication, Wijdeveld clearly stipulated that *Wendingen* would also address subjects other than architecture. The first issues were to cover a combination of art topics, but soon each number would be devoted to a particular theme. Of the latter, thirty-one were given over to Dutch architecture, and from 1918 to 1925 the Amsterdam School of architecture received the most attention. Then, after 1927, only sixteen issues would be devoted to architecture. This was largely the result of competition from *Bouwkundig Weekblad Architectura*, a new magazine on architecture created through a merger of *Architectura* and *Bouwkundig Weekblad*, the journal of the Dutch Association of Architects.

Among other subjects, ten *Wendingen* issues are devoted to sculpture, eight to theater and dance, three to poster design, three to stained glass, three to glass and ceramics, six to the graphic arts, five to interiors and one to statistical design. There were also issues devoted to the paintings of Toorop, Thorn Prikker, Lyonel Feininger, Pijke Koch, and Carel Willink, as well as Russian icons and Italian Renaissance painting. Although Austrian art and German architecture were included, German Expressionism and French Cubism were not, and, with a few exceptions, *Wendingen* remained fundamentally a Dutch publication.

When the applied arts were included, the subjects focused on architectural elements such as furniture design and stained glass. Most of the issues that were devoted to sculpture stressed its relation to architecture, and only in later issues was sculpture viewed as an independent art form. There were also issues, however, which centered on the glass and ceramic design of Lebeau and the industrial design of W. H. Gispen who later became known for his metal furniture and lighting fixture designs.

The double square shape of the *Wendingen* page spreads was adopted from the Japanese tatami mat proportions, and letters were frequently set vertically like Chinese characters. Although *Wendingen's* format was 33 x 33 centimeters, compared to the 30 x 23 size of *Ring*, the influence of *Ring* is at once apparent. Many of the sources for *Wendingen* can be seen in this publication, such as the Japanese method of binding where pages are printed on one side, folded, left uncut at the edges and sewn in the block book style with raffia. Also, as with *Ring*, there was a place in *Wendingen* designated for advertisements. Although the advertisements had to conform to an established grid, advertisers could use their own designs, unlike *Ring*, where advertisements had to follow Lauwerik's rigid specifications. *Ring* and *Wendingen* had other similarities including an exacting systematic approach, the use of geometrical forms, and thick vertical rules on the outside margins. The same sans serif Grotesque typeface is used, and at first Wijdeveld even employed triangular ornaments as decorative elements, in sizes close to those used by Lauweriks in *Ring*. However, *Wendingen's* layout was far less confined to one fixed system, and ornaments were used with greater freedom, while *Ring's* typography was never changed and followed an inflexible grid throughout.

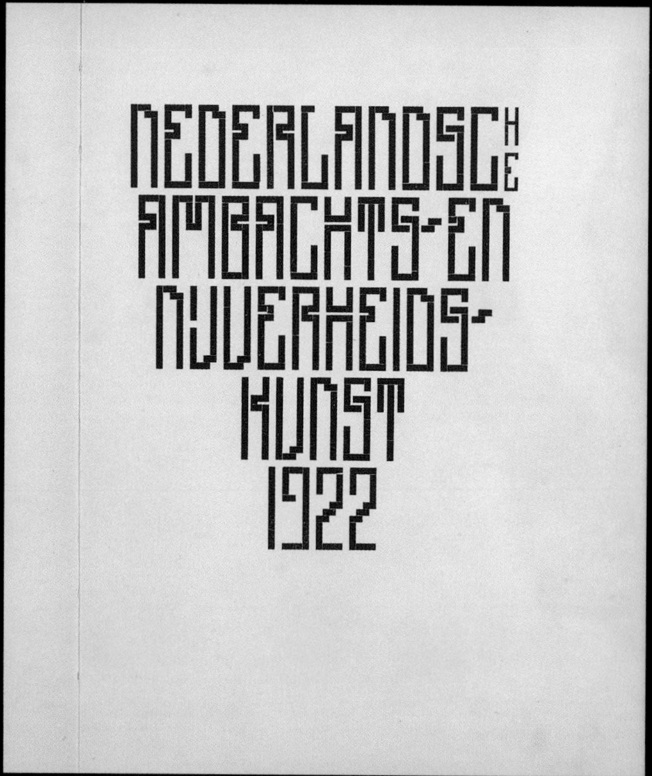

NEDERLANDSCHE
AMBACHTS-EN
NIJVERHEIDS-
KUNST
1922

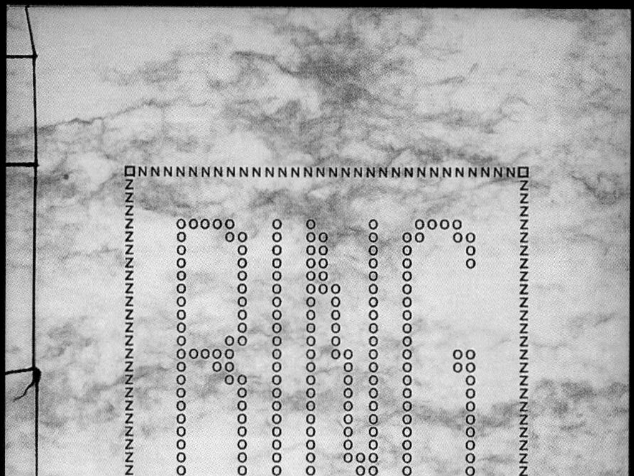

RING

ZEITSCHRIFT FUER KUENSTLERISCHE KULTUR

O   ERSCHEINT ALLE 2 MONATE   O

IM RING-VERLAG VON ERNST PIEPER DUESSELDORF

ZWEITES HEFT   · C · B ·   DEZEMBER 1908

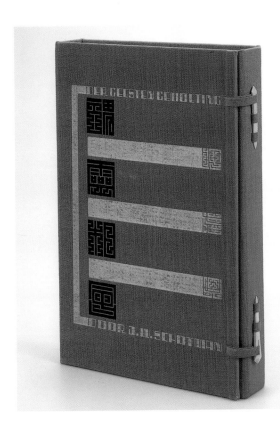

Opposite, above: J. L. M. Lauweriks, title
page for the *Dutch Crafts and Industrial
Art Annual*. Rotterdam, W. L. & J. Brusse,
1922. The architect Lauweriks
constructed letters from lines, a practice
that astounded traditional typographers.

Opposite, below: J. L. M. Lauweriks.
Cover for the bi-monthly magazine
Ring – Zeitschrift für künstlerische Kultur,
Düsseldorf: Ernst Pieper, 1908–9.

Above and right: H. Th. Wijdeveld,
cover and title page for *Der Geesten
Gemoeting, Vier morgenlandsche
dromen in verzen met orginele Chinese
illustraties van Moh Shi Chen* (The
Meeting of Souls, four Eastern dreams in
verse with original illustrations by Moh
Shi Chen) by J. W. Schotman, Amsterdam:
Van Holkema and Warendorf, 1927.

pages 108–109: El Lissitsky, cover of
Wendingen IV, no. 11, 1921.

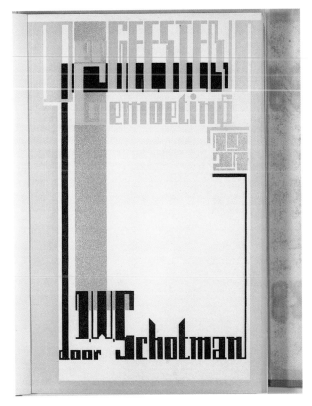

The use of a sans serif text typeface was in accordance with the then current tendency toward clarity, and it worked better with the constructed letters and ornaments. A sans serif, however, was considered by most typographers at that time to be unacceptable as a text type, mostly because it was thought that serifs were needed to visually join the letters. To use a sans serif typeface in an intellectual publication such as *Wendingen* was a revolutionary undertaking. The first commercial sans serif appeared as early as 1816 when William Caslon IV quietly introduced Two-line English Egyptian, essentially a slab-serif face with the serifs removed, yet until the publication of *Ring*, sans serif types were mainly limited to advertising.

Wendingen stressed decoration and eclecticism in its pages, while *De Stijl* moved in a far more progressive direction. *Wendingen* was also different from *De Stijl* in that its typography was indirectly related to its contents. In the early fall of 1917, Wijdeveld traveled to Leiden in an attempt to persuade Van Doesburg to become involved with *Wendingen*, then in its initial production stages. Van Doesburg declined by letter the very next day, and shortly afterwards the first issue of *De Stijl* appeared, preempting *Wendingen* by three months. With Van Doesburg's proclivity for self promotion, it is highly likely that he pushed *De Stijl's* publication date forward to have it appear before a possible rival.

Because of its profuse use of ornaments, *Wendingen* has often been called a consequence of Nieuwe Kunst. It is true that both styles displayed a lavish approach, and both stressed an all-inclusive control of form and a shared enchantment with the art of the Dutch East Indies. Also, by using solid, heavy borders built from right angles, Wijdeveld was consistent with one of the Art Nouveau approaches in the Netherlands. His intricate compositions were built exclusively from typographic elements, giving his designs a rigid and austere character. *Wendingen's* title pages, especially in the early issues, typographically reflected the brick architecture of the Amsterdam School. Not only did Wijdeveld create his ornaments out of printer's lines and bars, he used these elements to construct actual letters as a mason would use concrete blocks. The creation of type from these forms was often achieved at the expense of legibility. The Dutch type designer Gerard Unger derisively called the Amsterdam School 'a ponderous and earthy derivation of Art Nouveau and Art Deco that found expression chiefly in rich and varied brick architecture.'[1]

Besides Wijdeveld, others who designed covers for *Wendingen* included Lauweriks, Roland Holst, E. J. Kuipers, Lion Cachet, J. Sluijters, De Bazel, Toorop, M. De Klerk, Van Konijnenburg, Lebeau, Anton Kurvers, Jongert, Lissitzky, W. H. Gispen, Hahn, and Huszár. Lissitsky's 1921 design for the first Frank Lloyd Wright issue is by far one of the best known of the *Wendingen* series. It is also one of the most uncharacteristic of all the covers and the only time that Constructivism makes an appearance in *Wendingen*.

The Wright issues of *Wendingen* published at the end of 1925 and the beginning of 1926 made up a seven-part series extending from the third through ninth issues of the seventh edition. This came at a time when Wijdeveld was distancing himself from *Wendingen*, and he was determined to have the Wright issues be his crowning *Wendingen* achievement. Here he combined all his typographic skills, bringing *Wendingen* to its highest level both in design and content. Wright himself designed the title page for the first of the seven issues.

Huszár's 1929 *Wendingen* cover used a geometric rendering of the magazine's title with letters alternately aligned in a rectangular block on the top section of the page. Below, a square text block is an abstract composition made from the *Wendingen* letters set both vertically and horizontally, and the composition is repeated as rectangular shapes on the back. Clearly, Huszár's cover is intended to recall the content of this issue, which was devoted to the political murals of the Mexican painter Diego Rivera. The complimentary colors green and red are those of the Mexican national flag, and the patterns generated by the geometric letters suggest forms in Aztec architecture. This is also *Wendingen*'s only reference to De Stijl, and even though Huszár had cut his ties with De Stijl in 1921, the lettering resembles Van Doesburg's alphabet.

The *Wendingen* typography became less popular by the late 1920s, partially due to Wijdeveld's departure from the editorial board at the end of 1925, largely over cost and editorial concerns. Wijdeveld's dissociation from *Wendingen* diluted the strength of the magazine, and the repetitious typography that began in 1927 soon took on a tedious appearance. Concurrently, the Amsterdam School of archictecture had lost steam as the more traditional Delft School began to predominate. Another sign of a fall in interest in the magazine was a decline in advertising, and in the last issues there are no extra pages designated for this purpose; the few advertisements that do appear are relegated to the inside of the front and back covers. *Wendingen* was quietly laid to rest with number 116 in 1931, and the 'Omega' sign on the back indicated that it would be the last issue.

Wijdeveld's typography did not always reflect the *Wendingen* style, and his posters for the Stads Schouwburg (Municipal Theater) in Amsterdam are quite different in concept. Dominated by single harsh theatrical woodcut images, they are all completely symmetrical, with an exclusive use of capital sans serif letters, often in a combination of styles.

Although limited in number, Wijdeveld also designed books, bookplates, diplomas, alphabets, stationery, and other printed material. His later posters break away to some extent from the uniformity of the *Wendingen* layouts. In the 1929 poster for an International Exhibition on Economics and History, Wijdeveld's architecture background is evident, and the asymmetrical design resembles a solid building using the brick construction methods of the Amsterdam School. Unusual for Wijdeveld, his 1931 poster for the Frank Lloyd Wright Stedelijk Museum Exhibition has a symmetrical structure.

The finest example of Wijdeveld's book typography is J. W. Schotman's *Der Geesten Gemoeting*, a book on the subject of Japanese fairytales and Chinese legends. On the binding, Wijdeveld skillfully transforms Chinese characters into his own style. *Der Geesten Gemoeting* was printed in five separate sections, each with a different title page, and, as with *Wendingen*, Wijdeveld used the traditional Japanese sewn binding.

Wijdeveld's singular style produced both enthusiastic disciples and equally fervent critics. Traditional typographers such as De Roos and Jan van Krimpen considered *Wendingen* to be outright sacrilege and nothing less than a threatening adversary spreading a form of typographic plague. Referring to *Wendingen*, De Roos wrote in 1924, 'Really good typography cannot be achieved through inferior composition surrounded by yet another entanglement of lines, in the same way that a robe doesn't change a monkey into a church orator.' Others, though, saw it as a fresh start and Wijdeveld inspired some serious followers such as the Amsterdam designer Fré Cohen and the lithographer and decorative painter Kurvers. However, many imitators only managed to grasp its superficial side.

In *150 Years of Book Typography in The Netherlands*, G. W. Ovink wrote: 'While the people still lack some of the bare necessities of life, here comes Wijdeveld (Frank Lloyd Wright's

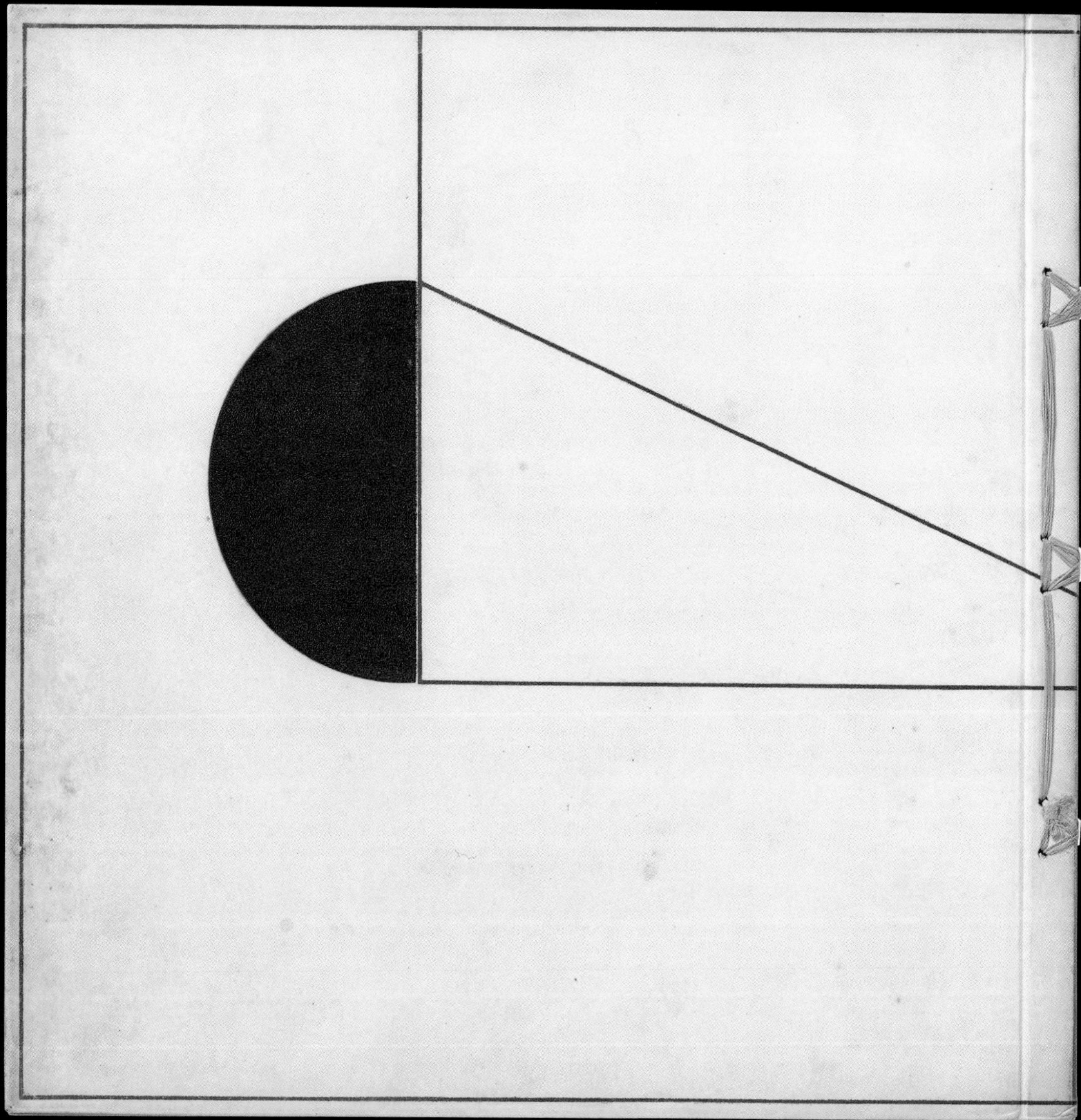

WENDINGEN

paladin in The Netherlands), who in his magazine *Wendingen* brought decoration ad absurdum, making the artistically minded élite lose their heads over his expensive, spectacular typographic constructions. This illegible rigid typography brought the entire art of printing into disrepute with average, sensible people....We are all now aware that Wijdeveld's typography and the whole Linear School (excessive use of brass rules) eventually expired of its own weaknesses.'[2] G. H. Pannekoek, Jr., in *De Herleving van de Nederlandsche Boekdrukkunst Sedert 1910* (The Revival of the Art of Dutch Printing from 1910) was also thinking of Wijdeveld when he wrote in 1925 that 'today people all too often influenced by architects, think that even though it is unreadable a letter must be constructed from pieces of lead.'[3]

The Constructivists were no less unkind, and Zwart belittled what he called Wijdeveld's extreme ornamental solutions. As evident in his Vickers House designs during the early 1920's and his early advertisements for the Nederlandsche Kabelfabriek, Zwart had ironically learned much from Wijdeveld. At the end of 1928, Paul Schuitema delivered his own assault in an article entitled 'advertising' for the progressive Amsterdam magazine *i-10*. Describing the role of a modern designer, he wrote, 'Yesterday was "artistic, decorative, symbolic, fantastic, antisocial, lyrical, passive, romantic, aesthetic, theoretical, craftsmanship-like," in other words "art." "Today" means: "real, direct, photographic, succinct, competitive, argumentative, active, actual, appropriate, practical, technical", in other words "reality."'[4] Both approaches were illustrated by designs, and even though Wijdeveld had also influenced Schuitema in the beginning, he used a title page from *Wendingen* to represent the past.

Wijdeveld's graphic design style, which both intrigued and shocked many of his contemporaries, was actually a combination of many approaches which had been earlier explored. Japanese printing and binding techniques had been used in Nieuwe Kunst books such as Van Hoytema's *Uilen-geluk* (The Happy Owls) in 1895 and *La Jeunesse Inaltérable et La Vie Eternelle* designed by Dijsselhof in 1897. The square format was used for *Ver Sacrum*, the official publication of the Vienna Secession, copies of which Wijdeveld had in his collection. As mentioned earlier, there are letter constructions in Lauweriks' designs which resemble those in *Wendingen*. In spite of both valid and unfounded criticisms, however, in the long run, *Wendingen* was one of the most graphically advanced magazines of its era. It differed from many other avant-garde publications such as *De Stijl* in that it conveyed the message rather than being a message itself. In addition, through its architectural structure and innovative typography, *Wendingen* constituted another valuable bridge between the nineteenth century and modern graphic design. It achieved its goals admirably within its inherent limits but went into decline once its design options were depleted. Unlike movements such as Constructivism, *Wendingen* typography provided little opportunity for further expansion once its objectives had been achieved. In spite of Wijdeveld's obvious enthusiasm for typography, he always found it a secondary discipline when compared to architecture. Although *Wendingen* had an impact on Dutch architecture, graphic design, and the applied arts, it did not leave an enduring impression. Wijdeveld was *Wendingen's* driving force, and the publication's highly personal style did not survive without its founder's active participation.

Wendingen was conceived as a post-war avant-garde publication, but its use of costly paper and tied string bindings was closer to the Arts and Crafts movement of the nineteenth century. It is significant that Wijdeveld went to England for three years beginning in 1905 where he met Eric Gill and became acquainted with the work of William Morris. Although

Wendingen was in many ways a progressive venture, its decorative approach was at odds with the international movement toward functionalism, and although the publication's covers exhibited a wide range of styles, its page layouts followed an established format. Although linked to the modern era, *Wendingen* had its foundations in the fin-de-siècle European culture of the nineteenth century.

Although never considered a monumental force in her own right, Fré Cohen was highly influenced by the *Wendingen* style and played an important part in the development of Dutch graphic design. She was born in 1903, the oldest of three children in a Jewish diamond-cutter's family in Amsterdam. After completing her secondary education she initially performed secretarial work in an office. However, after her artistic talents were noticed, she began producing advertisements for the same company. She joined the AJC (Workers' Youth Center), the youth organization of the S.D.A.P. (Social Democratic Workers' Party) and designed printed material for them as well as for other socialist organizations. Also, she made illustrations for the socialist book-dealer and publisher N. V. Ontwikkeling, which would later become the Arbeiderspers (Workers' Press). It was soon clear, though, that she was handicapped due to her lack of technical production skills. She then began to take night classes at the Amsterdamse Grafische School where the *Wendingen* style was very much in vogue. Cohen immediately fell under Wijdeveld's sway, and he would remain the strongest outside influence on her work for the rest of her career.

In 1927, Cohen received a scholarship for the Instituut voor Kunstnijverheidonderwijs (School for Applied Art) in Amsterdam, now the Gerrit Rietveld Academie. Upon completion of the two-and-a-half-year course, she was the first student to be awarded a prize for commendable achievement. Cohen's first significant typographic designs were AJC publications, mainly in the *Wendingen* manner using heavy lines, bold typefaces, and ornaments constructed from typographic material. She was also doing design work for the city of Amsterdam before completing school, and had produced her first printed piece for the municipal printing office in 1925. On September 1, 1929 she was hired by them full time, and worked there until 1932. At that time she was laid off due to budget reductions caused by the deteriorating economic climate. She did, however, continue working for them as a freelance designer until the Nazi occupation in World War II.

Cohen also worked for other municipal sectors such as the energy company, the housing service, the municipal theater, clean city campaigns, summer festivals, the education department, and the University of Amsterdam, as well as the Amsterdam publisher Querido. Her designs included posters, brochures, theater programs, books, diplomas, annual reports, logos, calendars, checkbooks, municipal reports, bookplates, and exhibits.

Although Cohen experimented with photomontage in the 1930s after encountering the work of Schuitema and Zwart, she was little affected by the trend toward functional typography taking place around her. She deftly adapted the *Wendingen* approach to government and socialist publications and never wavered as an adherent of Wijdeveld's design philosophy. Her suicide after being arrested by the Nazis in 1943 brought the *Wendingen* style to a final conclusion.

Above: H. Th. Wijdeveld, *International Economics and History Exhibition*, poster, 1929.

Opposite: Fré Cohen, cover of *La suppression des taudis et des quartiers insalubres à Amsterdam* (The elimination of slums and unhealthy districts of Amsterdam), Amsterdam Municipal Housing Service, 1930.

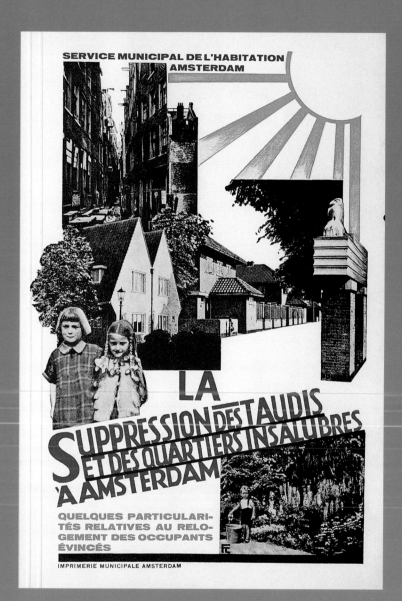

Chapter 3 Notes

1 Gerard Unger and Marjan Unger, *Hollands landschap met letters*, Utrecht:

Van Boekhoven-Bosch BV grafische industrie, 1989, p. 34.

2 G. W. Ovink, '100 Years of Book Typography in the Netherlands,' in *Book

Typography, 1815–1965 in Europe and The United States of America*, ed. Kenneth

Day, Chicago: University of Chicago Press, 1965, p. 269.

3 H. Pannekoek, Jr., *De Herleving van de Nederlandsche Boekdrukkunst Sedert

1910*, Maastricht: Boosten & Stols, 1925, p. 17.

4 Paul Schuitema, 'Reclame,' in *i10*, no. 16, vol. I, Amsterdam, November 1928.

R. N. Roland Holst, *Wendingen*, vol. 4,
nos. 4/5, Santpoort: C. A. Mees, 1921.

Opposite: R. N. Roland Holst, *Wendingen*, vol. 5, nos. 8/9, Santpoort: C. A. Mees, 1923.

Below, top: B. Essers, *Wendingen*, vol. 5, no. 10, Santpoort: C. A. Mees, 1923.

Below, bottom: S. Jessurum de Mesquita, *Wendingen*, vol. 5, nos. 11/12, Santpoort: C. A. Mees, 1923.

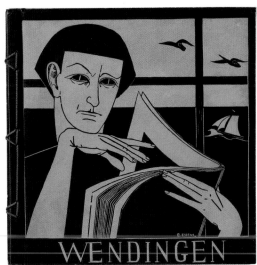

Below: W. M. Dudok, *Wendingen*, vol. 6, no. 8, Santpoort: C. A. Mees, 1924

Bottom: Anton Kurves, *Wendi*ngen, vol. 5, nos. 5/7, Santpoort: C. A. Mees, 1923

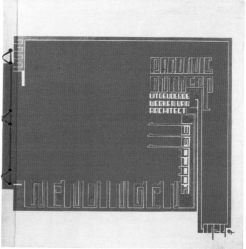

Below: H. Th. Wijdeveld, cover for *Wendingen*, vol. 7, no. 5, Santpoort: C. A. Mees, 1925. This was one of seven issues devoted to the work of Frank Lloyd Wright.

Bottom: Vilmos Huszár, cover for *Wendingen*, vol. 10, no. 3, Santpoort: C. A. Mees, 1929. This issue was devoted to the murals of the social realist Mexican artist Diego Rivera.

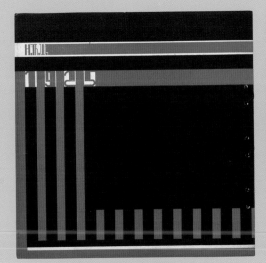
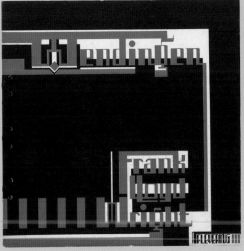

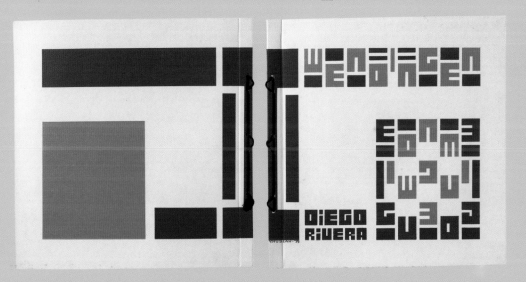

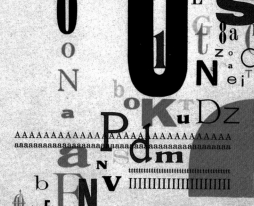

een kleine keuze uit onze lettercollectie

Piet Zwart, *Drukkerij Trio*
(Trio Printers), catalog page, 1931.

DUTCH CONSTRUC-TIVISM

During his highly prolific career, Piet Zwart embraced many fields of the visual arts, frequently at the same time. These encompassed graphic design, architecture, architectural criticism, furniture design, industrial design, painting, photography, and graphic design education. His involvement with avant-garde groups in other European countries and personalities such as Schwitters, Berlage, Schuitema, Van Doesburg, Huszár, Rietveld, Wils, Gerard Kiljan, and Lissitsky all helped to form his own philosophy and graphic design vision. The Bauhaus, De Stijl, Constructivism, Nieuwe Bouwen (New Construction), and Dada all played a role in Zwart's development.

Between 1902 and 1907 Zwart attended the Rijksschool voor Kunstnijverheid (National School for Applied Arts) situated at that time in the Rijksmuseum in Amsterdam. The student idols were then Berlage, Lion Cachet, and others in the Dutch progressive mainstream of architecture. There Zwart concentrated on architecture and drawing while also studying crafts such as copper embossing, weaving, batik, and woodworking. After graduating and completing the mandatory military service, Zwart moved to Leeuwarden in 1908 where he taught drawing and art history at the Industrie en Huishoudschool (Industry and Household School) for girls. In 1913 he moved to Voorburg to study architecture at the Technische Hoogschool (Institute of Technology) in nearby Delft. When the First World War began a year later, he was again called to serve in the army.

Time permitting, Zwart worked until 1918 mainly as a furniture and interior designer inspired by Wijdeveld and the Amsterdam School. It was then that he met Huszár and Wils, the latter of whom had studied under Berlage and was then working as an independent architect. Although Wils and Huszár had been among the founders of De Stijl, Wils left in 1919, feeling increasingly alienated from what he saw as its fixation on theory, and Huszár had severed his ties by the end of 1922. Zwart, Huszár, and Wils often got together at the Haagse Kunstkring (The Hague Art Circle) for exhibitions and lectures on contemporary art and music. This early connection with Huszár and Wils inspired a substantial change in Zwart's approach, but he never became part of De Stijl and became offended when anyone even dared to insinuate that he had anything at all to do with it. Zwart and the egotistical Van Doesburg both maintained strong opinions, often opposing, and they never shared any mutual affection: at times they engaged in acrimonious verbal altercations both privately and publicly. Zwart was indeed attracted to many of De Stijl's features such as its emphasis on purity, clarity, and use of primary colors. However, for him De Stijl's base was still insufficiently committed to modern technology, and, like Gropius and Wils, he opposed what he considered to be Van Doesburg's intractable ideology.

From 1919 until 1921 Zwart worked for Wils as a draftsman, and during this time they had an ongoing dialogue on subjects such Berlage, De Stijl, Wijdeveld, and Wright. Since Zwart's artistic educational background had been a product of both the Arts and Crafts movement and Nieuwe Kunst, he now found himself in another world entirely. However, his first work in typography, such as a 1921 bookplate design for E.G. de Roos, was still very much in De Stijl's shadow.

While still a student, Zwart was attracted by socialist idealism, and the writings of Karl Marx and Friedrich Hegel fueled his ideas regarding the artist's obligation to society. Zwart, as many in his generation, foresaw a social revolution as a result of the Russian Revolution and World War I. By discarding the past, they wanted to help bring about a fresh and improved world. Like those associated with De Stijl, they saw individualism, craft, and ornament as representing an old and tarnished society. For them, the future would be tied to technology, abstraction, Functionalism, and a new social order where art and daily life would be united. Zwart wrote in 1919:

Our time has become characterized by an enthusiastic desire for change, born out of a growing discontent over social conditions, determined and guided by new means of production, new spiritual insights, and new ideals.[1]

In 1921 Zwart began working for Berlage as a draftsman, and although Zwart was able to develop his individual path, it was Berlage's operation. Zwart later wrote:

At that time the relationship of architect to co-worker was completely different from today. Assistants are now usually mentioned, at least if they are of any importance. In those days not; you were the humble employee, the architect was your employer, and the relationship was quite fixed.[2]

His first design for Berlage was a pressed glass breakfast service for Hélène Kröller-Müller, the benefactress of the Kröller-Müller Museum at Otterlo. Other assignments included working on Berlage's design for the Gemeente Museum and the interior for the Christian Science Church, both in The Hague. The latter designs involved lecterns, the church organ, lighting, stained glass windows, and signage. In addition, he designed outdoor public furniture, signs, and street lamps for the city of The Hague.

In 1921, Zwart produced his first typographic work for the Dutch representative of the British importing firm, Vickers House. His use of horizontal and vertical bars recalls some of his earlier attempts at *Wendingen*-based lettering with architectural implications.

The year 1923 was pivotal for Zwart, for it was then that Berlage provided the contact with his son-in-law, then a member of the board of directors of the Nederlandsche Kabel Fabriek (Dutch Cable Factory). This initiated an unprecedented client–designer relationship that would continue uninterrupted for ten years. During this time, Zwart produced an estimated 275 advertisements for the publications *Tijdschrift voor Electrotechniek* (Magazine for Electrotechnology) and *Sterkstroom* (Strong Current). These advertisements would represent Zwart's most important contribution to Dutch typography and become one of the most innovative, bold, and challenging works by the Dutch graphic design avant-garde.

Zwart was self-educated in graphic design, and after being given the Nederlandsche Kabel Fabriek assignment he became acutely aware of his deficiencies in printing technology:

The first design that I made for the NKF was hand-drawn. I was still not finished with it when the publication had already been produced. At that time I realized this was not the best way to work, and then I plunged headfirst into typography. The good thing about all of this was that I actually learned it from an assistant in the small printing company where the monthly magazine on electrotechnology was being produced.... After going through the bitter experience of that piece being too late, I made more sketches and then played typographic games with the assistant in the afternoon hours, how we could make this and that. Actually, that's how I came to understand the typographic profession; I didn't know the terms, I didn't know the methods, I didn't even know the difference between capitals and lower-case letters.[3]

In the early stages, Zwart would first make simple sketches and then, after ordering the type, would proceed to consolidate the original concept. The earliest advertisements are still somewhat in the Dada manner, using as many as five different typefaces with a large bold letter as the dominant component. Later the advertisements become lighter and more simplified, with more white space, fewer typefaces, and an increased use of diagonals. In 1929, the NKF logo was changed from upper-case to lower-case letters.

By 1924 Lissitzky's influence was apparent, and some of the telephone cable advertisements in that year recalled pages from *El Lissitsky suprematisch worden van twee kwadraten in 6 konstrukties*. The NKF designs can be roughly placed in four categories: the magazine advertisements (1923–33); *Het Normalieënboekje* (The Normalization Booklet, a house-style manual) (1924–25); the 64-page catalog published in Dutch and English (1928–29); and the Delft Kabels information booklet (1933). With *Het Normalieënboekje* color was added as an additional graphic device.

Serving as his own copywriter, Zwart's use of language was both inventive and forceful, and with basic typographic elements, he visually interpreted the message. 'Alliterations, ambiguities, similes, allusions, metaphors, hyperbole, reiterations, inferences, and contrasts of direction, positioning, axis, size, shape, and weight were all used to heighten the meaning and activate the page with a new and provocative energy. Anything

VEREENIGING:EXPERIMENTEELTOONEEL

SECRETARIAAT:
ZEESTRAAT 82
TEL. 12292
DEN HAAG HOLLAND

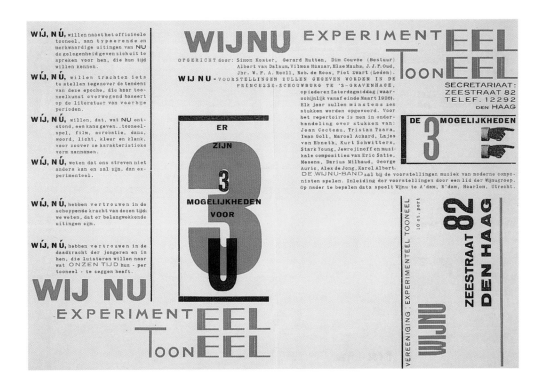

Piet Zwart, letter paper (**opposite**) and
publicity folder (**above**) for WijNu,
an experimental theater society,
The Hague, 1925.

extraneous was discarded, and only those parts that strengthened the meaning of the phrases were allowed.'[4]

Combining the terms 'typographer' and' architect,' Zwart called himself a 'typotekt,' a concocted label that represented his background in both fields. Le Corbusier referred to a house as a *machine à habiter* (machine for living in), and Zwart's typography could be called a 'machine for reading.'[5] Using the new typography, Zwart wanted to wipe the slate clean of what he found to be the tedious typography of the past.

Schwitters, Lissitsky, the French poets Mallarmé and Apollinaire, Paul van Ostaijen in Belgium, and the Italian Futurist Marinetti had already typographically interpreted words in their texts. Zwart, though, developed this into a practical typographic system.

Lissitsky introduced Zwart to the 'photogram' process in 1923. Here elements are placed on or above photographic paper, which is then exposed to light. Zwart included photograms in a *Normalieënboekje* in 1924, and although he rarely used photograms for the next several years, they would later appear in some of his designs for the PTT (the Dutch Post, Telephone, and Telegraph service).

In 1925, Zwart produced a number of abstract compositions printed by offset and designed while working on site with the printer. The use of color overprinting within these designs would often appeared in his later work as well. Although these compositions are in the same tone as the advertisements, they are not bound to any specific message. By now, Zwart's designs had become more concise, clear, and decisive, and the use of white space began to have an increasingly important role. Especially in the advertisements, contrast in the size and weight of letters reached new levels. Through what Zwart referred to as 'regulated dynamic tension,' he was able to attain a 'provocative asymmetrical elegance' while discarding previous rules.

Later Zwart would refer to his method as 'functional' typography, saying its purpose was 'to establish the typographic look of our time, free, insofar as it is possible, from tradition; to activate typographic forms; to define the shape of new typographic problems, methods, techniques and discard the guild mentality.'[6] The terms Constructivist and functional were similar; functional meant that it rejected previous artistic standards and was centered entirely on utilitarian motives; the Constructivist label implied a rational formation, a renunciation of subjectivity, and an embrace of technology.

By the middle of 1926 'phototypography' (the use of photographic images with typography) was part of Zwart's repertoire. He initially used photographs in the 1928–29 NKF catalog where he presented the product with total clarity through showing close-up cross-section images of electric cables. Here he achieved an energetic balance between text, image, and space, with double-page spreads functioning as single compositions. The 1933 Delft Kabels information booklet, the Brusse film monographs, and the postage stamp designs for the PTT represent his best achievements in photomontage.

In the beginning, Zwart used outside photographers, but the then-fashionable soft-focus approach was far removed from his own objectives. He quickly learned the photographic technique and by 1928 was producing his own photographs, distinguished by sharp, fine grain, close-up images. Zwart was designated secretary of the Dutch delegation to FIFO, the 1929 international photography exhibition in Stuttgart where Schuitema and Kiljan were also among the Dutch participants. When Zwart saw the work of photographers such as the American Edward Weston and the Russian Alexander Rodchenko, he considered contemporary Dutch photography to be inferior.[7]

Through its functionality, simplicity, and use of fundamental typographic elements, Zwart's typography satisfied most of Jan Tschichold's standards for 'Elementare Typographie,' published in *Typographische Mittelungen* in 1925. He preferred unpretentious sans serif typefaces usually set in lower case, considered unnecessary decoration to be taboo, and thought color should be used only for functional reasons.

There was a lively dialogue between European graphic designers on the purpose of the new typography and phototypography. In 1928, Schwitters founded a group of 'radical' designers, the Ring neue Werbegestalter. He asked Zwart to take part along with Tschichold, Willi Baumeister, Domela Nieuwenhuis, Robert Michel, Walter Dexel, George Trump, Vordemberge Gildewart, Max Burchartz, Hans Leistikow, Adolf Meyer, Richter, the Czech designer Karel Teige, and the Hungarian Laszlo Moholy-Nagy. Schuitema joined the group in 1929, but, unsurprisingly, Van Doesburg turned down the invitation. Using exhibitions, articles, and lectures, the Ring neue Werbegestalter's main goal was to advance modern advertising design, and both functionalism and Constructivism were compatible with its aims. After holding exhibitions in European cities including Berlin, Hamburg, Hanover, Basel, and Rotterdam, the Ring neue Werbegestalter was dissolved in the spring of 1931.

There were, though, many that did not view the new functional typography with enthusiasm, and in 1965 the Dutch design historian G. W. Ovink described the sentiments of its critics:

The evil did not bring on its own destruction. Van Doesburg was followed by hotheads such as Piet Zwart and Paul Schuitema, who, without a good typographical education, plunged in and made crude and noisy things for Kabelfabriek and Van Berkel.[8]

W. F. Gouwe, director of the Instituut voor Sier en Nijverheidskunst (Institute of Decorative and Applied Arts) and secretary of the VANK, also attacked functionalism in the 1929 VANK annual:

What principles guide the artist is a different question; it is not so very important these days if artists in their functionalism feel so detached from 'aesthetics,' craftsmanship and applied art.... The balancing of proportions, the controlling and dividing of space, the handling of the power of color, have always been and still are activities for which the power comes from another source other than the intellect. And this power, this ability, is so much needed and sought after by industry, in everyday life, and not least by advertising, because it is active where the other, the intellect, is powerless, and it completes the process of formation.[9]

Another onslaught came from the interior designer Paul Bromburg in response to a 1929 VANK lecture by Zwart:

Nowadays there is a new trend among artists to play the engineer. Everything has to look 'machine produced,' even if the machine has had nothing to do with the actual production. Everything has to look functional even in cases where there is no need for functionalism.[10]

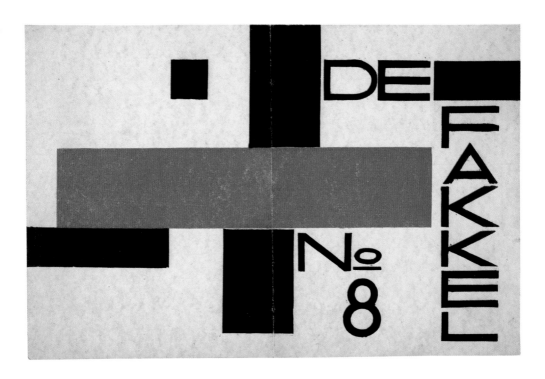

Above: Paul Schuitema, cover of
De Fakkel (The Torch), a student
magazine, 1926.

Opposite: Piet Zwart, four
advertisements for the Dutch Cable
Factory (NKF), 1926 (top row and
bottom left), 1930 (bottom right).

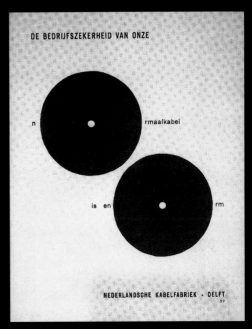

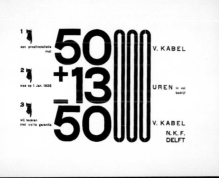

In Zwart's poster for the Internationale Tentoonstelling op Filmgebied (International Film Exhibition) in The Hague, the central element is the ITF logo which was also on the building facade while the exhibition was taking place. The red bars in the logo are repeated in a photogram made from a filmstrip, and in the lower center of the composition, part of a face showing two eyes is framed by a white square. Viewed as a unit, the white areas form an uppercase letter F.

The 1931 catalogue for The Hague printer Trio is one of Zwart's most successful designs. A page showing their type inventory is printed in black and the primary colors and contains over one hundred typefaces in a wide range of sizes. In spite of this typographic onslaught, Zwart brilliantly attained a feeling of unity and equilibrium with each element being allotted a role.

Zwart's most important works for the Rotterdam publisher W. L. & J. Brusse were the 1931 cinema monographs. This ten-part series combined many of his earlier experiments such as montage, multiple printing layers, and images distorted during the enlarging process. Another client from this period was the Rotterdam company Nijgh en Van Ditmar. In an advertising booklet for this firm, extreme contrasts of size and direction are employed in the design. Again, by serving as his own copywriter, Zwart was able to further experiment with his advertising concepts. His work for another important client, the PTT, will be addressed in Chapter Seven.

Design education was also one of Zwart's strong commitments, quite early he advocated giving more attention to teaching the skills of advertising, current reproduction methods, typography, photography, and film. In 1919, Zwart began teaching design and art history in the evening school at the Rotterdamse Academie van Beeldende Kunsten en Technische Wetenschappen (Rotterdam Academy of Fine Arts and Technical Sciences) where Dick Elffers was later one of his students. In 1931, Zwart introduced a plan for far-reaching changes in the curriculum, but this did not go over well with the board of directors, causing Zwart to be fired in 1933. In Zwart's opinion, design education in the Netherlands was still dedicated to training students for making useless ornamental objects, almost fourteen years after the beginning of progressive movements such as De Stijl and the Bauhaus. The main influence was still the *Wendingen* style, and only at the Rotterdam Academy of Fine Arts was there any inkling of anything else happening. The art academy in The Hague was not close to this stage, and in 1924 even the Applied Arts Department in the day school had been terminated. In the evening school the only subjects offered were lithography, metalwork, decorative painting, and furniture design.

In 1929, the Bauhaus invited Zwart to come as a guest lecturer, and, according to him, the overall tone was depressing and students were on the verge of leaving. Although he felt its greatest days had come to an end, he did enjoy meeting some of the important figures there such as Josef Albers.

Zwart felt that 'the greatest originality resulted from the tenacious search for restraint.... When students are given total license to create their own designs, the results are appalling. Rarely does one encounter an advertising exercise in which legibility has been given precedence. Triangles, squares and lines are arbitrarily used and simply to attract attention.... It is no small surprise that in all sectors of our discipline there is no advancement. The reason lies in the almost total dearth of proficient education.'[11]

At the end of 1933 Zwart became more involved with industrial and interior design, and after a twelve-year period of meteoric ascendancy, his career as a practicing graphic designer drew to a close. During this brief span, however, his impact on the graphic design field was nothing less than phenomenal.

Paul Schuitema, a native of the northern province of Groningen, studied drawing and painting at the Rotterdam Academy of Fine Arts from 1915 until 1920. Although he was awarded a Royal Grant for gifted young artists in 1923, he had already started to question the role of painters in the post-war society. As early as 1924 he ended up in the advertising and industrial design field, and in this year he met Zwart, a kindred spirit whose typographic knowledge had also been gained through practical experience.

Schuitema's earliest and most important clients were the P. Van Berkel Meat Company, the Van Berkel Patent Scale and Cutting Machine Factory, and the printer C. Chevalier, all in Rotterdam. In addition to designing Van Berkel's trademark, his work included booklets, brochures, advertisements, stationery, and exhibitions. Over a five-year period his designs for these companies raised mundane assignments to dynamic heights and had an unprecedented effect on the development of Dutch graphic design.

Schuitema's typography was initially unrefined and still under the sway of the Amsterdam School. He would soon felt, however, the influence of Russian Constructivism and the architectural group Opbouw (Construction) of which both Schuitema and Zwart were members. In 1920, Opbouw was started in Rotterdam by a group of functionalist architects who included Oud, Mart Stam, and the city planner Cornelis van Eesteren. Another group of Functionalist leaning architects founded the De Acht (the Eight), and in 1928 the two groups began to jointly publish the periodical titled *De Acht en Opbouw*. The first issue made it clear that *De Acht en Opbouw* would address 'the science of building instead of the art of building.' Opbouw members had already had contacts with Schwitters, Lissitsky, and the Bauhaus, and it was to a large extent through Opbouw that Schuitema became acquainted with the progressive graphic design of other European countries.

By 1927, the typography for Schuitema's Berkel designs had taken on a more functional and lucid approach largely through an increased contrast between light and bold letters and type sizes and through an inventive use of blank space within the page format. By a combination of vertical, horizontal, and diagonal positions of text, the reader was steered by strategically placed graphic signals. 'Through the free, asymmetrical, but rational grouping of words and the functional use of type, he created works of vibrant contrast, pushing designs to the very frontiers of instability.'[12] Schuitema used only sans serif or linear typefaces and restricted his palette to primary colors.

Like Zwart, Schuitema was affected by the ideas for a new society that arose in the radical social movements during the twenties. He was never active in any political party, but he was connected with leftist movements such as the Internationale Antimilitaristische Vereeniging (International Anti-Militarism Association) and the Genootschap Nederland Nieuw Rusland (Netherlands New Russia Society). His contribution to these organizations included covers and montages for the magazines *De Wapens Neder* (Down with Weapons), *Nieuw Rusland* (New Russia), and *Links Richten* (Aim Left). In August 1932, Schuitema joined the World Congress against War. His 1929 cover for the special number of *De Wapens Neder, 25 jaar Oorlog aan Oorlog* (Down with Weapons, 25 Years of War against War), prominently displayed the face of Ferdinand Domela Nieuwenhuis, a former Lutheran

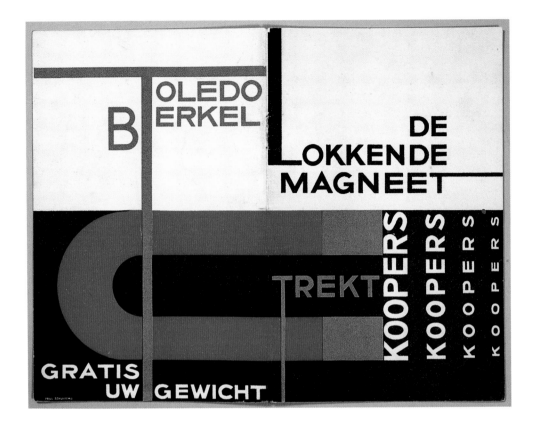

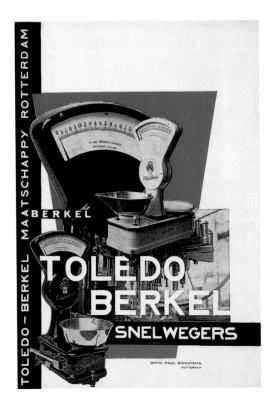

Above and left: Paul Schuitema, brochures for Toledo-Berkel weighing scales. Rotterdam, 1927.

Opposite: Sybold van Ravensteyn, poster for an exhibition by home crafts of mentally handicapped people, 1925.

GEEST

15·16·17 DEC

STEUNT DEN ARBEID ONDER DE MISDEELDEN VAN

VAN
10-6½
OUDE STADHUIS
8·10
UUR

BEZOEKT

DE

TENTOONSTELLING

VAN

REKKENS

25 CT
ENTR.

THEE
MET
STRIJKJE

HUISVLIJT

minister and fervent Dutch socialist who was the father of the painter and designer Domela Nieuwenhuis.

Schuitema later wrote about these years in a 1961 article for the Swiss publication *Neue Grafik*:

The 1914–18 war had shown us that everything, even the most beautiful expressions, were nonsense. Romance had gone under in mud and blood. Beauty, heroism, patriotism existed only for the sake of money and were dirty and untrue and full of false pathos. Art was the property of the rich. The socialist cry 'art for the people' was also seen as sentimental nonsense. It should not be the task and duty of society to grant commissions. The people should not wear secondhand clothing and become a new bourgeoisie.

He continued in the same *Neue Grafik* article:

Mondrian rang the death knell for painting, this creation on the easel, a product of super-individualists. The era of painting was over. Neither should one make socialist paintings, since in our opinion this type of art could not exist.[13]

Although Schuitema naturally accepted commercial advertising, he stressed strict guidelines for its ethical use, emphasizing artistic social accountability:

When producing printed material one must begin with the principle that the function of advertising is to sell. It should tell the truth and portray to the public the benefits of the products. We acknowledged industrial products as necessary. It was the duty of the artist to give them a clearer and more functional form. Through our work in the workplaces and factories we wanted to give the people better and more beautiful things. At that time we had already contributed to industrial design, even though the term had not yet been coined. We intended to give products a new functional form.[14]

Schuitema always felt that the typographer should visually imbue texts with more interpretative potential. He also believed that form must be derived from an objective assessment of the situation, or in his words, 'Order originates through making individual perceptions subordinate to the general issue.... The search for special forms for the sake of form is sheer nonsense.'[15] Schuitema saw the traditional arts and crafts as part of the past and modern industrial methods necessary to bring about new society.

In the Netherlands, Schuitema pre-empted Zwart by using photography as an essential design component. Through combining photographs and type, his goal was to convey information clearly, legibly, and instantly. This differed thoroughly from normal advertising of the time, which was distinguished by artifice, ornament, and trite illustrations. Beginning in 1926, photography was increasingly prevalent; and any drawn illustrations were abstracted and simplified. 'No golden section, no drawing, since that would be like painting. When we did draw, it would be abstract or aiming at an objective, greatly simplified, direct and without ulterior, romantic motives.'[16]

For Schuitema, photography was essential in advertising. Like Zwart, in the beginning he used an outsider for his images, in his case the Rotterdam photographer Jan Kamman. However, he soon became dissatisfied with using someone else's approach and in 1927 began making his own images. In his photographs he looked for the intrinsic aspects of objects and provided emphasis through color, type, and graphic elements. He felt that few words were needed if the product was well presented.

The diffusion of information was a primary goal for Schuitema, and photography was ideally suited for this purpose. Under the pseudonym S. Palsma in order to not offend his clients, he wrote an piece for the magazine *Links Richten* titled 'The Photograph as a Weapon in the Class Struggle.' Here he advocated the possibilities of using photography as a political weapon: 'No romanticism, no art, but vividly suggestive propaganda; tactically geared to the class struggle, technically attuned to the trade.... The photograph reports, gives the situation as it is, does not lie, is not dependent upon a special explanation, can never be disputed.'[17]

Schuitema thought that even though some people might find his designs to be austere and unfeeling, they were appreciated by simple folk such as factory workers and farmers. 'They had not been raised in an artistic cultural environment. They had never been bothered with these matters. They understood and grasped our work, not because they were smarter, but because their whole life was occupied with work, with the goal of saving their bare lives and supporting their families.' As Dick Dooijes observed, this resolute 'anti-romantic' hero had a brief romantic lapse, one with Marxist overtones.[18]

Although Schuitema did indeed at times display his photographs as artistic images, he and the designer and educator Gerard Kiljan presented their thoughts on the strict utilitarian role of photography in a 1933 article titled 'The Photograph as a Visual Element in Advertising.':

Through the influence of pacesetters in the design field and through the phenomenon of technological development and the tremendous increase in the influence of photographic illustration in dailies and weeklies, the photograph and also montage have materialized in advertising design.... We maintain from the beginning, however, that we regard the photograph merely as a formal or design element in the formal organization of an advertising assignment.[19]

For Schuitema, photographs were not only intended to augment the text but were treated as expressive elements and active participants in the design process. Photomontage, freed from the traditional photograph's rectangular format, provided new opportunities to integrate incompatible images into new and more flexible contexts. Clearly, Schuitema's work in montage was influenced by Russian and German artists, and some of his pieces reflect the work of the Russian Alexander Rodchenko.

Based in Amsterdam, the progressive magazine *i10* was published from 1927 until 1929 by Arthur Müller Lehning. Oud served as its architecture editor and Moholy-Nagy as graphic designer and editor for film and photography. Its goal was to afford an international medium to advocate the unity of art and society. Contributors included Huszár, Kandinsky, Mondrian, Roland Holst, Oud, Moholy-Nagy, Rietveld, Schwitters, Stam, Arp, and Schuitema. Writers also included some De Stijl dissidents and even some of its active associates. Unsurprisingly, Van Doesburg was furious and wrote in *De Stijl* that *i10* published items that he had tossed in his garbage can.

In 1930, Schuitema's association with the Van Berkel companies came to an end, thus completing the body of work that was one of the first examples of Dutch corporate design.

Left: Paul Schuitema, envelope (above) and letter paper (below) for Van Berkel, 1928.

Opposite, above: Cesar Domela, German brochure promoting coal dust as fuel, 1928.

Opposite, below: Cesar Domela, cover of a prospectus for the progressive Jutte Klamt Dance School, 1928. The De Stijl influence found in his paintings is combined with the principles of the 'new typography.'

KOHLENSTAUBFEUERUNG

G. M. B. H. **BERLIN** N 24, FRIEDRICHSTR. 110-112 (HAUS DER TECHNIK)

Wir sind Fachleute
auf dem Gebiet der Staubfeuerung

WIR BAUEN:

KOHLENMÜHLEN, STAUBPUMPEN
Verteilungs-, Meß- und Kontrollorgane
WIRBELBRENNER, STROMDÜSEN
KOHLENSTAUBFEUERUNGEN FÜR
Wasserrohr-, Schiffs- und Flammrohrkessel

Sie brauchen unsere Erfahrungen
für den Bau neuzeitiger Anlagen

DRUCK OTTO ELSNER, BERLIN S 42

Tanzschuler

JUTTA KLAMT SCHULE

BERLIN

In that year, Schuitema produced designs for the Rotterdam furniture and lamp producer W. H. Gispen that included catalogues and ads for *Wendingen*. Gispen met Schuitema through Opbouw and in 1927 he had already given Schuitema photography assignments. Since the early thirties, Schuitema had been connected with the film group Filmliga, and had designed covers for their magazine of the same name. Some designs for the printer Chevalier and the publisher Brusse concluded Schuitema's work in Rotterdam. His work in montage evolved into filmmaking, and he learned the entire process himself. He began his first film in 1931, a documentary on the Maas bridges in Rotterdam. Later he made documentaries on the Paris food market and De Bouwhoek, an area in Friesland. Schuitema later wrote that 'the meaning of film lay in its being a mass communication medium that directly stimulated the public's imagination and provided a propaganda tool of extraordinary power.'[20] After moving to The Hague in 1935, one of his new clients was N.V. De Vries Robbé/N.V. Betondak, for which he produced a photomontage brochure showing the company's production process. This client and work for the construction company Boele en van Eesteren brought his most productive period in graphic design to a conclusion.

In a 1961 article for *Neue Grafik*, Schuitema attempted to clarify the meaning of Functionalism:

Each object, each letter, each form, each sound, each color should have a function. Also, the artist should have a functional role in society... a letter should support the function of reading, nothing else. It should have a clear and functional form, and not be elegant or feminine. Its beauty is in its function, and nothing mysterious should be sought behind or beyond it.... This goes for the typeface as well, not because we consider this or that typeface more beautiful, squarer, rounder, straighter or more modern, but because we choose this or that typeface as the most appropriate for this objective, that is to say get the maximum result from a minimum of means, or in other words exploit every resource to the utmost.... the fact that well-organized printing sometimes looks empty is not due to the aesthetic choice to have it white but a necessary result of the economical use of the medium.... beautiful and ugly are notions that are impossible to rely on today. These are situations over which so many differences of opinion exist that they certainly cannot be applied as norms. As a standard for something good we proffer objectivity, not aesthetics, which is a matter of taste.[21]

Schuitema always insisted that he and Zwart were not attempting to establish a new design system:

Formalism was completely rejected by us. The new form should grow from itself and flow naturally from the matter at hand, resulting from the problems posed, the function, and the material. The form was not conditioned in advance but resulted from an attitude toward life.... It is a mistake to assume that the works stemming from this period are a new kind of design. Today we are referred to as pioneers, but we never thought of ourselves as pioneers, even though we obviously wanted to make a pioneering effort to clarify things. We did not want to make new conquests but instead to confirm that society as a whole was changing.... Evidently, there were always snobs who believed that we had created a new, exclusive, and sensational type of design. We are aware that misconceptions were bound to arise under the circumstances. However, clients understood our work as a new form of expression that was both economical and pragmatic. [22]

Although Schuitema's most influential work in graphic design ended by the mid-thirties, he continued working until his death in 1973. His greatest contribution lay in his application of visual hierarchy and concise design structure, and it was apropos that he referred to himself a 'visual organizer.' He was also active as a design educator, and through his teaching at the Koninklijke Academie van Beeldende Kunsten in The Hague, he influenced and inspired a new generation of Dutch graphic designers.

It has often been asked how graphic designers such as Zwart and Schuitema with socialist political convictions could produce most of their work for capitalist clients. However, they both always insisted that they did this also for idealistic reasons, and in addition to reforming typography, they wanted to help produce a change in society. In Schuitema's covers for the magazines *Wapens Neder* and *Links Richten* and posters such as the one for the *Centrale Bond, 30,000 Transportarbeiders* (Central Union, 30,000 Transport Workers), their talents were often used to serve this end. In their opinion, artists could make a meaningful contribution only through rejecting elitism. Schuitema alluded to these issues in a talk at Arti et Industriae in 1928:

The Arts and Crafts as hand work can only be sustained by a class of people who have enough money to pay the prices that these techniques demand; since this constitutes only a small segment of the present population, the arts and crafts are an absurdity and a personal hobby in this way inhuman.... Individual labor has had its day and has done its part to clear the way for something else.[23]

In addition to Zwart and Schuitema, other left-leaning designers worked for capitalist clients without feeling they compromised their political beliefs. Lissitzky designed ads for Pelikan Werke in Hanover, and Domela Nieuwenhuis produced anarchistic book covers and brochures and commercial ads simultaneously.

The legacy of Zwart and Schuitema mainly concerned advertising and had no noticeable impact on book design. As Dooijes stated, this was to some extent a consequence of conservative attitudes in book publishing and because book design had already been functional throughout the centuries. In the final analysis, however, it would be fair to say that with their ground-breaking work, Zwart and Schuitema substantially changed the course of graphic design in the Netherlands.

Piet Zwart, *Internationale Tentoonstelling op Filmgebied* (International Film Exhibition), poster and program, The Hague, 1928. Zwart created an overall style using the letters ITF as a basis.

Chapter 4 Notes

1 Kees Broos, *Piet Zwart, 1985–1977*, Amsterdam: Van Gennep, 1982, p. 16.

2 Kees Broos, *Piet Zwart, 1985–1977*, Amsterdam: Van Gennep, 1982, p. 26.

3 Kees Broos, *Piet Zwart, 1985–1977*, Amsterdam: Van Gennep, 1982, p. 38.

4 Alston W. Purvis, *Dutch Graphic Design, 1918–1945*, New York: Van Nostrand

Reinhold, 1992, p. 67.

5 H. L. C. Jaffé, essay in *Uitreiking van de David Röellprijs aan Piet Zwart.*

Een pictorale biografie van Piet Zwart door Pieter Brattinga, Amsterdam:

Prins Bernhard Fonds, 1964.

6 Paul Hefting, Piet Zwart, *Het boek van PTT* (facsimile), The Hague:

Staatsuitgeverij, 1985.

7 Paul Hefting, Piet Zwart, *Het boek van PTT* (facsimile), The Hague:

Staatsuitgeverij, 1985.

8 G. W. Ovink, '100 Years of Book Typography in the Netherlands,' in *Book

Typography, 1815–1965 in Europe and The United States of America*, ed. Kenneth

Day, Chicago: University of Chicago Press, 1965, p. 269.

9 Dick Dooijes and Pieter Brattinga, *A History of the Dutch Poster, 1890–1960*,

Amsterdam: Scheltema & Holkema, 1968, p. 36.

10 Dick Dooijes and Pieter Brattinga, *A History of the Dutch Poster, 1890–1960*.

Amsterdam: Scheltema & Holkema, 1968, p. 39.

11 Bruno Monguzzi, 'Piet Zwart,' *Graphis Magazine* no. 258, November–December

1988, p. 57.

12 Alston W. Purvis, *Dutch Graphic Design, 1918–1945*, New York: Van Nostrand

Reinhold, 1992, p. 82.

13 Paul Schuitema, 'Neue Typografie um 1930,' in *Neue Grafik*, 1961.

14 Paul Schuitema, 'Neue Typografie um 1930,' in *Neue Grafik*, 1961.

15 Paul Schuitema, 'Gisteren en Vandaag,' in *Schoonheid en Opvoeding*, 1929, p. 1.

16 Paul Schuitema, 'Neue Typografie um 1930,' in *Neue Grafik*, 1961.

17 Paul Schuitema (under the pseudonym S. Palsma), 'Foto als wapen in de

klassestrijd,' in *Links Richten*, 1933, p. 21.

18 Dick Dooijes, *Over typografie en grafische kunst*, Amsterdam: Lettergieterij en

Machinehandel voorheen N. Tetterode, 1966, p. 64.

19 Paul Schuitema and Gerard Kiljan, 'Foto als beeldende element in de reclame,'

in *Reclame*, 1933, p. 429.

20 Paul Schuitema, 'Neue Typografie um 1930,' in *Neue Grafik*, 1961.

21 Paul Schuitema, 'Neue Typografie um 1930,' in *Neue Grafik*, 1961.

22 Paul Schuitema, 'Neue Typografie um 1930,' in *Neue Grafik*, 1961.

23 Paul Schuitema, lecture for *Arti et Industriae*, 1928.

i10

AMSTERDAM 1928

16

PR. Fl. 0.90

Opposite: Laszlo Moholy-Nagy, cover for *i10*,
no. 16, edited and published by Arthur Müller
Lehning, 1928.

Below: Piet Zwart, NKF catalog pages, 1928–29.

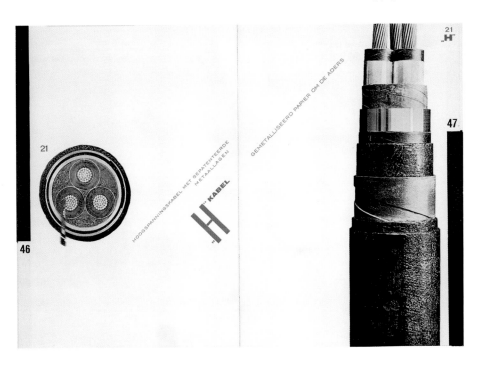

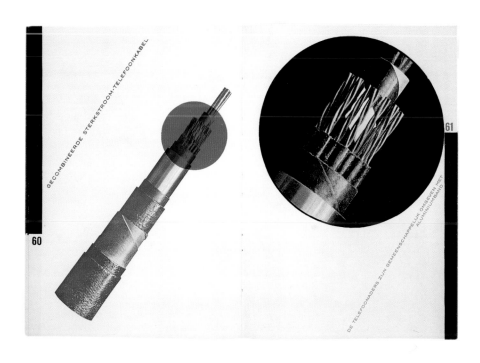

146

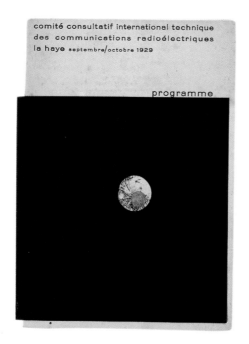

comité consultatif international technique
des communications radioélectriques
la haye septembre/octobre 1929

programme

Left: Piet Zwart, cover and spread
from the program for the
Conference on Radio-Electronic
Communications, PTT, The Hague,
1929. During this period Zwart
considered capitals unnecessary
and set all of the printed material
for the conference in lower case.

Opposite: Paul Schuitema,
advertisement for label-printing
services, C. Chevalier Printers,
Rotterdam, 1929.

lundi   **23** septembre
9   9 heures réunion
      après midi: excursion à rotterdam; un pro-
      gramme spécial sera mis à la dispositon de
      m.m. les délégués

mardi   **24** septembre
9.30   9 h. 30   réunion
14   14 heures réunion
20.30 20 h. 30 représentation de gala en langue
       française au théâtre „princesse schouwburg"
       de „la couronne de carton" de jean sarment.
       le texte de la pièce est à la disposition de m.m.
       les délégués dans la salle de lecture du comité

mercredi **25** septembre
excursion à eindhoven: visite des établissements
de la société anonyme philips

jeudi   **26** septembre
9.30   9 h. 30   réunion
14   14 heures réunion

vendredi   **27** septembre
9.30   9 h. 30   réunion
14   14 heures réunion
       soirée offerte par la délégation des indes néer-
       landaises

samedi   **28** septembre
excursion aux stations radiotélégraphiques de
kootwijk, huizen et hilversum en chemin de fer
et autocar. un programme spécial sera distribué

2

lundi   **30** septembre
9 h. 30   réunion   9.30
14 heures réunion   14
19 h. 30   dîner offert par l'administration des 19.30
postes, télégraphes et téléphones

mardi   **1** octobre
9 heures réunion   9
après midi: excursion à la station radiotélégra-
phique de noordwijk

mercredi **2** octobre
9 h. 30   réunion   9.30
15 heures clôture   15

P

l.g.

3

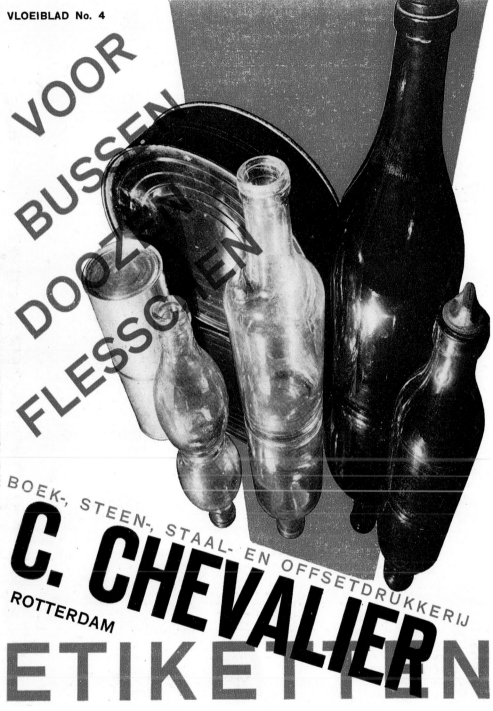

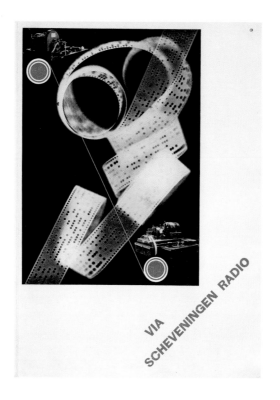

Above: Piet Zwart, *Via Scheveningen Radio*, information leaflet promoting the sending of telexes via the Scheveningen radio transmitter, PTT, The Hague, 1921. Here Zwart created a photogram from perforated telex paper.

Opposite: Paul Schuitema, *Centrale Bond 30,000 Transportarbeiders* (Central Union, 30,000 Transport Workers), poster, 1930.

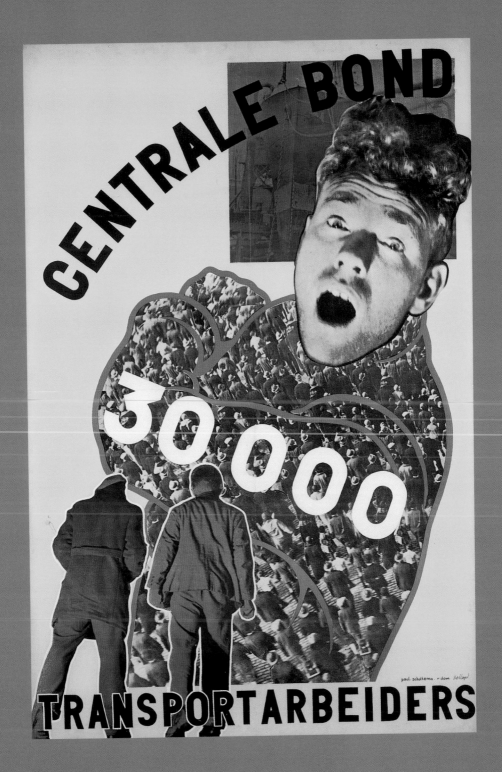

Below: Paul Schuitema, label for Van Berkel Patent cutting machine oil. Rotterdam, c. 1930.

Bottom: Paul Schuitema, leaflet for a late-night screening of *Sous les toits de Paris* by René Clair at the Rotterdam Filmliga, 1930.

Opposite: Paul Schuitema, advertisement for Nutricia powdered milk, 1929.

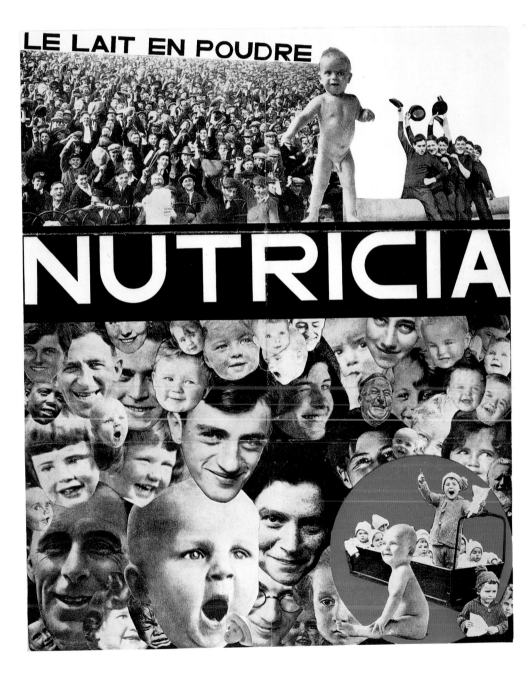

Above: Cesar Domela, brochure for Diesel
locomotives, Ornstein & Koppel AG, Berlin,
1930. The use of the diagonal was typical of
the new advertising typography.

Opposite, above: Paul Schuitema, brochure for
Berkel scales, Rotterdam, 1930.

Opposite, below: Cesar Domela, cover of *Hand
und Persönlichkeit* (Hand and Personality)
by Marianne Raschig, Hamburg:
Gebr. Enoch Verlag, 1931.

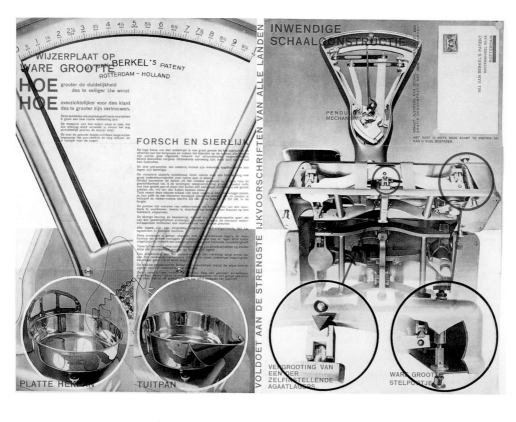

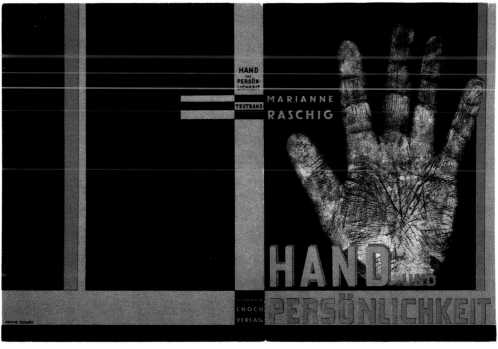

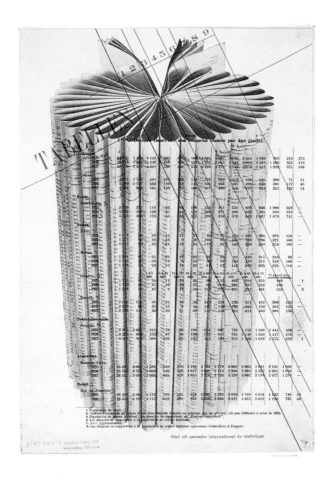

Above: Piet Zwart, page from Trio
Printers advertising brochure,
The Hague, 1931.

Opposite: Piet Zwart, *Het linnen venster*
(The Linen Window) by C. J. Graadt
van Roggen, from *Monografieën
over Filmkunst* (Monographs on
the Art of Film), series editor C. J.
Graadt van Roggen, Rotterdam:
W. L. & J. Brusse, 1931.

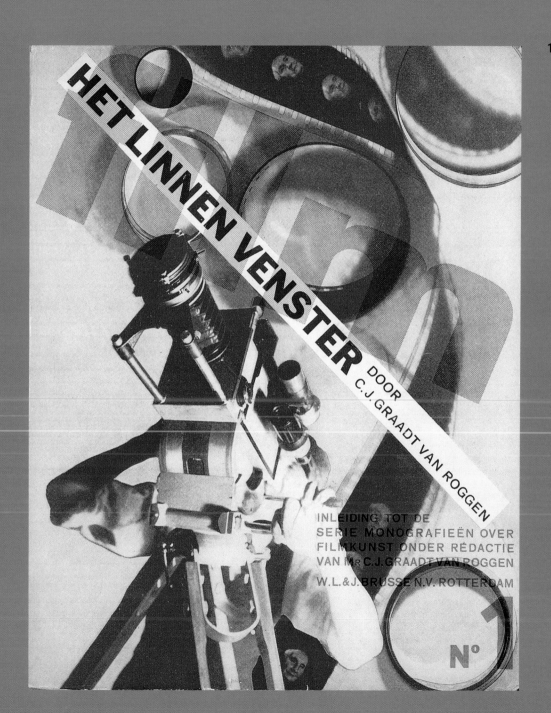

HET LINNEN VENSTER

DOOR
C. J. GRAADT VAN ROGGEN

INLEIDING TOT DE
SERIE MONOGRAFIEËN OVER
FILMKUNST ONDER REDACTIE
VAN Mr C. J. GRAADT VAN ROGGEN

W.L. & J. BRUSSE N.V. ROTTERDAM

N° 1

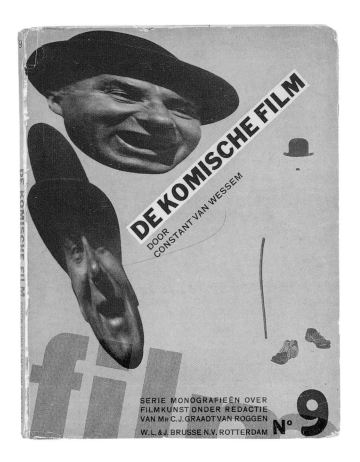

Above: Piet Zwart, *De komische film* (The Comic Film) by Constant van Wessem, from *Monografieën over Filmkunst* (Monographs on the Art of Film), series editor C. J. Graadt van Roggen, Rotterdam: W. L. & J. Brusse, 1931. Here Zwart combines a double self-portrait with a stylized image of Charlie Chaplin.

Opposite: Paul Schuitema, cover of *Filmliga*, an independent magazine on the art of filmmaking, March 1932. Diagonal photomontages were recurring devices in Zwart's use of photography. Here a focusing camera lens is implied.

film liga

ontw. paul schuitema

onder redactie van
Dr Menno ter Braak
L. J. Jordaan
Mr Henrik Scholte

Clive Brook en Marlene Dietrich in „Shanghai Express"

Maart 1932

5

Onafhankelijk maandblad voor filmkunst

Above: Paul Schuitema, magazine cover
for *de 8 en Opbouw*, 1932.

Opposite: Piet Zwart, cover and pages
from an advertising catalog for the
Dutch Cable Factory (NKF), 1933.
Instead of hiring an outside photographer,
Zwart now took his own photographs.

4 aders worden tot een kabel geslagen.

1 2 3 4

de papierkabel op de trekschijf.

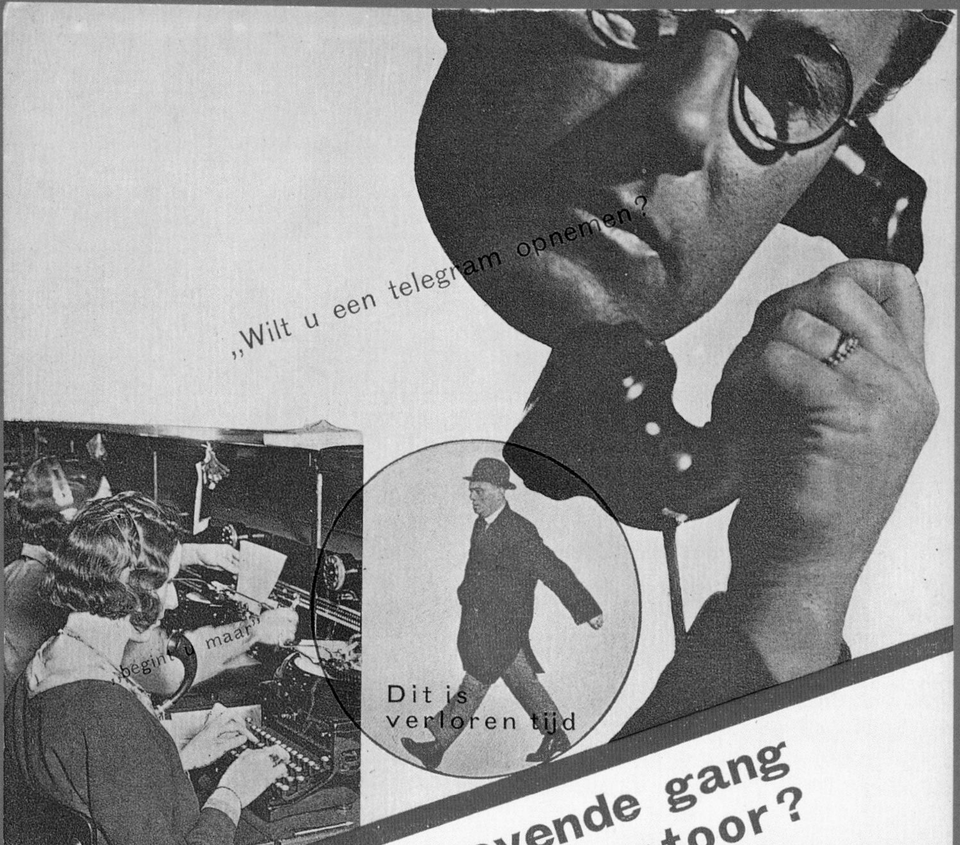

„Wilt u een telegram opnemen?

begint u maar

Dit is
verloren tijd

Waarom die tijdroovende gang
naar het telegraafkantoor?

Geef uw telegrammen
telefonisch op

Aanvragen en inlichtingen aan de telegraafkantoren

ontwerp: piet zwart

Mod. T 31. L 598 - '32

Op verzoek wordt een **afschrift
kosteloos** bezorgd in de
eerstvolgende postbestelling.

Opposite: Piet Zwart, *Send your
Telegrams by Telephone*, advertising
poster for the PTT, The Hague, 1932.

Above: Cas Oorthuys, pamphlet, *Plan
of Action for Work and Bread*, 1936.

Above: Wim Brusse, cover of *Mannen in leer* (Men in Leather) by A. J. Koenraads, Rotterdam: W. L. & J. Brusse, 1935. This photomontage is made from images taken at different angles.

Opposite: Wim Brusse, cover of *Nieuwe mensen in Moskou* (New People in Moscow) by Johan Huijts, Rotterdam: W. L. & J. Brusse, 1935.

nieuwe mensen
in moskou
door mr. J. Huijts

Brusse n.v. Rotterdam

Het boek van
PTT

Piet Zwart, cover and pages from
Het boek van PTT (The PTT Book),
The Hague, 1938.

COMITÉ VOOR DE VERKIEZING VAN ONAFHANKELIJKE KAMERLEDEN

MANIFEST

E VERWORDING VAN DEN STRIJD der politieke partijen — in Nederland toch reeds gegroepeerd naar verouderde en dus onwerkelijke scheidingslijnen — heeft bij ons volk de opvatting bevorderd, dat behartiging van economische belangen om hun zelfs wil een begeerlijk einddoel is.

※ Deze averechtsche opvatting werd de bodem, waarop de politiek der huidige partijen met haar scherp gevoerde onderlinge concurrentie kon tieren. Deze bestaat voor een groot deel uit het tegen elkaar opbieden om groeps- en andere kleine belangen te behartigen, omdat dit den luidsten weerklank vindt in den tegenwoordigen geestestoestand, die met stoffelijke wenschen is overvuld. Groote richtingslijnen zijn in deze politiek teloor gegaan. En de geestelijk belangrijke, doch in getal kleine groepen van kunstenaars en intellectueelen zijn van deze politiek meer en meer het slachtoffer geworden.

※ Wij achten het in 's lands belang, dat, nu aldus het materieele overmatig sterk naar boven is gekomen, de juiste verhouding van stoffelijke en geestelijke waarden worde hersteld.

※ Noodig oordeelen wij hiertoe, dat in de volksvertegenwoordiging afgevaardigden worden gebracht, die, los van knellend partijverband of -program, in de aangelegenheden van staatsbestuur zelfstandig zullen oordeelen en handelen, hierbij geleid en uitsluitend gebonden door de overtuiging, dat in laatste instantie de GEESTELIJKE VERHEFFING van een volk het einddoel van alle politiek is.

※ Ook wij achten economische welvaart een met alle kracht, ook in het staatsbeleid, na te streven goed. Die welvaart kome ten bate van alle lagen der bevolking. Wij ontkennen echter, dat dit een einddoel zou zijn, en oordeelen het noodzakelijk, dat de overweging van elken economischen maatregel van deze waarheid uitga, dat economische welvaart vooral van waarde is als een der voorwaarden voor den opbloei eener krachtige beschaving.

※ De politiek zal, juist in deze jaren van maatschappelijke en zedelijke depressie, van noodzakelijke sterke beperking der uit-

CHAPTER

05

J. F. van Royen, pamphlet
for the Committee to Elect
Independent Members of
Parliament, The Hague, 1922.

THE TRADITIONAL VANGUARD

In addition to De Stijl, *Wendingen*, and Constructivism, there was an additional search for a new beginning led by those who, largely inspired by the Arts and Crafts movement in England, remained committed to tradition-based typography. This classical vanguard mainly consisted of five important book designers. These were S. H. De Roos who worked for the N. V. Lettergieterij Amsterdam (Type Foundry Amsterdam), Jan Van Krimpen who served as art director for Joh. Enschedé en Zonen at Haarlem, Jean François van Royen, Charles Nypels, and A. A. M. (Sander) Stols. Although they recognized a need for a revival of Dutch typography, they were wary of the technological revolution and wanted to revitalize the art of printing by returning to time-honored printing values. They stressed symmetry, harmony, balance, classical page proportions, careful letter and word spacing, single fonts in limited sizes, letterpress printing, and an increasingly restrained use of ornament. They believed that book designers should first serve the writer and reader and not use typography as their own platform. These maxims were in direct contradiction to the Constructivist and *Wendingen* approach, and created an ongoing ideological conflict between the two factions.

Initially trained in lithography, De Roos studied at the Rijksacademie in Amsterdam from 1895 until 1898 with early signs pointing toward a painting career. In 1900, Het Binnenhuis (The Interior), a cutting-edge interior and industrial design business that manufactured and displayed high-quality industrial products, was founded in Amsterdam by Berlage, the silversmith W. Hoeker, and the interior designer J. van den Bosch. De Bazel and Lauweriks maintained an association with the firm as well. Het Binnenhuis engaged De Roos as an assistant draftsman at the age of 23 to work mainly in furniture and fabric design. While there, De Roos became conscious of the dire condition of current typography, and from then on the revitalization of Dutch book design became his single objective. In 1901 his first binding design was for the poet C. S. Adama van Scheltema's *Uit den Dool* (Out of the Thaw), quietly initiating his career in typography.

In 1903 De Roos resigned from Het Binnenhuis to design labels for a tin can maker. Also in that year he received his first break into book design when the Social Democrat publisher A. B. Soep commissioned him to design *Kunst en Maatschappij* (Art and Society), a Dutch translation of William Morris's essays. Although largely in the Nieuwe Kunst mode, this was thought to be one of the first modern Dutch book designs of the twentieth century. Although to some extent influenced by Morris, it was not De Roos's intention to emulate book designs of the past. *Kunst en Maatschappij* was set in a new typeface produced by the German foundry Genzsch & Heyse and named for its designer, the Swiss-born French architect and graphic designer Grasset. Although De Roos continued to design a number of bindings in the Nieuwe Kunst style, this was the only complete book designed by him in that manner. Its simplicity and refinement made it unusual for Dutch book designs of that time. However, it bore little resemblance to his later achievements inspired by the American book designers Daniel Berkeley Updike and Bruce Rogers, and the writings of J. W. Enschedé, the Dutch librarian and writer on printing and the book arts.

De Roos's design for *Kunst en Maatschappij* was admired by Modderman, director of the Amsterdam firm that printed it, Ipenbuur & Van Seldam. In 1907, Modderman and Enschedé asked De Roos to design the second *Drukkersjaarboek* (Printers' Annual) for which De Roos produced seven initial letters, the layout, and binding stamps. Set in a new typeface, Nordische Antiqua, later called Genzsch Antiqua, the *Drukkersjaarboek* demonstrated a unique visual harmony. This resulted in De Roos's appointment as artistic assistant at the Type Foundry Amsterdam, a relationship that would last until 1941.

Without question, De Roos considered type to be the basis of book design. For him, a book should be well designed and easily readable, and the typographer should endow the page with an aesthetic appearance. He stressed that 'legibility must not be impaired by beautiful form, and that beauty in type design must not be achieved at the expense of the total image.'[1] In an article titled 'American Book Art' for the 1908 *Drukkersjaarboek*, De Roos defined some of his beliefs on type design:

The eye desires balance. The greater the refinement of the viewer, the more insistent the need for equilibrium, proportion and harmony. If these requirements are not met, a technically perfect design is not in a position to be called a thing of beauty.[2]

De Roos wanted a new Dutch typeface to meet his requirements and one that would encapsulate their entire historical and cultural tradition. In January 1912, the Type Foundry Amsterdam released De Roos's Hollandsche Mediaeval in ten sizes, a 'heavy and solid'[3] text face largely derived from fifteenth-century Venetian fonts, Morris's Golden Type, and the Doves type of Emery Walker and T. J. Cobden Sanderson. De Roos's Hollandsche Mediaeval was, however, the first significant Dutch typeface for over a century and remained immensely popular until World War II. It was used by Stols, Van Krimpen, and Nypels for their first book designs, and in 1913 Van Royen wrote a flattering assessment of

Hollandsche Mediaeval for the magazine *Onze Kunst* (Our Art): 'In circles where typography was never even considered, De Roos's typeface has become a familiar sound.'[4]

De Roos's first type design, also for the Type Foundry Amsterdam, was actually a Javanese font designed in 1909 for the State Printing Office for use in publications in the Dutch East Indies. In addition to Hollandsche Mediaeval, De Roos designed Ella Italic and Zilvertype in 1915 for Van Royen's press, De Zilverdistel; Erasmus Mediaeval in 1923 followed by its semi-bold version Grotius in 1925; Meidoorn in 1926 for his private press, De Heuvelpers (The Hill Press); Nobel, a sans serif face, in 1929; the Egmont series in 1932; the uncial Simplex in 1937; and his least successful face, Libra, in 1938.

Between 1907 and 1942 De Roos produced no less than 193 articles on type design and typography, and he provided typographic guidelines for other designers in the Type Foundry Amsterdam's journal. In addition, he was a popular lecturer and planned exhibitions such as one on good and bad typography at the Amsterdam Stedelijk Museum in 1913. De Roos also made hand-drawn letter designs for posters, letterheads, labels, book jackets, bindings, title pages, and chapter openings.

De Roos had no use for the *Wendingen* style and considered Zwart just another architect playing with typography. De Roos derisively named him 'Piet Blok,' referring to Zwart's logo, a P next to a black square. However, Zwart found De Roos's typography anachronistic and tedious and his type designs second-rate variations on previous faces.

An important client for De Roos was the innovative Rotterdam publisher W. L. & J. Brusse who published Berlage's *Een drietal lezingen in Amerika* (Three Lectures in America) in 1912, the first book set in Hollandsche Mediaeval. Around the same year, Brusse commissioned De Roos to provide its publications with a new look, resulting in a lengthy professional relationship. The Brusse brothers worked more closely with their designers than most others in their field and published an imposing range of books designed by diverse figures such as De Roos, Zwart, Schuitema, and Van Krimpen. One sees the wide-ranging tastes of the Brusse brothers when contrasting Zwart's designs for the *Monografieën over Filmkunst* (Monographs on the Art of Film) and P. C. Boutens's translation of Aeschylus's *Smeekelingen* (The Suppliants), published around the same time. For this and other translations of Aeschylus and Plato by Boutens, De Roos designed the binding and many of the initials, but it is unclear if he was responsible for all of the typography. De Roos was, however, the designer of Adama van Scheltema's *De Tors* (The Beetles) in 1924, one of his most successful publications for Brusse.

Clearly, one of De Roos's finest book designs was Dante Gabriël Rossetti's *Hand and Soul* for De Heuvelpers in 1929. Not only did De Roos design the pages, he also designed the typeface Meidoorn and initial letters as well as personally printing the book on a small press. For De Roos, clarity was always a primary consideration, and decoration was eventually phased out. The Type Foundry Amsterdam produced his last typeface, De Roos Romein, in 1947, and the early fifties concluded his typographic work.

Born in Gouda, Van Krimpen received his artistic education at the Royal Academy of Fine Arts in The Hague, a school that would years later kindle a revolution in modern type design under the auspices of Gerrit Noordzij. At first Van Krimpen planned on being a calligrapher, and this indeed played a significant role in his later work as a book designer. Van Krimpen's brother-in-law, the poet and critic Jan Greshoff, brought him into literary

RALPH·WALDO·TRINE

HET·LEVEN EEN·ZEGEN

✵DE·WEG·TOT✵
WAAR·LEVEN
WARE·GROOTHEID
VREDE·KRACHT
✵ EN·GELUK ✵

MET·EENE·VOORREDE·VAN
∷P·H·HUGENHOLTZ·Jʀ∷

Opposite: S. H. de Roos, book design for *Het leven een zegen* (In Tune With The Infinite) by Ralph Waldo Trine, 1915

Right: Jan van Krimpen, title page for *Het jaar der dichters, muzenalmanak voor 1915* (The Year of the Poets, an Anthology for 1915) by Jan Greshoff. This was the yearbook's fifth edition and had a German-inspired hand-drawn title page.

Below: J. F. van Royen and P. N. van Eyck, opening spread of *Over boekkunst en de Zilverdistel* (Book Design and the Silver Thistle), The Hague: De Zilverdistel, 1916. Here De Roos's Zilvertype (1915) was used for the first time. The initials were hand-drawn.

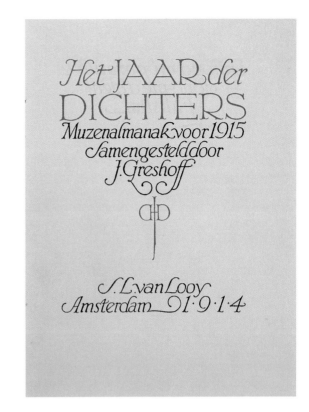

Het JAAR der DICHTERS Muzenalmanak voor 1915 Samengesteld door J. Greshoff

S. L. van Looy Amsterdam 1·9·1·4

¶OVER BOEKKUNST.

DE ZILVERDISTEL WIL BOEKKUNST GEVEN. ¶IN DEZE VERSCHIJNT HET BOEK ONS ALS EEN EENHEID, WELKE HET BUITEN HAAR niet bereikt en die het nochtans, wil het een kunstwerk zijn, bereiken móet. Deze een/heid is die van geest en materie, bepaald door de uit het begrip 'boek' af te leiden wet/ten en door het karakter van den geschreven inhoud. Vrucht eener kunstarbeid, is het boek in dit saamtreffen van geest en materie een nieuwe schepping, een nieuwe persoon/lijkheid, die door de volmaaktheid van haar lichaam te beter de volmaaktheid van haar innerlijk doet erkennen. Als zoodanig moet het in de eerste plaats voor de constitutieve vereischten der soort eene technisch en aes/thetisch op het volmaakte gerichte verwer/

kelijking vinden; in de tweede plaats dient het, als species van zijn soort, persoonlijk be/paald te zijn. Deze persoonlijke bepaling kan slechts het gevolg zijn van een zorgvul/dige aanvoeling en verbeelding van datge/ne, welks middelaarschap de bestemming van het boek is: het wezen van den geschre/ven inhoud. Slechts dàn, wanneer in een boek tegelijkertijd de technische en aesthe/tische eischen van het boek op zichzelf be/vredigd zijn en de persoonlijkheid der door den inhoud bepaalde species harmonisch belichaamd is, mogen wij ons over een goed en schoon boek verheugen. ¶Alleen op de/zen grondslag kan men spreken van boek/kunst, omdat alleen hierbij sprake is van een geestelijk voorstellen en van een vormend verwerkelijken dezer voorstelling door den maker. De geestelijke voorstelling omvat in de boekkunst chronologisch vooreerst een inzicht in het wezen en de saamstellende

Over Boek/kunst.

2

3

circles, and this engendered a profound and lifelong fondness for books and was a factor that led to his work in typography. He began by designing bookbindings, at first influenced by De Roos, but he soon established his own singular path.

Van Krimpen's first work in typography is considered to be a title page in 1912 for Greshoff's *De Witte Mier* (The White Ant), a bibliophile journal on the printing arts published in two separate series: volumes 1–2 from 1912 until 1913 and volumes 1–3 from 1924 until 1926. Van Krimpen's first known book design was the 1914 *Het Jaar der Dichters, Muzenalmanak voor 1915* (The Year of Poets, Muse Almanac for 1915). His personal approach began to take shape with his 1917 design for *Sonnetten* (Sonnets) by Albert Besnard. This was the first of five books that would later be called 'pre-Palladium,' although they were eventually included as part of the Palladium series dedicated to contemporary poets. The publication of Roland Holst's *Deirdre en de zonen van Usnach* (Deirdre and the sons of Usnach) actually began the 21-book Palladium series in 1920. Those involved included Greshoff, the Flemish poet Jan van Nijlen, the Dutch poet J. C. Bloem, and Van Krimpen as the designer. In 1922 they printed a brochure announcing Palladium's purpose:

The goal pursued by Palladium is quite simple. Palladium wants to produce books in which the form is sound and which serve the text... what we mean by a sound book is one which is printed on good paper in a beautiful typeface and which, as much as possible, has all of the qualities which a good craftsman can provide through his labor. A good book is one that does not offend the good taste of the reader and does not disturb the pure intellectual pleasure that the text provides him. Thus, it is not necessary and even undesirable that we produce a book with the aesthetic intentions that characterize many deluxe editions.[5]

The design for *Deirdre en de zonen van Usnach*, the first under the name Palladium, demonstrated that at first Van Krimpen did not adhere to these rules. Here the red titles and initial letters still display a design extravagance that would soon be replaced by a more refined approach. The five 'pre-Palladium' publications were all set in Hollandsche Mediaeval. However, some of the decorative aspects of Hollandsche Mediaeval began to annoy Van Krimpen who also thought it was over used. In a 1920 article titled 'S. H. de Roos, Book Artist and Type Designer,' Van Krimpen wrote that 'a handsome book seems a bit strange printed in the same type that a butcher uses for his price list.'[6] In the design for *Deirdre en de zonen van Usnach*, Hollandsche Mediaeval was replaced by Caslon. Among the most successful Palladium designs are Jan Veth's *De Zwerver spreekt en andere gedichten* (The Wanderer Speaks and Other Poems) in 1920, Arthur van Schendel's *Safija* in 1922, André Jolles's *Idylle* in 1924, and the majestic design for Karel van de Woestijne's *Het zatte Hart* (The Drunken Heart) in 1926. *Het zatte Hart* displayed some of Van Krimpen's most elegant initial letters and is set in Lutetia, making it the only Palladium book where he used one of his own typefaces.

In 1923 Van Krimpen's work on a commemorative PTT stamp series put him in touch with the stamps' printer, Joh. Enschedé en Zonen in Haarlem. After impressing the firm's director, Dr. Johannes Enschedé, with his ideas on type design, Van Krimpen began a prolific association with the company that would continue for thirty-five years. As art director he was in charge of the design and printing of books, the design of specimen sheets of types from the Enschedé archives, and designing new typefaces in collaboration with Enschedé's German master punch-cutter, P. H. Raedisch. Lutetia was Van Krimpen's first type design for Enschedé. Produced between 1923 and 1924, it was later was revised on two occasions. Lutetia was the Latin term for Paris, and Van Krimpen chose this name because of the typeface's use in publications for the International Exhibition of Decorative Arts in Paris in 1925. In 1926 Stanley Morison reviewed Lutetia for *The Fleuron* V, and, except for some critical observations on details such as the diagonal crossbar in the lowercase 'e', his comments were quite favorable. The design of Lutetia decisively established Van Krimpen's position in type design.

Porter Garnett, then director of the School of Printing at the Carnegie Institute of Technology at Pittsburgh and its Laboratory Press, asked Van Krimpen in 1928 to change some of the Lutetia letters to be used in a catalog for the Frick Museum in New York. Although the main changes only involved adjusting some of the character proportions, one request was to make the crossbar in the lowercase 'e' horizontal instead of diagonal, an adjustment that surely must have pleased Morison.

After Lutetia, Van Krimpen designed the Greek font Antigone in 1927; Romanée Roman in 1928 to accompany Christoffel van Dijck's seventeenth-century italic; the chancery italic Cancelleresca Bastarda in 1935; and the unfinished Romulus font family in 1936. The initial version of Spectrum, by far Van Krimpen's most popular font, was commissioned by the publisher Het Spectrum in Utrecht for a Bible and was designed between 1941 and 1945 during the Nazi occupation. All in all, Van Krimpen designed eight Romans, seven italics, three majuscules, four sans serifs, and three Greek typefaces. His last complete font was Romanée Italic in 1949, meant to supplant Van Dijck's italic. Shortly before he died in 1958, Van Krimpen had begun a new typeface specifically designed for phototypesetting, an indication that he saw a positive side to new technology.

Van Krimpen saw typography as only serving the book, and he designed his typefaces accordingly. He looked upon advertising and those involved in the field with contempt and never wavered in protecting what he thought to be valid typographic values. Van Krimpen believed that the reader should not be aware of a book's design and that a designer's task was to facilitate reading and serve both author and reader. For Van Krimpen, *beautiful* and *aesthetics* were irrelevant terms when applied to book design, and he often quoted Eric Gill's statement that 'beauty will look after herself.'[7] This reflected what Morison believed as well, as both he and Van Krimpen insisted that beauty was not their objective. De Roos expressed similar sentiments in a 1955 newspaper interview when he said that ' ....if the book looks beautiful, it is not yet beautiful. I am against experimentation with the book and the intrusion of the designer. I believe that too much of this is happening today. A problem in book design solved within the traditional boundaries leaves ample latitude.'[8]

Although Van Krimpen promoted exact rules, he often transcended his own formulas. All of his book designs display subtle differences, and his refined initial letters provide the pages with a sublime ambiance. Ironically, Van Krimpen's fundamental approach and rejection of superfluous decoration to some extent connected him with the Constructivists he so despised.

In many respects De Roos and Van Krimpen were kindred spirits, yet in their work after 1920 some dissimilarities are evident. De Roos began fifteen years before Van Krimpen and in 1925 was far into his career as a designer with socialist leanings. Although Van Krimpen and De Roos were close to the same generation, Van Krimpen's work as a designer was less effected by World War I. Van Krimpen was essentially a patrician intellectual, and his

Right: Jan van Krimpen, page from *Idylle* by André Jolles, Palladium series no. 19, 1924.

Below: Jan van Krimpen, double-page spread from *Deirdre en de zonen van Usnach* (Deirdre and the Sons of Usnach) by A. Roland Holst, Palladium series, 1920.

Opposite: S. H. de Roos, decorative and calligraphic initials for Hollandsche Mediaeval (1915, 1914) and two series of initials for Erasmus (1923), published by the Type Foundry Amsterdam.

IDYLLE

I.

Bedelaar. SLAAPWEL, MIJN OUDSTE BROE-
der Zon, slaap wel.
Wij hebben beide onze plicht gedaan;
Gij wandelt zonder doel den hemel langs
En ik de aarde. — In tevredenheid
Willen wij beide van dit wijze werk
Rusten op welverdiende lauweren —
Gij in de zee en ik bij deze bron.
Vriendlijk daalt schemering in 't moede dorp.
Daar komt een meisje dat zich heeft verlaat
Zich wiegend als een jonge wilgeboom
Met slanke heupen; op het donkre hoofd
De roode waterkruik. Nu schrik maar niet,
Ik ben geen faun al is mijn wang behaard.
Mijn voet is ongespleten en geen hoorn
Versiert mijn menschelijken zwerverskop.
Meisje. De steen is hard. Aan de ingang van het dorp
Honderd schrêe verder staat een herberg. Bed. Duifje,
Ik zag er veel maar nergens zoo gastvrij
Als deze vrije nacht. Mei. De wijn is goed!
Bed. Een verre wijn is altijd minder goed
Dan water in de buurt. Mei. De koele lucht....
Bed. Zoo is uw vader dan de herbergier?

4

DEIRDRE &
OE ZONEN
VAN USNACh

ONVERMOED DOOR DE TAL-   I. DE
LOOZEN KOMT DE STORM   VLUCHT.
VAN DE GROOTE ONDER-
GANGEN. ALS DE DUISTER-
NISSEN STIJGEN UIT HET
OOSTEN EN OVER DE WA-
TEREN VAN HET WESTEN
de groote schaduwen al waaiende zijn en het schuim
bleek wordt, zijn zij nog onbekommerd, en weten
niet, dat onder het zwarte weer zij de wapenen tegen
elkander zullen heffen, noch vermoeden zij de schemering van het einde, waarin de schilden en de
zwaarden gebroken zullen liggen naast de doode li-
chamen. Zonder meedoogen, onafwendbaar, komt de
storm over de onwetenden.
Maar soms, over de landen en de windrige heuvelen,
nadert een teeken tot aan den voet onzer muren en
den drempel onzer poorten. Van een enkele wordt
dan het leven overschaduwd. Verwijdering en don-

3

Hollandsche Mediæval Sier-Initialen Serie 2, Corps 66

A F G N P S

Hollandsche Mediæval Initialen, Aansluitend bij Corps 48

G H N U V

Erasmus-Initialen Serie I, Corps 36

P Q R

Erasmus-Initialen Serie II, Corps 48

typography was more elegant, polished, and austere than that of De Roos. Van Krimpen's purpose was to make text easy and quick to read, and expressing personal emotion or in any way affecting the reader's feelings was not part of his agenda. Even though De Roos had a more artistic nature, he never equaled Van Krimpen's aesthetic achievements. De Roos's type designs eventually fell out of favor with Van Krimpen who considered them 'too round, too self seeking and excessively decorated.'[9] In a 1930 article for the English publication the *Fleuron,* Van Krimpen was so disparaging toward De Roos that the editor, Morison, felt it necessary to tone down the wording. Still, Van Krimpen held little back when discussing De Roos's type designs:

More and more, it seems to me, they have something too much: they have become drawings, and their details have become so minutely worked out that to my mind they no longer seem to be types which will satisfy the book printer. They certainly do not lack personality but theirs is a personality that seems to have been superimposed upon their essence. Their curves would have been better less rounded, their endless undulations charm one at first, but after a time become tiresome.[10]

In the same essay Van Krimpen belittled De Roos's book designs as well, calling them regressive and De Roos's use of expensive handmade paper and wood-engraved initial letters frivolous. Three years later however, in an article for *The Dolphin,* De Roos ridiculed what he called Van Krimpen's 'sterile perfection.'[11]

Another cause of the rivalry between De Roos and Van Krimpen had to do with their employers, the Type Foundry Amsterdam and Enschedé, who had been bitter competitors since 1850. In 1856 the Enschedés had gone so far as to accuse the founder of Type Foundry Amsterdam, Nicolaas Tetterode, of theft for reproducing their Javanese typeface using a new electrotype process. Although there was some shared esteem between De Roos and Van Krimpen, the never-ending competition and bitter reproaches engendered a professional obstacle between these two great traditional designers.[12]

Crowning his career, Van Krimpen's design for the *Eerste Nederlandse Systematische Encyclopedie* (First Dutch Systematic Encyclopedia) was chosen as one of the best Dutch book designs in 1948. Until his death in 1958, he would fervently defend his principles of book typography.

Charles Nypels's initial connection with Maastricht printing went as far back as 1786 when his great-great-grandfather Theodoor Nypels assumed control of the remnants of the French firm Roux et Dufour. In 1914, Nypels began as a proof-printing assistant at the Type Foundry Amsterdam where De Roos became his mentor. In 1917 he began working for his family firm Leiter Nypels and by 1920 was made a partner. Nypels's approach as publisher, printer, and designer, became early evident. Reflecting the influence of De Roos, his first book designs, *Verzen en Fragmenten* (Verses and Fragments) by F. J. H. Lousbergh, and *Poésies* (Poems) by Gérard de Nerval, both published in 1920, were set in Hollandsche Mediaeval.

Nypels's career in book design spans roughly three segments. The first was from 1920 to 1932 at the family company, where he also worked as director for the last three years under his brother's guidance. This was a prolific period, and in 1924, in partnership with the French publisher La Connaissance, he published the first of a French series, Pierre de Ronsard's *Les sonnets pour Hélène* (Sonnets for Hélène).

Through his use of color and initial letters in the title and text pages, Nypels gave a fresh look to his books. His best design from this period is Constantijn Huygens' *'t Voorhout ende 't Kostelick Mal* (The Voorhout and the Delightful Comedy), published in 1927, in which De Roos's red and blue initial letters create lively typographic pages. The elegant *Don Quichotte*, also embellished by De Roos's initials, was published in four instalments between 1929 and 1931. In spite of its exceptional quality, the high cost of producing *Don Quichotte* caused such ill will that Nypels eventually had to leave the family firm.

Nypels's book designs covered a wide range, and he was able to work with ease in various spheres. Another distinguishing aspect of Nypels was his collaboration with a number of renowned illustrators. Of the five traditional designers discussed in this chapter, Nypels was the one who intentionally sought originality and dared to break with many of the established conventions. In doing so his designs were often visually enhanced, but at other times they did not live up to expectations. However, Nypels was never a dilettante as he has sometimes been unfairly called. In the 1933 article for *The Dolphin*, De Roos gave a fair appraisal of Nypels's achievements:

He experiments with each new book in an effort to suit dress to content, and although the result is not always satisfying, what he achieves is invariably and entirely unique and pleasing to the eye, which, after all, is the object every book producer has in view. The books he has issued vary greatly in style.[13]

Nypels also fell within Van Krimpen's target sights. The fact that De Roos had been Nypels's mentor was not in his favor, and, in Van Krimpen's eyes, Nypels's use of decorative elements tied him to the typography of the past. As Van Krimpen stated in his 1930 *Fleuron* article, a 'book is really a book only when it has shaken itself free from the influence of the decorative artist.'[14]

In 1930, Nypels designed a book together with Schuitema, one of the rare occasions when a traditional designer and a Constructivist worked on a joint project. For *Balans* (Balance), a publication on Dutch art, Schuitema's photomontage was used for the cover and Nypels designed the title page. In 1925 Nypels became connected with the magazine and publishing house De Gemeenschap (The Community), an association of young poets. From 1927 until 1934 he designed many of their publications aimed at the trade book market.

Nypels entered the second phase of his book design career when he began working for De Gemeenschap and, often moving away from his earlier classical approach, his book designs displayed a greater freedom. The more prominent ones included: *Songs of Kalua* by Albert Kuyle, 1927; *Hart zonder Land* (Heart without a Country) by Albert Helman in 1929; *Sine Nomine*, by Jan Engelman in 1930; *Het Wereldorgel* (The World Organ) by Anton van Duinkerken in 1931; and *Porta Nigra* (Black Door) by H. Marsman in 1934. Although he began his association with De Gemeenschap while still in Maastricht, his amount of work for them increased after moving to Utrecht.

The third phase of Nypels's career lasted from 1938 until 1948 when he was typographic advisor to Het Spectrum, a publisher that bought the book section of De Gemeenschap. It was then that he was able to use all of his printing and design skills in a wide range of publications. In 1948 he was awarded the State Prize for Typography with his design for *De Heilige Schrift* (The Holy Script), a Het Spectrum publication. Following a long period in a sanatorium, Nypels died in January 1952.

NIEUWE LOTEN

LENTE.

Alles vernieuwt zich, alles herleeft !
Ik wil ook nieuw zijn en mij vervormen.
Al wat ik won in vreugden en stormen
wil het nieuw kleed, dat de lente geeft.
Hooger groeit de boom van mijn leven,
wijder breidt zich zijn innerlijk streven.
Ik blijf dezelfde, maar rijker spreidt
zich mijn ervaring
tot openbaring
van wat tot diepere wijsheid leidt.

DE GROET.

Lichtende oogen, die groeten van ver
als een heldere bloem en een vriend'lijke ster,
in u is pijnen noch schrijnen.
Blijdschap is in uw glanzend strelen
als van verre vogel het blinkend kwelen
en vrede blijft na uw verdwijnen.

2

HET EGELTJE.

Achter mijn tuin in het eikenhout
zie ik soms in het avondgoud
een onbewegelijke egel schuiven.
Hij ziet er uit als een despotisch koning,
gehuld in zware pels. Waar is zijn woning ?
Ik zie hem na in 't stille takken-wuiven.
Zijn snoetje is spichtig.
Hij doet gewichtig.
Hij heeft iets van een schuwe zonderling,
die zich toch vorstlijk voelt. Hij heeft een eigen
wereld ; en hij peinst in ontoeganklijk zwijgen.

HERLEVING.

Ik dacht dat mijn leven ten einde liep,
totdat een nieuwe stem mij riep
uit de roerlooze droom, waarin ik sliep
De rozen lachten, de dorens staken :
't Was vreugd en pijn, wat mij deed ontwaken.
Toen zag ik een nieuwe horizon,
die ik strevend en strijdend bereiken kon ;
en als 't paard dat voelt de sporen
drijft mij liefdes wreede doren.

3

A PAROLE DU SEIG-
NEUR QUI FUT FAICTE A
IOEL FILS DE PHATHUEL.
VOUS ANCIENS ESCOU-
TEZ CES CHOSES CY, & EN-
TENDEZ DES OREILLES,
VOUS TOUS QUI DEMOU-
REZ EN LA TERRE : SI
TELLE CHOSE A ESTE
FAICTE EN VOZ IOURS OU
és iours de voz peres. Racomptez à voz enfans
telle parole, et voz enfans à leurs enfans, et leurs
enfans à une autre generation. La fauterelle a
mangé le refidu de la chenille, et la chenille a mangé le refidu de la fauterelle, et l'enrouillure a mangé le refidu de la chenille. Entre vous yurongnes,
refveillez vous, et plorez ; et vous tous qui beuvez
le vin en doulceur, hurlez : car il eft ofte de voftre
bouche. Pourtant qu'une gent eft montee fur ma
terre, forte, et fans nombre. Ses dents font comme
les dents d'un lion, ses groffes dents font comme
celles du petit lion. Elle a mis ma vigne en friche :
et a ofté l'efcorche de mon figuier. Elle l'a def-
pouillé tout nud, et l'a ietté au loing : fes branches
fe font blanchies. Plains toy comme la vierge vef-
tue d'un fac, fur le mary de fa ieuneffe. Le facri-
fice, et la libation eft oftee de la maifon du Seigneur : et les preftres ferviteurs du Seigneur ont
ploré. La contree eft defpeuplee : la terre a ploré,
pource que le froment eft gafté, le vin eft confus,
l'huile default. Les laboureurs font confus, les
vignerons ont lamenté fur le froment et le vin
et l'orge : pource que la moiffon des champs eft

OOSTERSCH,
DE DAUW HANGT PARE-
len aan takken en aan blaren
in kettingen en snoeren;
de kusmond van den
wind, als hij ze aan wil roeren,
doet ze ontstellen, sidderen zonder bedaren
en stort ze allen neer, de wankelbaren.

De beek is een velijnen blad,
een boek, een open letterschat,
een gulden labyrinth, waarin
de vogels komen lezen, dat
de wind beschrijft,
de wolk, die overdrijft,
zet er de stippen en de tittelteekens in.

Mijn boom heeft kweeën tegen ooft,
dat glanzend was en honingzoet.
De top is over en het pad
ligt afwaarts voerend voor mijn voet.

Gedronken is wat van den wijn
de klare opperbloesem is.
Er rest mij nu nog ééne slok,
een slok, die niets dan droesem is.
4

Een lichte lente is de jeugd,
een winter is de ouderdom,
Maar is een winter zonder meer
en brengt geen nieuwe lent' weerom.

Waar zijn de vrienden van voorheen
in fleur en frischheid hunner jaren?
Waar zijn de bruiden met de krans
en de juweelen in de haren?

Onder de aarde hebben ze al
hun tent gebracht en heengebeurd
En nu de zefir spelend heeft
de winterwa vaneengescheurd,

Nu tilt de eerste amandelbloem
een hoofdje popelend en stout,
Een tenger, zilvren vrouwenlijf
te voorschijn uit het doodkisthout.

En de violen zijn een lok
van zwart en muskusgeurend haar,
Dat viel, o liefste, liefste, en zeeg
onder der dagen valsche schaar.

Ik meen, de lelie is een kind,
een feeënkind en opgeleid
Tot hooge kieschheid van gevoel
en adel van welsprekendheid.
5

Opposite, above: A. A. M. Stols, double-page spread from *Nieuwe Loten* (New Shoots) by Marie Cremers, 1923, third book in the Trajectum ad Mosam series.

Opposite, below: Charles Nypels, decorative vignette from *La prophétie de Joël* (The Book of Joel), Maastricht: Leiter-Nypels, 1923. Set in Plantin, this is an example of Nypels's early typographic style. The woodcuts are by Henri Jonas.

Above: J. F. van Royen, double-page spread from *Oostersch, Verzen naar Perzische en Arabische Dichters* (Oriental, Verses after Persian and Arabian Poets) by J. H. Leopold, 1924. title, initials and design by Van Royen. Set in Disteltype by Lucien Pissarro.

Although limited in quantity, Van Royen's book designs were of considerable merit. His main contribution to Dutch graphic design, however, came through his innovations as general secretary of the Dutch PTT, a subject that will be addressed in Chapter Seven. After graduating from the University of Leiden in 1903 with a doctorate in law, Van Royen worked for The Hague publisher Martinus Nijhoff before being hired by the the legal department of PTT as a clerical assistant in 1904.

In early December 1909, two young poets, J. C. Bloem and Jan Greshoff, began a private press in The Hague called De Zilverdistel (The Silver Thistle). The purpose of the press was to publish principally Dutch literature in well designed editions. A few months later the poet (and later critic) P. N. van Eyck also joined De Zilverdistel followed in 1912 by Van Royen whose designs gave the press a unique visual character.

Two new typefaces were designed for De Zilverdistel. The first was De Roos's Zilvertype, a refined version of Hollandsche Mediaeval. The second was Disteltype, essentially a new rendering of Carolingian Minuscule lettering, was designed in England by Lucien Pissarro, the son of the Impressionist painter Camille Pissarro. Although De Roos also designed initial letters and titles for De Zilverdistel and advised Van Royen on typography, he became highly annoyed when Van Royen attempted to influence the design of Zilvertype. The first three books for De Zilverdistel were designed and printed by Enschedé. Around September 1912, Van Eyck, increasingly involved with typography and intending to make the press a successful commercial operation asked Bloem and Greshoff to leave De Zilverdistel.

Van Royen learned printing as an apprentice at Enschedé, and was self educated in typography. In the beginning, he printed everything on a handpress at Enschedé, but with the De Zilverdistel catalogue in 1915, he began printing on a press in his home. *Over Boekkunst en de Zilverdistel* (Concerning Book Arts and The Silver Thistle) by Van Royen and Van Eyck, the first book set in De Roos's Zilvertype, was published in 1916 as was the book Cheops, also set in Zilvertype and designed by Van Royen. De Roos designed the initial letters and titles complying with Van Royen's recommendations.

Never having liked the name De Zilverdistel, Van Royen changed it to De Kunera Pers (The Kunera Press) in 1923. Van Royen designed the layouts, initials, and titles for De Kunera Pers and Pissarro designed the trademark, and after the name change, Van Eyck and De Roos were no longer involved. The first book issued by De Kunera Pers was J. H. Leopold's *Oostersch, Verzen naar Perzische en Arabische Dichters* (Oriental, Verses after Persian and Arabian Poets) in 1924, which contained poems inspired by Persian and Arabic verse. The book was set in Pissarro's Disteltype, and Van Royen's title and initials were based on Pissarro's type inspired by Carolingian lettering. Only four more books were published by De Kunera Pers: François Villon's *Oeuvres* in 1926; Arthur van Schendel's *Maneschijn* (Moonlight) in 1927; Charles Péguy's *La Tapisserie de Nôtre Dame* (The Tapestry of Notre Dame) in 1929; and Boutens's *In den Keerkring* (In the Tropics) in 1942. With the exception of *Maneschijn*, all were set in Disteltype.

Van Royen's title and initial designs were more ornate than those of either Van Krimpen or De Roos. Van Krimpen did not think much of De Zilverdistel, and considered Van Royen's use of the handpress to be elitist. For him De Zilverdistel's publications were of little typographic value, and the only two books that he found at all praiseworthy were actually designed by Van Eyck.[15] Van Krimpen was totally opposed to the interpretation of text through typography, and his feelings about Van Royen were linked with his opposition to decorative book design in general.

Like Nypels, Stols was part of a Maastricht printing dynasty. While studying law in Amsterdam in 1921, he and his younger brother Alphonse had earlier decided to remain in the family publishing business, Boosten & Stols. They were critical of what the firm had produced in the past and wanted to introduce the best design quality. Stols's canon was clarity, legibility, classical typography, a discerning choice of texts, and fine printing. Although Stols admired the work of his friend Nypels who advised him on his first publications, he never veered from the traditional approach. Garamond and Bembo were among his favorite types, although at times he used Hollandsche and Erasmus Mediaeval. Nypels was a devoted follower of De Roos, while Stols admired Van Krimpen whom Nypels could not abide. Sadly, the friendship and professional connection of Stols and Van Krimpen created a rift between Nypels and Stols.

Van Krimpen designed several books for the Halcyon Press, which Stols began in 1927. The 1929 edition of *The Sonnets of John Milton*, set in Christoffel van Dyck's Italic, exemplifies Van Krimpen's work both in its typography and its initial letters. In 1932, Boutens's *Strofen en andere Verzen uit de Nalatenschap van Andries de Hoghe* (Stanzas and other Verses from the Estate of Andries de Hoghe), set in Van Krimpen's Romanée, was designed by Stols with initial letters by his brother Alphonse. Valéry's *Existence du Symbolisme* (Existence of Symbolism) in 1939 was another collaborative design in which Alphonse again designed the initials.

Like Van Krimpen, Stols' view on the designer's role was clear and to the point:

Providing the form in which a book will be printed, the designer must nevertheless satisfy a number of requirements for the book, knowledge of its history and technology, artistry and taste, and insight as to production costs. In short all those factors which make it possible to make a written text into a printed book that satisfy the greatest demands of legibility.[16]

Stols never attained the design heights of De Roos, Van Krimpen, Nypels, and Van Royen, yet at their best his large number of book publications are outstanding, both in typography and printing quality. Because of the high costs, few printers were able to give so much effort to producing finely printed books, making Stols's achievements even more extraordinary.

Stols remained in publishing until 1951 when he was appointed typographic advisor for UNESCO in Ecuador, Guatemala, and Mexico. He served as cultural attaché at the Dutch Embassy in Mexico City from 1963 until 1965, and while there gave talks on printing history. He later moved to Spain where he died in 1973.

Although there were at the same time other notable Dutch typographers working in the classical tradition, De Roos, Van Krimpen, Nypels, Van Royen, and Stols formed the traditional vanguard. Having firmly placed their stamp on the development of Dutch graphic design, they were later appropriately referred to as De Grote Vijf (The Great Five).

Above: S. H. de Roos, binding for
De Tors, zeven zangen (The Beetles,
Seven Songs) by C. S. Adama,
Rotterdam: W. L. & J. Brusse, 1924.
For this publication, De Roos
used his own typeface Erasmus,
published a year earlier by the
Type Foundry Amsterdam.

Opposite: R. Gerbrands, cover of
Plastische kunst in huis (Plastic
Art in the Home) by Jan Lauweriks,
one of a 24-part series on Dutch
applied arts. Rotterdam:
W. L. & J. Brusse, 1924.

DE
TOEGEPASTE KUNSTEN
IN NEDERLAND

EEN REEKS MONOGRAFIEËN
OVER HEDENDAAGSCHE
SIER- EN NIJVERHEIDSKUNST

PLASTISCHE KUNST
IN HUIS
DOOR JAN LAUWERIKS
MET 45 AFBEELDINGEN

UITGEGEVEN BIJ
W.L. & J. BRUSSE'S
UITGEVERS MIJ
TE ROTTERDAM

Chapter 5 Notes

1 Dick Dooijes, *Over typografie en grafische kunst*, Amsterdam: Lettergieterij en

Machinehandel voorheen N. Tetterode, 1966, p. 62.

2 Dick Dooijes, *Over de drukletterontwerpen van Sjoerd H. de Roos*, Zutphen:

Bührmann-Ubbens Papier BV, 1987, p. 7.

3 Gerard Unger and Marjan Unger, *Hollands landschap met letters*, Utrecht:

Van Boekhoven-Bosch BV grafische industrie, 1989, p. 34.

4 J. F. van Royen, 'De Hollandsche Mediaeval van S. H. de Roos', in *Onze Kunst* 12,

1913, p. 132.

5 Jan van Krimpen, *Palladium* prospectus, 1922.

6 Jan van Krimpen, 'S. H. de Roos, Boekkunstenaar en Letterontwerper,' in *Nieuwe

Arnhemsche Courant*, 1922.

7 Mathieu Lommen, *De Grote Vijf,* Amsterdam: M. M. Lommen, 1991, p. 38.

8 S. H. De Roos, interview in *Haarlems Dagblad*, 1955.

9 Gerard Unger and Marjan Unger, *Hollands landschap met letters*, Utrecht:

Van Boekhoven-Bosch bv grafische industrie, 1989, p. 34.

10 Jan van Krimpen, 'Typography in Holland,' in *The Fleuron*, no. 7, 1930, pp. 5–7.

11 S. H. de Roos, 'Holland,' in *The Dolphin*, vol. 1, 1933, p. 336.

12 Dick Dooijes, *Sjoerd H. de Roos, zoals ik mij hem herinner*, The Hague: Rijksmuseum

Meermanno-Westreenianum, Museum van het boek, 1976, p. 30.

13 S. H. de Roos, 'Holland,' in *The Dolphin*, vol. 1, 1933, p. 336.

14 Jan van Krimpen, 'Typography in Holland,' in *The Fleuron*, no. 7, 1930, pp. 1–2.

15 Mathieu Lommen, *De Grote Vijf*, Amsterdam: M. M. Lommen, 1991, p. 11.

16 Dick Dooijes, *Wegbereiders van de Moderne Boektypografie in Nederland*,

Amsterdam: De Buitenkant, 1988, p. 50.

L'ART HOLLANDAIS
À L'EXPOSITION INTERNATIONALE
DES ARTS DÉCORATIFS
ET INDUSTRIELS
MODERNES
PARIS
1925

Jan van Krimpen, title type and
page from *L'Art Hollandais à
l'Exposition Internationale des Arts
Décoratifs et Industriels Modernes*
(Dutch Art at the International
Exhibition of Modern Industrial and
Decorative Art), Paris, 1925. Van
Krimpen's Lutetia typeface is used
for the first time in the year that it
was released by Enschedé. The
open capitals were hand-drawn.

C'EST de 1880 qu'en Hollande on fait partir la grande rénovation artistique. Elle fut surtout sensible à cette date dans le domaine de la littérature, mais un mouvement parallèle dans les arts industriels s'était déjà dessiné en Angleterre sous l'inspiration de William Morris, et ne tarda guère à se répandre en Europe.

Il convient toutefois de signaler un courant précurseur: le rationalisme, dont Viollet-le-Duc fut l'initiateur en France et Cuypers l'introducteur en Hollande. En architecture ce rationalisme, utilisant les formes gothiques traditionnelles, fut confusément interprété. On prêta en effet plus d'attention à l'expression formelle du gothique qu'au solide principe de construction rationnelle sur lequel il s'appuyait. Cuypers notamment remit en vogue la voûte et chercha en outre à obtenir de nouveau dans les divers métiers une pure exécution du détail.

C'était là une tâche fort difficile, exigeant de nombreuses années de préparation, ne permettant d'ailleurs pas d'espérer la possibilité de porter la pratique professionnelle au degré de perfection qu'elle atteignit au moyen âge. Cuypers ne la poussa pas plus avant parce que, s'il faisait lui-même les dessins, il n'exécutait pas de ses propres mains. Elle fut reprise par des artistes œuvrant dans diverses branches des arts industriels et qui s'inspirèrent des idées de William Morris et de Semper. Les sculpteurs taillèrent eux-mêmes leurs statues dans le bois ou la pierre, les céramistes moulèrent et tournèrent leurs vases, procédèrent à leur émaillage et à leur cuisson, les fresquistes et les peintres verriers exécutèrent leurs travaux, les artisans du batik, les graveurs, les imprimeurs, les tisserands et les relieurs étudièrent leur métier, se familiarisèrent avec les matériaux et la technique et consacrèrent toute leur activité à l'exercice

8

QUELQUES LETTRES CONCERNANT
LA PREMIÈRE ÉDITION DU
DE IVRE BELLI AC PACIS
DE HUGO GROTIUS
(PARIS 1625)

AMSTERDAM 1926

VAN uit een bleeken morgen
het blozend avond-uur genaêrd;
aan 't voorhoofd alle zorge
gezengd bij zuiverende klaart';
ter leên (alwaar ze 't stoeiën
en 't hijgend worstel-spel van de' arbeid kwam vermoeiën,)
ter leên den milden gloed der rust:
zóo treedt de groote zon Ge tege', in trager trippen,
die, naauw-gekloven abrikoos, Uw rooz'ge lippen
tot eene kleine en trippend-trage zonne kust.

De dag schoot Uw gedachten
met lichte en schicht'ge draden door;
de olie der zilvren vachten
doopte Uwe hand in gulden gloor;
van spinne-wiel en kaarde
die snorde aan Uwen voet of uit Uw vingren schaarde,
trilt rechtend en verschiet Uw leest;
nòg kromt tot kroon de garve Uwe armen, die ze torschten;
de sikkel die ze sneed en rond is als Uw borsten
is nimmer onder 't werk zoo flitsen-rijk geweest.

6

Maar — plots-ontwaakt verbazen —
thans staat Gij gansch van last geleêgd;
geronne' uit de avond-wazen,
Uw aêm een zinder-vlam beweegt:
de zoete zinder-vlamme
die klimt aan iedre kim en loopt aan alle kammen
en vlak ten lagen dale vloeit
aldaar Gij treedt, aldaar Ge wijlt, aldaar ze Uw dijën,
de koele, Uw kuiten langs, met glanzen komt beglijën
en naar den hollen boog van Uwe ribben groeit.

En, zwaait de nacht heur huive
de curve uit van haar wijd gebaar:
als glinstrend gruis gaan stuiven
de sterren om Uw duister haar;
als snoeren-rij'n, als booten
slaan om Uw hals, slaan om Uw polsen hemel-klooten;
terwijl de schacht van beide scheen
rijst in het mane-licht tot dubblen stam, tot schrage,
tot levens-boom die klaar de hemel-kruine drage
waar de openbaring bloeit van Gods verborgenheên.

7

Opposite: S. H. de Roos, title page for *Quelques lettres concernant la première édition de De Ivre Belli Ac Pacis de Hugo Grotius* edited by A. Lysen, Type Foundry Amsterdam, 1926. Grotius, a semi-bold version of Erasmus, was used here for the first time.

Above: Jan van Krimpen, double-page spread from *Het zatte Hart* (The Drunken Heart) by Karel van de Woestijne, Palladium series no. 25, 1926.

Above: J. F. van Royen, double-page spread from *Oeuvres* by François Villon, set in Disteltype, The Hague: Kunera Press, 1926.

Opposite, above: Jan van Krimpen, page from *Inkeer* (Repentance) by P. N. van Eyck, Palladium series, 1922. Printed by G. J. van Amerongen, Amersfoort, and set in Caslon with hand-lettered titles and initials.

Opposite, below: Jan van Krimpen, double-page spread from *Oeuvres* by François Villon, 1929. This is part of the fine book series first published in 1927 by A. A. M. Stols and printed by Enschedé in Haarlem for the Halcyon Press. Van Krimpen used a 15th-century Gothic typeface by an unknown typecutter from Enschedé's historic collection.

INKEER

I. MET ZOOVEEL drift van de aarde weg te stormen
En dan, niets méér dan slechts dit smartlijk lied
Uit smaadlijk leed en bitterheid te vormen, —
Waarom, mijn ziel, waarom berust gij niet?

Droom niet de vrede die gij zoekt daarbuiten,
Pijnend als gij terugvalt op uw zelf,
Kunt gij dan nóg die blinde drang niet stuiten,
Die zich te bloeden stoot aan 't laag gewelf?

Gij wilt het licht maar 't licht is niet de waarheid,
Alle gesternten zijn gelijkenis,
Beeld, onverhuld voor de innerlijke klaarheid,
Onvruchtbre praal voor 't duister van gemis.

Wat nut u al dat wemelend geflonker
Als 't niet de bloem is van wat in u groeit?
Delf dan geduldig, kernwaarts door uw donker,
Naar 't vuur dat in uw diepste gronden gloeit.

4

Les Lais

Puis que mon sens fut a repos
Et l'entendement demeslé,
Je cuidé finer mon propos;
Mais mon encre trouvé gelé
Et mon cierge trouvé soufflé;
De feu je n'eusse peu finer;
Si m'endormis, tout emmouflé,
Et ne peus autrement finer.

Fait au temps de ladite date
Par le bien renommé Villon,
Qui ne menjue figue ne date.
Sec et noir comme escouvillon,
Il n'a tente ne pavillon
Qu'il n'ait laissié a ses amis,
Et n'a mais qu'ung peu de billon
Qui sera tantost a fin mis.

16

Le Testament

EN l'an de mon trentiesme aage,
Que toutes mes hontes j'eus beues,
Ne du tout fol, ne du tout sage,
Non obstant maintes peines eues,
Lesquelles j'ay toutes receues
Soubz la main Thibault d'Aussigny...
S'evesque il est, seignant les rues,
Qu'il soit le mien je le reguy.

Mon seigneur n'est ne mon evesque,
Soubz luy ne tiens, s'il n'est en friche;
Foy ne luy doy n'hommage avecque;
Je ne suis son serf ne sa biche.
Peu m'a d'une petite miche
Et de froide eau tout ung esté;
Large ou estroit, moult me fut chiche:
Tel luy soit Dieu qu'il m'a esté!

17

ALBERT KUYLE
DE BRIES

DE WINGERD No. I
DE GEMEENSCHAP
UTRECHT, MCMXXIX

Above: Charles Nypels, title page from
De Bries (The Breeze) by Albert Kuyle,
Utrecht: De Gemeenschap, 1929.

Opposite: Charles Nypels, title page from
Don Quichotte by Miguel de Cervantes,
book I, 1929–31.

CERVANTES

QDon QUICHOTTE

I

LEITER·NYPELS S.A. · MAASTRICHT
MCMXXIX

HET TIENDE
POORTJE GAAT OPEN

XXXVIII

Leonidas beschermt de Thermopylen

Tot al zijn helden op dit slagveld vielen.

DE VELDHEER LEONIDAS ZEGT:

Wat is de dood dan een volstreden strijd?

Wacht dus uw laatsten stond met dapperheid,

Zoo zal uw nederlaag de goden overwinnen

En 't roemvol sterven spaart u levens spijt.

Charles Nypels, pages from a book
of poetry by Anton van Duinkerken,
Utrecht: De Gemeenschap, 1931.

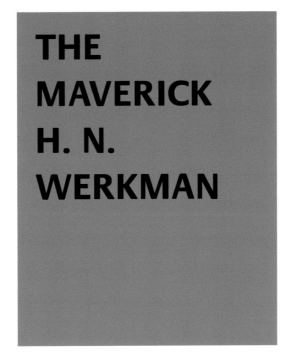

THE MAVERICK H. N. WERKMAN

Hendrik Nicolaas Werkman was by far the most significant visionary force in modern Dutch graphic design. A reclusive and singular outsider, his existence was one of solitude and introspection, and for most of his life he remained semi-isolated in the northern part of the Netherlands. He created no school and had no real followers, nor was he an active participant in the international dialogues taking place at that time. He has never fitted comfortably into any section of graphic design history, and, for this reason, most graphic design historians have allotted him a minor role; in general art history, he is not included. Yet, by helping to free type from its conventional role, Werkman gave a new definition to its artistic and symbolic function. Or as the Dutch printing historian and type designer Dick Dooijes later wrote, Werkman 'used common things in a completely uncommon manner and in this way achieved a very uncommon, innate artistic form.'[1]

Abstraction for its own sake was never Werkman's objective, and words were not used phonetically as with Schwitters and Van Doesburg. Instead he sought the poetic side of typography. Much was implied, and when contemplating his work we often have to provide our own interpretation. Living in an enchanted world of his own concoction, Werkman later commented that he considered the secluded paths to be the most beautiful. He was reserved by nature and, until the war years, had few close friends. Indeed, in August 1943, he wrote to his friend and collaborator Henkels '.... In my heart I am a loner who occasionally feels the need of some companionship.'[2] Herbert

Spencer described him as 'honest, simple, contemplative yet passionate – and above all, intensely human.'[3]

Although aware of Dada and Constructivism, Werkman remained outside of the European artistic graphic design mainstream. Although Van Doesburg, Lissitsky, Marinetti, Tschichold and others broke with established rules of typography, they all strove to initiate new systems. Werkman, though, rejected all formulas and had no interest in introducing fresh ones, and stylistically there is little to equate with his work.

Werkman was born on April 29, 1882, in Leens, a small town in the northern province of Groningen, the middle son of three for Klaas Pieter and Grietien Alingh Louwes Werkman. His father, a veterinarian, died from an accident in the fall of 1891, and in 1895 the family moved to the city of Groningen. This city was Werkman's home for the remainder of his life.

In the early fall of 1900, Werkman found a job at a printer, publisher, and bookseller in a nearby town, starting as a type-sorter, more commonly known as a 'printer's devil.' In addition, he wrote a number of pieces for their newspaper and later helped to set type as well. Around this time he also became interested in photography, taking his attempts in this field seriously enough to print a business card with the text, 'H. N. Werkman Amateur-Fotograaf Groningen.'

In 1903 he began working as a journalist for the local newspaper *Het Groninger Dagblad*, writing under the pseudonym 'Farao,' and then transferred to the *Nieuwe Groninger Courant*. Werkman spoke very little about this period, but later he wrote: 'For four years I also worked as a correspondent.... it was a dog's occupation for little money, and when I finally left I could not even look at a newspaper for an entire year.'[4] However, this time engendered a love for the world of printing, and his brief encounter with the field helped him to get a job as shop supervisor for the printer Knoop in Wildervank near Groningen.

In 1907, Werkman became engaged to Jansje Cremer, a member of a prosperous Groningen family involved the hardware business. In spite of misgivings on the part of her family, they married on April 10, 1909. Even though Werkman had bought a small Groningen printing business in 1908 with help from his mother, he had few other resources of his own, and was therefore not deemed an ideal choice by Jansje's family.

Shortly after their marriage, the newlywed couple decided to establish a larger and more modern printing business. Financed by Jansje's own personal means and with the financial participation of other Cremer family members, the business was launched in early 1913 in new and larger facilities, albeit on a modest scale. The company began with a staff of ten that included the young Wybren Bos, who continued the business after Werkman's death. The firm flourished from the very outset, and by 1917, it had a staff of twenty-seven and was one of the larger printing businesses in Groningen. Although Werkman was a highly capable professional printer, he had little interest in making money, and the fiscal advice provided by members of the Cremer family was an important factor in the commercial success of the business. Werkman, however, saw this as meddling, and for him it became an increasing source of annoyance.

Werkman's early work in typography displayed indications as to how it would later manifest itself, and there was little to distinguish his work from that of other printers from the same period and region. However, a few items such as *Museum van Plastische Verzen* (Museum of Plastic Verse), a book of poetry written by his younger brother, Martinus Hendrik Werkman, were commendable accomplishments, but as a traditional designer he was not on the same level as luminaries of the period such as De Roos, Van Royen, Van Krimpen, Stols, and Nypels.

On April 2, 1917 Jansje died of a stroke, leaving her husband with a five-year-old son and daughters aged two and six. In the course of that year Werkman got to know Pieternella (Nel) Supheert, who, as one of Werkman's clients, had provided advice on the printing of a feature article she had written for an educational magazine. The business relationship gradually developed into a deeply felt affection, which, led to their marriage a little more than a year after Jansje's death. This turn of events and the fact that Werkman was designated sole heir to the printing business, was something that Jansje's family resented, and as a result they severed all ties with Werkman. Werkman then had to repay the Cremers in one lump sum for their investment in the business and in doing so was forced heavily into debt. The rupture also brought an end to the Cremer family's influence on the management of the printing business, a prelude to financial difficulties.

The diverse Groningen art circle De Ploeg (The Team) was launched in a local café on June 5, 1918 to bring artists together and encourage regional art. Notable founding members included the painters Jan Wiegers, Johan Dijkstra, Jan Altink, and the photographer Simon Steenmeijer. They were later joined by, among others, Jan G. Jordens and Jannes de Vries, both drawing instructors; Jan van der Zee, a house painter; Johan van Zweden, a teacher; and Wobbe Alkema and Job Hansen, who worked as architectural draftsmen. Werkman joined in 1919 and in that year printed their first catalogue.

Although he first became interested in painting in 1896 after attending an exhibition of work by Vincent van Gogh, Werkman did not begin painting himself until 1917, when he was encouraged to do so by Nel. Van Gogh, Ernst Ludwig Kirchner, and Edvard Munch were his principal influences in this medium. Like these three artists, Werkman had a melancholy strain to his character that was reflected in his paintings. Since over half of his paintings were destroyed at the close of World War II, it is impossible to adequately evaluate their significance, but compared to his printed pieces, his paintings were lesser achievements. As he had not been trained in painting, he instead seized the tool with which he was most familiar, his printing press.

Although the name of the art circle was not used, from October 1921 until March 1922 Werkman printed and published, at his own expense, a monthly magazine for De Ploeg titled *Blad voor Kunst* (Publication for Art). Although its literary value was insignificant, it was the first publication in Groningen devoted to modern art. Through woodcuts and photographic reproductions, it provided a venue for De Ploeg members to show their work and publicize their views on art. After seeing an exhibition in Groningen of works by Huszár, Van Doesburg and Van der Leck in February 1922, Werkman, inspired by Huszár, designed the title page and abstract cover for the last *Blad voor Kunst* issue. This provided an early clue as to how his work would eventually evolve.

B B

EEN RIL

GRONINGEN
1923 Groote Verzoendag

Tot deze AANVANG was besloten reeds voor de
eerste symptomen van de jubileumgolf met de ont-
eerende persoonsverheerlijking zich voordeden.
Meen dus niet dat gebeurtenissen van al te recen-
ten datum die ge in Uw beperkt gezichtsveld mocht
bespeuren, aanleiding gaven tot het rose pamflet.
Het ontstond uit den drang des tijds en is geen
aardigheidje. Het is geen herhaling van het Da-
daïstisch grapje; het is geen hoon.
Het ontstond met moeite, want wij zijn traag, hoe-
wel de tijd dringt. Het zomerlanterfanten is gedaan.
Mocht het een REVEILLE zijn in den tijd van
afwachting.
Meewarig of verachtelijk, het zou in elk geval
verachtelijk zijn, langer te zwijgen.
Getuigen en spreken.
Maar 't GELUID KAN NIET SCHOON ZIJN en de
TAAL KAN NIET VERSTAANBAAR ZIJN voor
wie niet luisteren WIL als hij niet spreken KAN.
Wat zij van ons verlangt kunnen wij U niet geven.
Dit is de AANVANG.
Voet voor voet. Stap voor stap.
Uit de beklemming van de kunst, het parool.

Above and opposite: H. N. Werkman,
The Next Call 1, pages 2–7, 1923.

BERLIN
Am dritten Montag

Heute habe ich mich frisch rasiert.
Ich hasse die Weiber, weil ihre Schönheit mich banget.
Einen wirklichen Freund habe ich nie besessen.
Die Einsamkeit ist nicht mild.
Ruhmlos ist die Ehre.
Die Augen sehen mich an.
Der Mensch glaubt ein psychologisches Rätsel zu sein,
statt eines banalen Säugetiers. Sein Instinkt nennt er
Verstand. Das verständige Raubtier. Das Automobil.
Censoren gibt es noch immer. Sie schleichen durch die
Sälen und spüren ängstlich mit der Nase ob irgendwo
die Kunst verletzt wird. Diese Dummköpfe. Man sollte
sie alle auffangen und ihnen in der Stillen Südsee die
Ohren waschen. Und noch etwas anderes.
Das publikum meint das zum Feiertag die Freude gehört
und fängt beim Leiden an zu weinen.
Also am nächsten Feiertag.

MOSCOW
Saxophoon en fagot

Nauwelijks is de nacht gedaald of gij verlangt den dag
te zien. Wees stil met Uw vrees. De wit-gesteven
opretteugel zal U thans niet kwellen voor een poos en
de spiegel is geho005d te Uwer eer. De verzenbouwer
is naar 't gemaskerd bal en laat zijn hoofdhaar streelen
door schoone vrouwen. Begeef U naar den achtergrond
en hoor de stem die in de kamer komt. Zij zal U lafaard
noemen, maar gij behoeft niets te vreezen. Eens zal de
dageraad U wekken. Dan zult ge Uself weer kennen
en Uwe vrienden zullen niet meer bij U zijn. Als Uw
middenrif zal reageeren op den klank der dagen, kunt
ge veilig gaan, verlost van 't koord waaraan ge U leiden
liet. Dan wordt Uw naam gedragen en zult ge sterk
staan en niet vluchten. Uw weg moet ge zelf zoeken.
Val niet. Hier is Uw kruis.

HET LIJF DAT VREEST

PARIS
Le lendemain

Il fait un temps horrible.
C'est l'exécution de l'été. La neige douce et la pluie
sont les sanglots et les larmes de la foule autour de l'é-
chafaud. L'immense vent hurlant est le cri effroyable
du peuple au moment que la hâche est tombée.
J'aimerais mieux assister à l'exécution de l'art. Ça serait
une scène touchante.
Imaginez-vous que tous les gens qui se disputent sur
l'art seraient témoins de cette cérémonie. Je me méfie
de cette foule qui se mettra à crier et à pleurer. Savez
que les mêmes bouches chanteront au lendemain et se
disputeront de nouveau sur l'art. Ces messieurs parlent
de l'amour et adorent la cochonnerie, ces farceurs qui
n'ont jamais eu d'autre aspiration que de se préparer
pour un bon dîner avec du bon vin et une belle femme.
Assez de ces méditations sentimentales, l'histoire se ré-
pète toujours. L'été prochain sera encore plus beau et
mourira au fin. L'art se rend et ne meurt pas. Rien
de nouveau sur ce monde.

LEVENS VREUGD

Smeek om smart,
Geen liefdesverkwijnen;
Verwoestingswee,
Weelde van lijden.

Haat overwinning
Ruiters roes.
Morgen de wroeging,
Dood in de kroes.

DE VRIJHEID VAN DE GEEST

Around the same time, Werkman began to pay less attention to the running of his business, and the unexpected cost of a new printing press ordered from Germany was especially damaging to his finances. In the purchase agreement, the price of the press was tied to inflation in the Weimar Republic, and Werkman eventually had to pay far more than anticipated. This, together with the absence of the Cremer's financial expertise, adversely affected the firm's financial position to such an extent that on December 21, 1921, Werkman was forced to sell his once flourishing company. The collapse of the business was largely a result of Werkman's indifference toward business affairs. Willem Sandberg later described Werkman as someone for whom anything utilitarian was beyond comprehension. Bos later said that when some new stationery had been printed for the company, someone noticed they had forgotten to include the telephone number. Werkman's casual response was, 'Oh well, just leave it as is. I've already had enough bother with that telephone.'[5]

After the sale Werkman was compelled to dismiss all of his employees except for Bos and moved what was left of the company to a seventh-floor attic space above a warehouse on a canal called the 'Lage der A.' Since his work area could only be reached by climbing several long flights of stairs, it was not a location conducive to attracting customers. Although Werkman managed to make ends meet by taking on commissions such as wedding and birth announcements, invitations, brochures, stationery, and posters, the new business never prospered.

In the long run, however, these setbacks became a means of liberation, or in the words of his friend Job Hansen, 'Werkman's art is the result of unemployment.'[6] Werkman later wrote that until then his life had not been his own but that he had been a prisoner of convention. From this time on he increasingly tried to distance himself from anything not related to the poetic nature of printing, and even his commercial pieces reflected this attitude. After using typography for so many years to serve his clients, he suddenly realized that he had never used type in the way that he wanted.

Years later, he wrote to his war-time friend Paul Guermonprez that in spite of his destitution during this period it was then, at the age of forty-one, he 'realized the better purposes in life are to be found somewhere else.'[7] Beginning in August 1924, The Belgian artist Michel Seuphor, pseudonym of F. Berckelaers and publisher of *Het Overzicht* (The Review), became an important correspondent for Werkman as well as his connection with the European avant-garde. In 1930, Werkman wrote to him: 'It seems that my objective in life has become to redress myself for all that I have overlooked until now and could have done.'[8]

On September 12, 1923, a printed flyer was delivered to Werkman's colleagues in De Ploeg. Commencing with the phrase 'GRONINGEN BERLIN PARIS MOSCOW 1923 – Beginning of a Violet season,' it announced the advent of the new avant-garde publication soon to be named *The Next Call* and candidly proclaimed a new era in the arts. It stated: 'It must be attested and affirmed... Art is everywhere.'[9] Berlin, Paris and Moscow were then centers of new art movements, and by having Groningen head the list, Werkman contended that similar achievements were possible there as well. It was signed 'Travailleur & Cie' ('Workman & Co.' in French) which gave a clue as to the writer's identity, but the recipients knew that it was Werkman from his address.

The year 1923 was pivotal for Werkman, and as Ad Petersen wrote in his book *De Ploeg*: 'To view *The Next Call* as a *cri de coeur* is no exaggeration.'[10] Werkman later wrote: 'Like a wet poodle I shook off everything that for me was annoying and stood then for a while virtually alone. To tell the truth I did not understand it myself at times. Still I continued: everything that you now lose is gain....'[11]

From 1923 until 1926, *The Next Call* was published in nine random issues in editions of forty with no subscription charges. Although it did not bear the name *The Next Call* until the second issue, the first issue of publication was mailed on September 22 with Travailleur & Cie cited as the publisher. In large, rough upper-case sans serif letters, it boldly displayed a phrase that reflected Werkman's philosophy for the rest of his life:

EEN RIL DOORKLIEFT
HET LIJF DAT VREEST
DE VRIJHEID VAN DE GEEST

(A CHILL SEEPS THROUGH
THE BODY THAT FEARS
THE FREEDOM OF THE SPIRIT)[12]

Including the front and back covers, the issue consisted of eight pages. The front page was one of Werkman's first non-objective typographic compositions where two lower-case 'r's and a larger lower-case 'e' are combined with the impression of a lock plate taken from the side of a door. The letters are not intended to convey a message, and the lock plate assumes a new identity as an upper-case 'E'.

The first of the series ends with the cryptic text:

JOY OF
LIFE

Pray for Anguish
No Languishing from love;
Wasting worry,
Luxury of Woe.

Loathe triumph
Horseman's glow
Tomorrow the regret
Death in the cup[13]

With the first issue of *The Next Call*, Werkman combined traditional printing with an unconventional method where the paper was placed face up on the bed of the press, which enabled him to freely arrange previously inked separate design elements.

Werkman used a Christian Dingler handpress manufactured in Germany in 1850, which he pushed beyond any previous capabilities. Every printed nuance played a role in Werkman's work – idiosyncrasies of wood grains, scratches on damaged type, thickness of ink, different ways of inking, and paper textures all became part of his design. Totally captivated by the printing process, Werkman often referred to his materials as animate beings: 'There is paper so beautiful that one only wants to caress it and otherwise leave it unblemished.'[14]

Below: H. N. Werkman, *The Next
Call* 2, cover, 1923.

Opposite: H. N. Werkman, *The Next
Call* 2, pages 2–5, 1923.

204

Groeiende Lach

October 1923

Ondanks de kunst. Want de kunst heeft veel op haar geweten.
Ondanks de pers. Want de pers is nog schuldiger domper.
Altijd hebben ze samen geprobeerd elke goede kiem te verstikken,
elke goede gedachte te verslijmen en elke goede daad te vermodderen.
De epidemische hersenverweeking en de ontzettende leververdorring
komen voor beider gezamenlijke rekening.
Maar desondanks wordt er reeds tamelijk veel gelachen in deze wereld.
Vergeet dat niet bij 'tgeen gij doet en beschouw deze lach niet als
een hebbelijk verschijnsel dat zich thans aan de hoeken der straten
openbaart.
Het heeft natuurlijk niets gemeen met het gedoe van den oppassenden
burgerman die met zijn weldoorvoede vrouw in de stijlvolle kamers
hokt, welke noodig een uitmesting behoeven.
Het is de lach van de vrijgeworstelde bij het zien van de pogingen
om de vrijgaande geest het evolueeren te beletten.
Nog flaneert het geganteerde officiertje ridicuul door de hoofdstraten.
Nog imponeert de bureaucraat en handhaaft zijn gezag.
Nog duldt de beer de ketting om zijn hals.
Nog gaat in schijnvertoon en onder inmaakleus de snijboon door de
straten.
Nog gaapt de kloot zich suf aan elke gouden kar en weet z'n functie
niet.
Zoo lomp gaat deze tocht door het moerasland voort en stoort zich
niet aan and'rer ergernis en sjoeksjakt naar z'n einde en vindt op
't laatst de dood.
Hoor de lach.
Over alle bajonetten heen, over alle gouden kragen gaat de vrije
geest de wereld door.
Alle handhavers, alle deurwaarders, ijdeltuiterige veldwachters en
griffiers, alle beffen, toga's en baretten zullen aanhooren den lach
van de gesomberde en vervolgde die zoo luid zal klinken in hun
rechtzaal dat zij hunne kaken na de stompzinnige aangaping nooit
meer kunnen sluiten.

Compared to the more urbane centers of Amsterdam, Rotterdam, Utrecht and The Hague, in 1923 Groningen was still a parochial and somewhat insular city. Werkman wrote to Seuphor in 1924: 'Much to my regret I have to admit that Groningen sits in a corner which almost no sound penetrates.'[15]

As evidenced by the Dutch proverb '*Wat de boer niet kent, dat vreet hij niet*' (What the farmer doesn't know, he doesn't eat), by temperament, the people of Groningen were inherently cautious, and the first issue of *The Next Call* did not impress his De Ploeg colleagues. Hansen and Wiegers, who contributed to five of the issues, were the only ones who seemed to comprehend what Werkman was attempting. For the most part the others reacted more with curiosity, as they were suspicious of their colleague's sudden plunge into the avant-garde. Werkman later lamented: 'In spite of the fact that many of the things produced in this period seem somewhat mad in retrospect, *The Next Call* was never intended as a joke. Otherwise, with vacillating self-confidence, I would never have been able to continue.'[16]

The second number of *The Next Call*, now officially using the series' name, appeared on October 6, 1923, again with the lock plate as the dominant element on the cover. Puppet-like figures constructed out of type appeared on pages 2 and 4, and in a vertical column on the back page the author was again listed as Travailleur & Cie.

On page 6, the word 'Paris' is covered with a rectangular paper fragment, indicating that Werkman altered pieces even after they were printed. Although he sometimes made preliminary sketches, Werkman never worked from pre-determined designs or as he later wrote, 'the subject proclaims itself and is never sought.'[17] With Werkman, the design did not precede the type-setting and printing, and the three processes were combined into a single creative procedure, allowing him to discover his configurations through the printing procedure itself. Werkman wrote in 1941: 'Do you know the difference between me and others? They are designers who do not work at a press and instead leave the production to others, while I produce designs during the course of printing.'[18]

No two copies of *The Next Call* are exactly the same. The printing is irregular, the letter-spacing arbitrary, and the inking inconsistent. Werkman did not concern himself with the aesthetic aspects of typeface design and used what was available in his printing shop. Werkman was never interested in exact printing, and details assumed a secondary place in his design process. He was prepared to use any means necessary to achieve his results.

In 1923 Werkman printed his first series of over six hundred monotypes employing techniques similar to those used in *The Next Call*. To describe them, he coined the term *druksel*, a derivative of the Dutch infinitive 'drukken' meaning 'to print.' Until the early thirties, the druksels usually were primarily made from type material, and by controlling the printing pressure, inking procedures and consistency, Werkman achieved an intricate arrangement of tone and layers. Werkman later elaborated on his procedure: 'I use an old hand press for my prints; so the impression is done vertically, and the impression can be regulated instinctively. Sometimes you have to press hard, sometimes very lightly, sometimes one half of the block is heavily inked, the other half sparsely. Also, by printing the first layer of ink on another sheet of paper you then get a paler shade, which is used for the definitive version.... Sometimes a single print goes under the press fifty times.'[19] The procedure could be repeated indefinitely with an unlimited number of shapes and colors, and in this way his printing technique touched upon the milieu of painting.

Werkman's druksels bring to mind abstract prints that Zwart was producing at the same time. However, Werkman used a traditional letterpress while Zwart preferred modern printing technology. Werkman allowed the druksels to evolve during the printing process, while Zwart maintained a strict control from the conception stage until the end product. Werkman's youngest daughter Fie remembered her father's excitement when he came home with the first of these prints. However, they were never displayed until included in a Prinsenhof Gallery exhibition in Groningen during the fall of 1925. A reviewer in the *Provinciale Groninger Courant* dismissed them as pleasantries rather than serious work.

The druksels could be partially defined as printed collages and were analogous to what Schwitters was doing during the same period. Both worked from pre-existing elements, but instead of using fragments of paper and other found components, Werkman combined materials available in his type shop.

Although Werkman's approach could not be called functional, there was a similarity between his approach and that of Zwart. Through respecting the inherent qualities of the printing elements, Werkman did approach the constructivist view that art should reflect the character of its material.

In addition to the druksels, between 1926 and 1927 Werkman produced a series of typographic drawings created on the typewriter. He labeled them *tiksels*, a play on the word 'tikken' meaning 'to type' in Dutch. These tiksels were produced around the same time as comparable pieces in *De Stijl* (vol. VII, nos. 75/76 and 77, 1926–27) by Pietro (de) Saga, a nom de plume of the Austrian artist Stefi Kiesler. Werkman's tiksels, however, were abstract designs rather than word poems.

The fourth issue of *The Next Call* appeared at the end of January 1924. With this issue the typography became more experimental, and the pages were filled with movement and tension. Both the front and back pages consist of numbers within a grid made from typographic rules, and page 6 alludes to a machine and suggests a 1920 collage by Moholy-Nagy. The compositions seem to have randomly fallen into place, and the harmony of double-page spreads is more pronounced.

On the second and third pages, the death of Lenin on January 21 is commemorated by two columns of type constructed from 'O's and 'M's. These letters suggest soldiers standing in vigilance around a casket, and the word 'OOM' means 'uncle' in Dutch, so this could have been intended as a term of endearment.

Although Werkman was fundamentally apolitical, he admired the Russian avant-garde and viewed the Russian revolution as an artistic rebirth. He often remarked that he wanted to visit Russia before he died. When asked about the absence of social issues in his work, however, Werkman said that he had no interest in such matters.

When the fifth issue of *The Next Call* was distributed in June of 1924, the lock plate appeared on the first page for the last time. Boldly printed in orange, blue and black, this was by far the most colorful issue of the publication. The typography in issue five was more animated than in prior issues as the pages alternated between text and image. On page 2, an ampersand seems to be perched atop a vertical rectangle like a typographic parrot, while on page 3, one sees the juxtaposition of a wide variety of typefaces which manage to achieve a visual harmony.

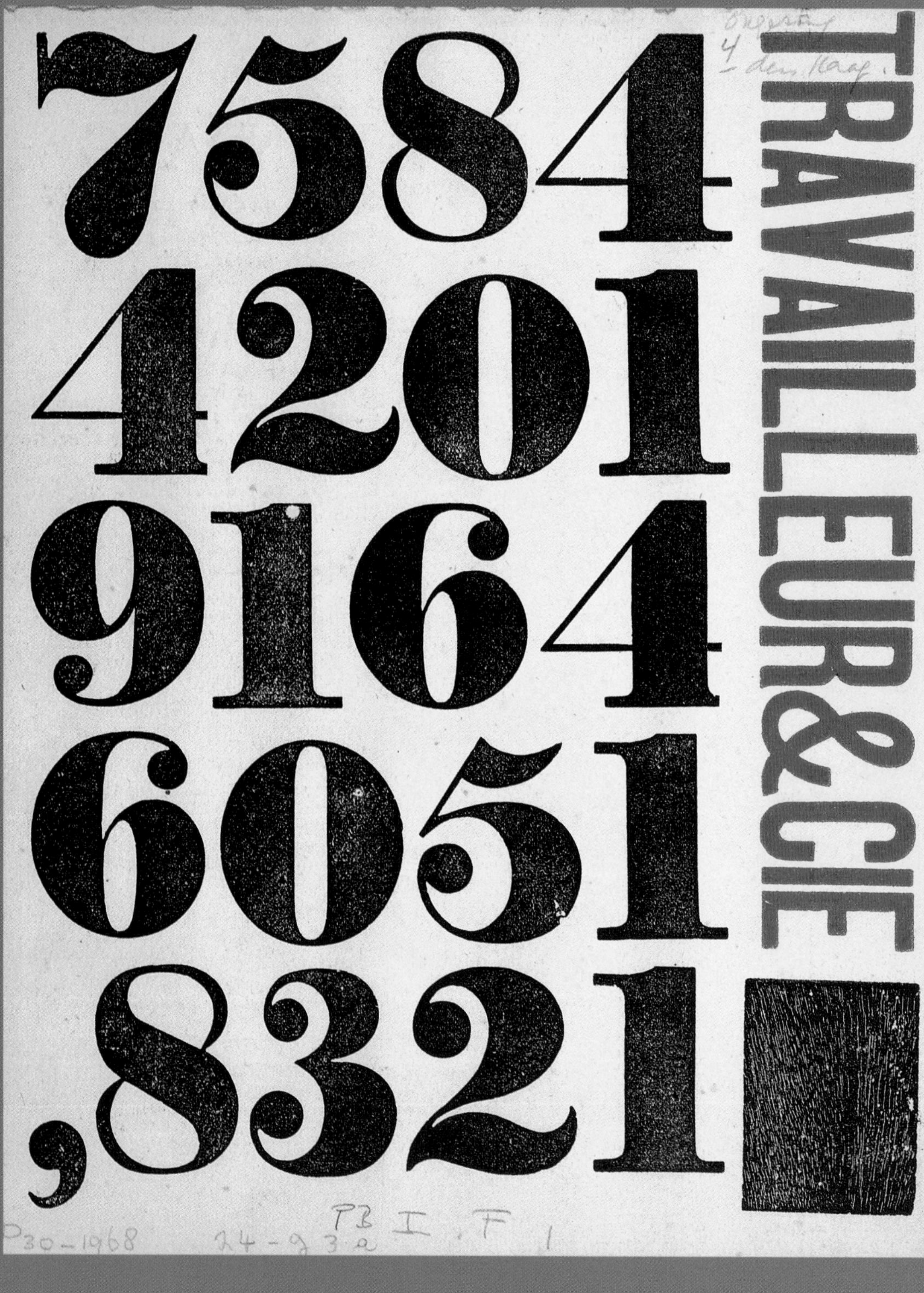

7584
4201
9164
6051
,8321

TRAVAILLEUR&CIE

H. N. Werkman, *The Next Call* 4,
front and back, 1924.

Significantly, this was the first issue of *The Next Call* to be sent to recipients outside of Groningen. Werkman received a letter from 'I. K. Bonset' in response to the receipt of a copy of the fifth issue, but was unaware that Van Doesburg was the writer. Obviously Van Doesburg did not understand Werkman's tongue-in-cheek humor in using the term Travailleur & Cie, and he replied with typical pomposity:

210　　When and however it would be plausible to restructure your magazine in a more dadaist path I would be glad to help you, also in sending it to addresses of conceivable interest such as: Picabia, Tzara, Arp, Schwitters, Richter, etc.... Typographically I find a lot to admire in your publication, notably page 4. However, it does not make a good impression when you neglect to mention the names of the collaborators at the beginning of your magazine. Every clandestine action is a priori rejected.[20]

Known for his competitiveness, it is clear that Van Doesburg saw Werkman as a rival when he did not include *The Next Call* in a list of books and magazines published in *De Stijl* in 1924 and 1926. Van Doesburg's letter, however, did produce a response, for in the next issue 'Travailleur et Cie' was replaced by 'Edit. Publisher H. N. Werkman, Lage der A 13, Groningen, Holland.' By then Werkman had discarded any hope of getting much understanding from De Ploeg members, which was an additional reason for eliminating Travailleur et Cie.

The sixth issue, which was the first of two printed as foldouts on a single sheet, was mailed on the first of November 1924. Rectangular fragments of type from discarded posters were pasted on the top of the front and back pages adding to the uniqueness of each copy. When the sheet was completely unfolded, the typographic construction 'Plattegrond van de Kunst en Omstreken' (Map of Art and Environs) appeared.

The text on the back page states that Werkman was now in contact with other avant-publishers and editors.

The Next Call sustains international communication with the editors of numerous avant garde publications and subscribes to: *Het Overzicht*, F. Berckelaers and Josef Peeters, Antwerp. *De Stijl*, Theo van Doesburg, Leiden. *Mécano*, I.K. Bonset, Paris. *Merz*, Kurt Schwitters and El Lissitsky, Hanover. *La Zone*, A. Cernik, Brünn Jullanov, Belgrade. *Zenith*, L. Mitzitch, Belgrade. *Blok*, H. Stazewski and others, Warsaw. *Disk*, K. Teige, Prague, and many others.[21]

Except for Seuphor, there is no indication that Werkman ever met any of those outside of Groningen to whom *The Next Call* was mailed, nor is there any indication as to how they perceived the publication.

The typography in the eighth number from September 1925 has a strong association with industry. The cover suggests a factory while other constructions depict machinery, a fork-lift, and a truck.

The ninth and final issue of *The Next Call* was published in November of 1926. Typographically this was the most elegant and refined issue of them all. The center spread on pages 4 and 5, constructed with large lower-case 'a's and black rules, had a melodic feel with its type forms freely meandering through the white space. Werkman began with a poem that suggested the end of the series as well as his disillusionment:

struggling is useless
struggling is not useless
not struggling is useless
not struggling is not useless
useless struggling is useless
useless struggling is not useless
not useless struggling is useless
not useless struggling is not useless
It is about a motto
because a good motto is part
of the renown
of the house, as a pendant of the
excuses
whoever can not congratulate
himself with an excuse
will be severely depressed
by a heavy mind
how else would he be able to get above
the belief in or the fear of
ideals that are within reach.[22]

The Next Call concluded with Werkman's pensive poem:

once when the earth was still not round
once when art was still not art
once when the ant was not yet diligent
once when he was still young
once when she was still small
once when my mother still sang
once when it was summer
once when it was still the day before yesterday
once when yesterday was not yet today.[23]

One of Werkman's objectives for *The Next Call* was to agitate some of the De Ploeg members out of their complacency and make them question the validity of their academic training. Although it did produce an initial jolt, most of the group soon considered the publication little more than an oddity. *The Next Call* did give Werkman a venue to display his experimental typography and to communicate with the international avant-garde, and it also helped to keep him spiritually creative in what he felt to be a provincial environment.

By 1926, Werkman had given up trying to affect the stances of those in De Ploeg. Van Zweden wrote about this subject after Werkman's death in 1945: 'For members of De Ploeg, Werkman served as a kind of artistic conscience; he protected them from becoming bourgeois too early and with his astute vision he breached the limitations of a menacing parochialism.'[24] De Vries also stated in 1945 that, 'his colleagues in De Ploeg had as much admiration for him as their pedestrian states of mind would permit.'[25]

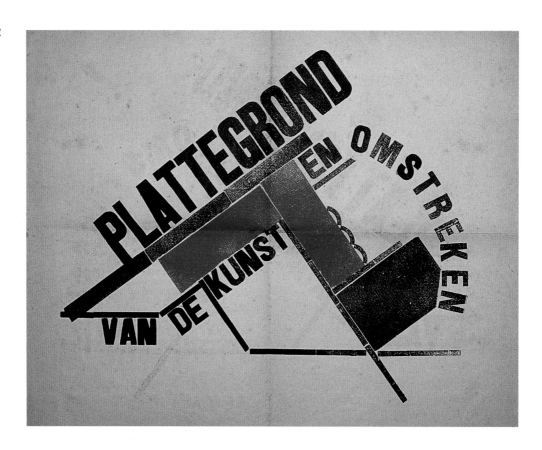

Above: H. N. Werkman, *The Next Call* 6,
unfolded, 1924.

Opposite: H. N. Werkman, *The Next
Call* 6, front and back, 1924.

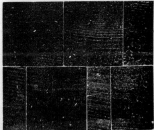

The Next Call
onderhoudt internationaal verkeer met redacties van onderscheidene Tijdschriften van de avant-garde en neemt abonnementen aan op:
Het Overzicht, F. Berckelaers en Jozef Peeters, Antwerpen. De stijl, Theo van Doesburg, Leiden. Mécano, I. K. Bonset, Parijs. Merz, Kurt Schwitters en L. Lissitzky, Hannover. La Zone, A. Cernik, Brünn Julianov, Zenith, L. Mitzitch, Belgrado. Blok, H. Stazewski e.a. Warschau. Disk, K. Teige, Praag, en vele andere.

Redact.-Uitgever H. N. Werkman, Lage der A 13. Groningen, Holland.

Hans van Straten elaborated on this in his biography of Werkman:

For him, *The Next Call* was a rebellious act against everything, against his existence, against the dire circumstances associated with his printing business, against Groningen and in a certain sense against De Ploeg. What he did as a member of the circle was, in effect, 'out of order': he began there to formulate an artistic ideal in a strictly personal manner; and that in an organization that had never had an artistic program, only statutes (approved by the government in 1921) and regulations.[26]

In the first issue of *The Next Call*, Werkman stressed that the publication 'arose from the tempo of the times and is not a triviality. It is not a repetition of the Dada joke; it is not a mockery.'[27] Also, unlike the Dadaists who insisted they were not creating art, Werkman saw the aesthetic relevance of his creations.

Even though Werkman criticized the academic stances of De Ploeg, he remained on good terms with its members. Part of his company space was always made available as a studio where De Ploeg members could print etchings and draw and paint from live models.

Consecutive with the first issue of *The Next Call*, Werkman continued to print other material using a similar approach. This included De Ploeg posters and invitations, birth announcements, calendars, bookplates, and cards. These are consistently characterized by the same playfulness, innocence, and boldness seen in his experimental work.

With a few interruptions, the next years were productive for Werkman. He was never able to fulfil his dream of leaving the business world, but by investing in a more modern letterpress in 1927, he was able to continue working as a commercial printer. In 1929 he began using the printer's ink roller as a drawing and painting tool, applying it directly to the paper, and in 1934 he introduced stencils as well. In addition, he incorporated a method where pieces of wood type were individually inked and pressed onto the paper surface. An avid jazz fan, in 1935 he named this new series of druksels 'Hot Printing' after a then-popular term 'Hot Jazz.'

In 1945, Ate Zuithoff, whom Werkman met in 1940, described his new method of working.

When I saw him in later years busy with a sheet of paper and an old razor blade with which the form was quickly and flexibly cut out, it seemed as if he was working with a pencil, so skillfully did he manipulate the contours. The cut-away as well as the cut-out piece were both used. Applying the ink to the roller was done by rolling it back and forth over a zinc pallet on which the ink had been mixed. The manner of rolling and the separation of the ink provided diverse nuances and made it possible to spread out the colors. This resulted in a colored form or a recess in a colored area that eventually could be filled with another color.... With most of the prints he first made a small sketch with a fountain pen on a calendar page. The colors were already envisioned in his imagination....[28]

Werkman's financial situation often affected what he produced, and the tiksels, for example, were certainly economical. Also, because of defaulted payments to suppliers, he sometimes had to resort to printing on wrapping paper and using whatever ink colors were on hand at the time.

During the fall of 1927, Seuphor wanted to arrange for an exhibition of Werkman's druksels in Paris. This never took place, but in August 1929 Werkman made his one trip outside of the Netherlands, and accompanied by Wiegers, he traveled to Essen, Cologne, and Paris. Although visiting museums and galleries made the trip worthwhile, Werkman was deeply disappointed in not being able to see Seuphor who happened to be away at the time. In April 1930, however, Seuphor included two of Werkman's druksels in an exhibition that Seuphor organized at Galerie 23 in Paris. Although his work made little impact, it was an important event for Werkman, since he was included among artists such as Hans Arp, Sophie Taeuber-Arp, Huszár, Wassily Kandinsky, Antoine Pevsner, Le Corbusier, Fernand Léger, Mondrian, Schwitters and F. Vordemberge-Gildewart.

Werkman's marriage to Nel fell apart in 1930, and, inspired by Gauguin, he made serious plans to move to Tahiti. With this in mind, he resigned from De Ploeg on January 15, 1932, but on Van der Zee's initiative was kept on as an honorary member. After the Tahiti dream failed to materialize, Werkman was again made an active De Ploeg member.

Werkman's approach changed significantly with the introduction of new techniques in the 1930s, and, while retaining its candid simplicity, his work became more refined. The *Proclamatie* manifesto posters, an abortive attempt to promote a new version of *The Next Call*, were exemplary of this subtle change.

His 1933 poster for *De Rekenmachine* (The Adding Machine), a drama by the progressive American playwright Elmer L. Rice, depicted an adding machine constructed out of typographic material. Years later Rice saw the poster for the first time at a Werkman exhibition at the Stedelijk Museum in Amsterdam.

Preludium was published in September 1938, and was one of the few pieces that was printed, illustrated and written by Werkman. *Preludium* was created as a protest to De Ploeg members who wanted to accept twelve new associates whom Werkman and some other members feared would introduce a bourgeois and conservative influence. When they were eventually accepted, some of the more progressive De Ploeg members resigned, but Werkman retained his membership.

Between 1926 and 1945, Werkman created nine calendars which were in line with his other experimental typography. These calendars served two important functions. Firstly, they were yet another means to explore experimental typography. Even more significantly, however, was that they heralded the coming years and were therefore spiritual manifestations of Werkman's unyielding optimism.

When Werkman married for the third time in 1936, his printing company was still surviving, but only on a shoestring. His career, however, came to a climatic conclusion with his clandestine publications produced during the German occupation.

Part of Werkman's legacy was: 'to teach us that type could function independently without communicating a message; that graphic design need not be bound to new technology.... that it can come from the heart and transcend craftsmanship; that it does not have to rely on systems, modes, or rules; that in the end the transcendental can prevail.'[29]

Above: H. N. Werkman, *The Next Call* 9,
back and front, 1926.

Opposite: H. N. Werkman, poster for
the play *De Rekenmachine* (The Adding
Machine) by Elmer L Rice, 1928.

Chapter 6 Notes

1 Dick Dooijes, *Over typografie en grafische kunst*, Amsterdam: Lettergieterij en

Machinehandel voorheen N. Tetterode, 1966, p. 72.

2 H. N. Werkman, letter to F. R. A. Henkels, August 4, 1943. In *Brieven van*

H. N. Werkman, 1940–1945, ed. Jan Martinet, Amsterdam: De Arbeiderspers,

1982, second edition.

3 Herbert Spencer, 'H. N. Werkman, Printer-Painter', in *Typografica*,

old series no. II, 1955, p. 20.

4 H. N. Werkman, letter to F. R. A. Henkels, May 12, 1941. In *Brieven van*

H. N. Werkman, 1940–1945, ed. Jan Martinet, Amsterdam: De Arbeiderspers,

1982, second edition.

5 Adriaan Venema, *De Ploeg, 1918–1930*, Baarn: Het Wereldvenster, 1978, p. 74.

6 Hans van Straten, *Hendrik Nicolaas Werkman*, Amsterdam: Meulenhoff, 1980, p. 61.

7 H. N. Werkman, letter to Paul Guermonprez, May 22, 1942. In *Brieven van*

H. N. Werkman, 1940–1945, ed. Jan Martinet, Amsterdam: De Arbeiderspers,

1982, second edition.

8 Hans van Straten, *Hendrik Nicolaas Werkman*, Amsterdam: Meulenhoff, 1980, p. 78.

9 H. N. Werkman, announcement for *The Next Call*, 1923.

10 Ad Petersen, *De Ploeg*, The Hague: Uitgeverij BZZTôH, 1982, p. 56.

11 H. N. Werkman, letter to F. R. A. Henkels, May 12, 1941. In *Brieven van*

H. N. Werkman, 1940–1945, ed. Jan Martinet, Amsterdam: De Arbeiderspers,

1982, second edition.

12 H. N. Werkman, *The Next Call* 1, 1923.

13 H. N. Werkman, *The Next Call* 1, 1923.

14 H. N. Werkman, letter to Paul Guermonprez, September 25, 1942. In *Brieven*

van H. N. Werkman, 1940–1945, ed. Jan Martinet, Amsterdam:

De Arbeiderspers, 1982, second edition.

15 See Venema, *De Ploeg*, 1918–1930, p 18.

16 See Hans van Straten, *Hendrik Nicolaas Werkman*, p. 67.

17 H. N. Werkman, letter to F. R. A. Henkels, January 24, 1941. In *Brieven van*

H. N. Werkman, 1940–1945, ed. Jan Martinet, Amsterdam: De Arbeiderspers,

1982, second edition.

18 H. N. Werkman, letter to F. R. A. Henkels, July 23, 1941. In *Brieven van*

H. N. Werkman, 1940–1945, ed. Jan Martinet, Amsterdam: De Arbeiderspers,

1982, second edition.

19 H. N. Werkman, letter to F. R. A. Henkels, January 24, 1941. In *Brieven van*

H. N. Werkman, 1940–1945, ed. Jan Martinet, Amsterdam: De Arbeiderspers,

1982, second edition.

20 See Hans van Straten, *Hendrik Nicolaas Werkman*, p. 73.

21 H. N. Werkman, *The Next Call* 6, 1923.

22 H. N. Werkman, *The Next Call* 9, 1923.

23 H. N. Werkman, *The Next Call* 9, 1923.

24 Johan van Zweden, 'H.N. Werkman, De Groningse Drukker-Schilder,'

in Han Steenbruggen and Sjoukje Posthuma (eds.), *Hendrik N. Werkman*, catalog

published on the occasion of the exhibition 'Werkman,' November 9, 1995 to

January 14, 1996, Groningen: Groninger Museum, 1995, p. 14.

25 Hendrik de Vries and Dr. A. J. Zuifhoff, *Werkman, Drukker-Schilder*, Amsterdam:

Stedelijk Museum, 1945, p. 3.

26 See Venema, *De Ploeg, 1918–1930*, p. 141.

27 H. N. Werkman, *The Next Call* 1, 1923.

28 De Vries and Zuifhoff, *Werkman, Drukker-Schilder*, p. 5.

29 Alston W. Purvis, *H. N. Werkman*, London: Laurence King, 2004, p. 7.

Above: H. N. Werkman, De Ploeg
calendar, 1923. Only the November
page was designed by Werkman.

Opposite, above: H. N. Werkman,
cover for *De Ploeg*, 1927. **Below:**
H. N. Werkman, *Proclamatie* 1, 1932.

N.V.V. S.D.A.P

'T GAAT OM DE TOEKOMST — VAN UW KIND — KIND TOT GELUK GESCHAPEN

14 SEPTEMBER
ROTTERDAM

FRÉ COHEN '30

Fré Cohen, *The Concern is for Your Child's Future*, SDAP (Labor Party) poster, Amsterdam, 1930.

THE 1930S, A PERIOD OF TURMOIL AND CHANGE

The unstable economic and political climate in Europe during the thirties had a regressive effect on the expectations and aspirations of the 1920s. As National Socialism emerged in Germany, and to a lesser extent in the Netherlands, the stimulating international exchanges diminished, and an outlook of isolation began to take hold within the artistic and intellectual communities. Although Dutch society continued to be relatively stable, unemployment and inflation increased as the depression continued. As the political and economic situation became increasingly dismal, a new and sometimes retrogressive realism in painting emerged parallel to Constructivism. Apathy, despondency, and irony largely replaced the optimism of the twenties. In one way, this was exemplified through Surrealism and its submission to the subconscious, and in architecture, a reactionary movement developed as a counter-force to functionalism.

Graphic design was not immune to these political and social upheavals. Embellishment, which had been largely rejected during the twenties, began to appear more frequently, and conventional illustration regained some of its popularity. These changes were evident in the exhibition 'Art et Technique' at the Paris World Fair in 1937 where few of the graphic design innovations of the twenties and early thirties were on display.

Prior to 1930, no graphic design schools existed as they do today; most graphic designers also worked in other disciplines such as painting, architecture, industrial design, or the printing industry. However, even though graphic design was still not viewed as a distinct profession, after 1930 those in industry began to recognize its value more than before. The VANK, the Vereniging voor Ambachts Nijverheidskunst (Association for Crafts and Industrial Design), founded in 1904, became steadily more important in the thirties. This was an organization open to both progressive and traditional designers and encompassed all design fields. The VANK had three basic objectives: to advocate topics relevant to these diverse disciplines; to advance the arts and crafts in industry; and to inform the public regarding their agenda. It also staged exhibitions, and members were involved in industrial fairs. In addition, the VANK provided advice and information, encouraged member participation in international exhibits and trade shows, procured commissions for members, and set pricing standards. Its magazine *New Arts* advocated the collaboration of artists and craftsmen, and from 1919 until 1931 the VANK printed an annual that published the work of members and articles on their professions. The VANK remained an active force until dissolved by the occupying Nazi administration in 1942.

Prominent Dutch graphic designers whose careers began to flourish in the late twenties and thirties included Willem Sandberg, Gerard Kiljan, Wim Brusse, Hendrik Josef Louis (Henny) Cahn, Nicolaas P. de Koo, Cesar Domela, Peter Almo, Dick Elffers, and W. H. Gispen. Gispen, both a manufacturer and industrial designer, was first attracted to the *Wendingen* style and later converted to Functionalism. Another often overlooked figure was Andries M. Oosterbaan, manager of the printer Lumax in Utrecht, which produced many of the books for De Gemeenschap. Oosterbaan was initially trained as a bookbinder before focusing on typography, and from 1930 until the end of 1933 he supervised the design for at least eight books for Lumax, the most prominent of which was *Blokken* (Blocks) by F. Bordewijk. Although small in number, his designs exemplify some of the most innovative book typography of the period.

Although Willem Sandberg's most significant work in graphic design did not appear until after World War II, his accomplishments during the thirties gave a clear indication of his developing talents. Raised in a traditional Calvinist environment, he had detached himself from religion by his sixteenth year. At first he was determined to become a painter, and, since his family had for generations been lawyers and civil servants, this was difficult for his parents to accept. He persisted, however, and in 1919 entered the Rijksacademie in Amsterdam. After six months time, Sandberg became disillusioned with the art school milieu and decided to leave the program. Among other reasons, he found it particularly irritating and insulting when his instructors made corrections directly on his drawings. After marrying a year later, Sandberg and his wife went to Italy, Switzerland, and Germany, and for a brief period in 1922 he studied at the Académie de la Grande Chaumière in Paris. His painting ambitions had all but evaporated by 1923, however, and he later remarked that Mondrian had already achieved what he wanted to do. Sandberg and his wife then returned to the Netherlands where he earned a law degree. A born intellectual, Sandberg also studied philosophy, art history, psychology, and statistics in Vienna and later in Utrecht. While in Vienna he encountered Otto Neurath's pictograms, which helped to stimulate his interest in graphic design.

Almost unknowingly, Sandberg entered the graphic design field in 1927 when he designed a calendar for the publisher Ploegsma. As with most others of the period he was self-taught, and although his initial inspiration came from De Stijl, Constructivism, and Dada, his ultimate work in graphic design was based on experimentation, spontaneity, and intuition.

When Sandberg became increasingly involved with graphic design at the end of the twenties, he joined the VANK and De 8 en Opbouw where he came into contact with progressive young designers. The latter group included architects and graphic designers who were keenly aware of new developments in Germany and Russia and who were committed to progressive industrial design and to the idea that housing should serve society. Mart Stam, one of the members, was an important force in the formulation of Sandberg's artistic vision. Beginning in 1934 the two friends collaborated on a number of exhibitions, and during World War II they worked together in the Dutch resistance.

In 1928 Sandberg produced a statistics chart for a Work for the Disabled exhibit, his first design for the Stedelijk Museum. Early clients also included the State Insurance Bank, the Economic Information Service, the Stadsschouwburg (Municipal Concert Hall), Spin Printers, and the PTT. In 1931 he created geography charts for the publisher Nijgh & Van Ditmar, and in 1933 he designed window displays for the PTT in The Hague. In 1935 he began working as an exhibitions consultant for the Stedelijk Museum and in 1936 was hired as a curator. He succeeded D.C. Röell as the museum's director in 1937 and also began designing Stedelijk exhibition catalogs. The 1939 catalogue for the *Rondom Rodin, Honderd jaar Fransche Sculptuur* (Around Rodin, A Hundred Years of French Sculpture) exhibition became a prototype for his later post-war catalogs.

During the winter of 1938–39 Sandberg became acquainted with Werkman and later described his first meeting with the man who became his mentor:

It came about in that I was a friend of the painter Jan Wiegers. Originally from Groningen, he had worked for a time in Switzerland and Germany and had become friends with Kirchner. He was instrumental in bringing expressionism to Groningen. I had not been at the museum very long before he arrived with a portfolio under his arm and said: 'I have a few things here that I don't know quite what to do with. You do a bit with typography and design and will like them.' He then produced the large sheets by Werkman.... I was so curious and intrigued by these large pieces that I wanted to actually see the man and learn about other things he was doing. Shortly afterwards I took a train to Groningen and looked him up at his small home. I then encountered a reserved Groninger with whom it was not easy to start a conversation. A really taciturn person. However, having grown up under the shadow of Groningen in Assen I understand this type. After the first cigarette things went better and, I believe, we became friends that day.... I was fascinated by him and by his work. And then to think that this man was once the head of a book printing establishment.[1]

For both Werkman and Sandberg the 1940–45 occupation years were a time of spiritual and artistic renewal. After being forced to go underground for most of the war, Sandberg returned to his position as the Stedelijk Museum's director and continued to supervise the design of its publications.

Gerard Kiljan studied decorative drawing at the Quellinus School of Applied Arts at Amsterdam from 1904 until 1907 and worked as a lithographer at the Steen-en Boek Drukkerij Faddegon (Faddegon Lithography and Book Printers) from 1909 until 1911. He then became a draftsman and retoucher at the Van Leer Printing Company while following evening courses at the Rijksacademie. After teaching at several Amsterdam technical schools, he joined the faculty at the Academy of Fine Arts in The Hague in 1918 and in 1920 began teaching at the Rotterdam Academy as well. This was Kiljan's first

Below: Stephan Schlesinger, cover of a Christmas catalog for Metz & Co., Amsterdam, 1928. Schlesinger's designs of the 1920s were inspired by decorative Austrian calligraphy.

Opposite: Jacob (Jac.) Jongert, advertisement for Van Nelle's Prisma tea, Rotterdam, 1928. During the 1920s, Jongert, as director of the company's advertising department, changed to a more functionalist design style using primary colors.

VAN NELLE'S
PRISMA
THEE
DE
THEE
VAN 34 ct
PER ONS PAKJE

112 JAC. JONGERT, RECLAMEBILJET

contact with Zwart, who had been hired as an instructor at the Rotterdam Academy a year earlier.

Although principally involved in design education, Kiljan began to accept design commissions in 1926. However, design theory, photography, and visual tonal scales were his real interests, and his work in design production was mainly brochures, advertising, and stamps for the PTT.

Kiljan's designs were based on elementary shapes, sans serif letters, and contrasts as employed by Zwart and were distinguished by an exacting structure, overprinting, photography, and a graduated use of tones. Instead of Constructivism and Dada, Kiljan was more inspired by the Bauhaus. He wrote in 1935:

This devotion (to functionalism) is hardly of value....whenever we really need it, without a doubt the next day it would again be modified both in the theoretical and practical aspects and the next day again, and further on. That is evolution.[2]

In 1930 Kiljan's plan to establish a Department of Advertising at the Academy of Fine Arts in The Hague was approved by the school's board of directors. Although this department was far removed from the school's traditional approach, it was strongly supported by its director, Dr. J. H. Plantenga. In spite of Kiljan's Bauhaus leanings, this was the first Dutch graphic design department largely based on functionalist principles, but Bauhaus principles were indeed taught by the former Bauhaus student, Paul Guermonprez. This was also the first program at a government art school where photography was given official status. However, while teaching in the drawing and painting department, Kiljan had already exposed students to photography by having them create montage images using photographs from magazines.

In 1929 Schuitema came as a guest instructor on several occasions and officially joined the faculty in 1931. Schuitema did not have the required academic credentials but was appointed due to his 'special capacities.'[3] Although some of their colleagues in other departments derisively referred to Schuitema and Kiljan as the 'maniacs,'[4] together they constituted the Dutch avant-garde in graphic design education. Teaching there until the 1960s, Schuitema and Kiljan trained an entire generation of graphic designers and photographers, among the more prominent of whom were Wim Brusse and Henny Cahn.

Brusse studied at the Academy of Fine Arts from 1928 until 1933, and even though he was not in their department, was strongly influenced by Schuitema and Kiljan. After graduation, he became Schuitema's assistant while also working as a freelance graphic designer. His clients included the Spain Help Commission, and the PTT, and his family connection with W. L. & J. Brusse provided him with some early book cover commissions. He soon broke away from the influence of Schuitema and Kiljan and developed an independent style. This shift was partially due to the influence of Dick Elffers who was also working with Schuitema at the time. Together he and Elffers produced the contentious 1939 'Grafiesnummer' (Graphics Number) of *De 8 en Opbouw*, which was openly critical of Constructivism.

Cahn began studying with Kiljan and Schuitema in 1930 and in 1934 began his career as a freelance photographer and graphic designer. His most important clients included the PTT, the N.V. Nederlandsche Huistelefoon Mij (Dutch Home Telephone Company), the N.V.

Handelmaatschappij Reforma (Commercial Company Reforma), and the Dutch Communist Party. Also, in 1937 he participated in the design of the Dutch Pavilion at the Paris World Fair. Although Cahn remained a follower of Schuitema, he never became a die-hard Constructivist. Drawings were used in addition to photographs, and following Kiljan, he exploited overprinting and graduated tones of color. He also used Zwart's system of leading the viewer through the composition. In 1942 Cahn taught at the Ecole d'Humanité in Schwarzsee and Goldern in Switzerland. A few years after the war he returned to the Netherlands where he continued his work in graphic and industrial design.

Nicolaas P. De Koo is one of the lesser-known Dutch graphic designers who played a role during the twenties and thirties. From 1902 to 1907 he studied interior design at the State School for Applied Arts in Amsterdam and moved to Rotterdam around 1910. He found it difficult to earn a living as an interior designer, and thus graphic design soon became his principal discipline. In addition to the PTT, he produced printed material such as stationery and reports for the Rotterdamse Schoolvereniging (Rotterdam School Association) and designed a corporate image for the Phoenix Brewery. His illustrative charts for the International Chamber of Commerce in Rotterdam display a fresh and lively approach and the pictograms recall the 'Vienna Method' of Gerd Arntz and Otto Neurath who had moved to The Hague in 1934. De Koo's typography was not experimental in the manner of Zwart or Schuitema, and he was known for his use of solidly constructed sans serif letters and traditional illustrations instead of photographs.

Peter Alma was another Dutch graphic designer who worked with pictograms, having seen the work of Neurath while doing practical training in illustration in Vienna. After working in Moscow Almo returned to Amsterdam in 1935 where he established a design studio specializing in pictograms.

Dick Elffers was active in many different fields including graphic design, interior and architectural design, tapestry design, ceramics, photography, illustration, and painting. Wim Crouwel later called Elffers a 'grensbewoner' (one living on the border) who 'lives in the no-man's-land between the professions.'⁵ Unlike his earlier mentors, Zwart and Schuitema, Elffers never attempted to create specific theories and manifestos about his work.

For a short span Elffers attended the evening school at the Rotterdam Academy before he was accepted by the day school of Decorative and Industrial Arts in 1927. There he studied under Zwart, Kiljan and Jac. Jongert, the latter playing an important role in Elffers's development as a graphic designer. Jongert studied first at Quellinus and then at the Rijks Academy in Amsterdam. Initially inspired by Roland Holst and De Roos, he soon received commissions from the VANK and began designing posters and ads. Beginning in 1919 he produced posters, packaging and the corporate image for the coffee, tea and tobacco manufacturer De Erven de Wed. J. van Nelle and for the annual Utrecht Industrial Fair. Although his work eventually became more functionalist, Jongert advocated subjectivity. He contended that individuality was a crucial part of the creative process, and that a subjective approach went far deeper than simply arranging functional elements. He was constantly at loggerheads with Zwart who believed that personal expression had no place in functional design.

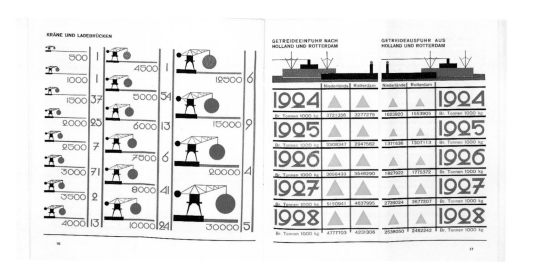

Above: N. P. De Koo, information
booklet for the International Chamber
of Commerce, Rotterdam, 1929. A
fine example of pictograms, although
strictly speaking incorrect by Otto
Neurath's standards, since the variations
in size are not proportionate.

Opposite: L. C. Kalff, poster advertising
the seaside resort of Scheveningen,
The Hague, 1930.

Elffers soon became Jongert's protégé, and was introduced by Jongert to many artists and clients concerned with social issues. In 1931 during his final year at the academy Elffers became Schuitema's assistant and was able to gain from both Schuitema's functional approach and the expressive concepts of Jongert; he saw a need for personal expression in Constructivism and in Expressionism he found a necessity for practical structure. Even though Schuitema was trained as a painter, he disparaged any such tendencies by Elffers, saying that painting was something that you do in your spare time. Elffers, though, took painting quite seriously and exhibited his work at the outset of his career.

An early bloomer, Elffers received graphic design commissions while still a student and won an award for a book jacket design when he was nineteen. One year after leaving school he began teaching at the Rotterdam Academy and became a member of De 8 en Opbouw during the same year. Elffers left Schuitema's studio in 1934 and became Zwart's assistant, having known Zwart as an art history instructor at the Rotterdam Academy. Staying on at Zwart's studio until 1937, Elffers worked on many highly diverse assignments with apparent ease.

Obviously targeted toward Zwart, Schuitema, and Kiljan, Elffers wrote an article in 1937 for the magazine *Prisma der Kunsten* that addressed the work of the three designers and expressed Elffers's ideas on the limitations of photography as the sole visual element in graphic design:

Although it was logical to overrate the value of photography in the discovery of the new design possibilities, we consider it of interest to point out that with photography no renewal in design has taken place.... We would like to see photography placed on the same level with all the other techniques and suggest that in the future the visual artist or designer will, for example, use photography in contrast with other techniques in the same image. How the image came into being is not so important to the observer; what it says to him is the decisive factor.[6]

Zwart, Schuitema, Kiljan, and Cahn fired back in the next issue, saying that Elffers and other 'young Turks' were living in the past:

Do the hearts of these juniors have such small desires? If the answer is yes, then it is to be hoped that these young ones are not the only young ones, for this does not raise great expectations.... In spite of the fact that modern art generates new symbols there is still a great shortage, according to Elffers. Common sense says that the 'young ones' still have a lot to do in filling this shortage, or have they lost confidence in modern art? Or would they rather evoke the past?[7]

In an article for the 1939 'Graphics Number' of *De 8 en Opbouw*, Elffers wrote that he was happy to be called a 'young one' by Zwart but no longer wanted or needed Zwart's methods. Elffers added that *Het boek van PTT* was far too overpowering and ponderous.

Much of Elffers's early graphic design was destroyed during the bombing of Rotterdam in May 1940, concluding the first period of his career. His design during the occupation years and after the war would represent an entirely new phase in his work.

One of the important Socialist designers was Cesar Domela, son of the fiery Socialist Ferdinand Domela Nieuwenhuis. Domela spent his most creative years in Berlin where he met figures such as Richter and Schwitters, the latter of whom asked him to join the Ring neue Werbegestalter. Unable to make a living as a Constructivist painter, he adopted graphic design as his medium. In the late twenties and early thirties he began using photomontage for book covers, ads, and brochures. After being forced to leave Berlin in 1933, he moved to Paris where he set up the first silk-screen studio for printing advertisements. Then, in 1936 he returned permanently to painting. Using montage with extraordinary power, Cas Oorthuys was, like Domela, another designer who vehemently served socialist and anti-Nazi causes.

Van Royen's early years at the PTT were frustrating, as new concepts faced the opposition of the conservative directors. While working as a legal aide to the PTT in 1912, he condemned official printing in an article for the first issue of *De Witte Mier*: 'Three words suffice: government printing is ugly, ugly, ugly, thrice ugly in form, composition, and paper, the three main elements which give printing its character.'[8] Then, in 1920, Van Royen became secretary general of the PTT, and reforming its overall design approach became his passion. He eventually brought about a total transformation of the PTT's official design.

Van Royen's two goals were to completely change the design of the PTT and to provide better and clearer service for its clientele. He commissioned young original and progressive designers and never let his personal approach to typography interfere with that of the PTT. De Roos's relationship with Van Royen was always reserved, most likely because De Roos felt he had not been given adequate credit for his contribution to De Zilverdistel and Kunera Pers publications. Also, De Roos was uncomfortable with Van Royen's enthusiastic acceptance of the Industrial Revolution and new printing innovations. De Roos had respected Van Royen as a proponent of traditional typography, and now Van Royen was giving PTT assignments to Zwart and others like him. For De Roos, this was unacceptable.

Beginning in 1920 the PTT began to produce increasing amounts of advertising and informative material including stickers, folders, posters, booklets, and instruction manuals. Designs were also needed for lettering on vehicles, forms, stamps, symbols, and logos, furniture, telephone booths, mailboxes, and architecture. Although the press on occasion referred to what was taking place as 'official anarchy,' the design section of the PTT continued to expand both in quantity and variety.

In 1924 Van Royen, W. F. Gouwe, and W. Penaat, director of the Museum van Kunstnijverheid (Museum of Industrial Art) in Haarlem, together with a number of industrialists, formed the BKI (Association for Art in Industry) to promote the production of high-quality design in industry. Many important executives and companies in the industrial sector joined the BKI, including Joh. Enschedé en Zonen and W. L. & J. Brusse. This provided an ideal platform for Van Royen in his initiative to improve PTT design standards.

Making the public aware of PTT services became increasingly important, and in 1927 a new division, the PPD (Press and Propaganda Service), was established for this purpose. Whenever a new design project was proposed, the PPD's director, P. G. de Pater, would ask Gouwe, director of the ISN (Institute of Decorative and Industrial Art), to suggest an appropriate designer, for which the ISN would get a ten percent commission. Van Royen had the authority to reverse any decisions, but for the most part he went along with their recommendations. Although Van Royen tried to involve staff at the PTT on all decisions, his word remained final. In spite of Van Krimpen's outspoken criticism of De Zilverdistel,

Below: A. Oosterbaan, cover,
8.100.000m³ Zand by M. Revis,
De Gemeenschap and Lumax, 1932.

Opposite: A. Oosterbaan, cover,
Blokken (Blocks) by F. Bordewijk,
De Gemeenschap and Lumax, 1931.

BLOK

LOK

BORDEWIJK

KEN

DE GEMEENSCHAP

UTRECHT

BLOK

BORDEWIJK

KEN

Van Royen commissioned him to work on stamp designs in 1923, initiating a connection that endured until 1937. Van Krimpen's first assignment was to design the lettering for stamps illustrated by Van Konijnenburg for Queen Wilhelmina's Silver Jubilee. Another designer who worked for the PTT was De Koo who was initially given an interior design assignment in 1918. During the thirties De Koo worked for the PTT mainly as a graphic designer and helped to create the PTT's image during this period. He also worked closely with Van Royen as secretary of the VANK.

In spite of his preference for classical typography, Van Royen never hesitated to use progressive designers. Zwart received his first PTT assignment in 1929, a four-page brochure for Scheveningen Radio. By using photomontage and photograms, he contrasted small photographs of ticker tape machines with a large photogram made from the actual punched paper tape. This design began a long relationship that included stamps, brochures, posters, printed forms, and displays. Zwart refused to use the typefaces Van Royen favored, asserting that 'the typefaces to avoid are those which have a conceited, personal, and particular touch; the more uninteresting the letter, the more useful it is typographically. A typeface is more uninteresting in proportion to its having less historical leftovers and is derived from the true tense spirit of the twentieth century.'[9]

Also in 1929, Zwart's use of only lower-case letters for the airmail promotion booklet *ook post voor U* (also post for you) generated controversy, and some even called it a desecration of the Dutch language. Zwart's humorous reply was that he could not have predicted that there would be 'such a close semblance between Roman capital letters and pure, undiluted Dutch blood.' In the same year Zwart caused another uproar when he used only lower-case letters on an invitation card and other printed material for a PTT convention. Some delegates thought it was insulting to be invited in lower-case, and the invitation was reprinted using upper-case letters. Using photomontage, Zwart designed his first two postage stamps in 1931, reluctantly including a mediocre state portrait of Queen Wilhelmina as a central element. However, Zwart selected his own material for the next two stamps, and his use of asymmetry and lack of borders added to their originality.

Het boek van PTT (The PTT Book), concluded Zwart's major work in graphic design. Although the booklet did not appear until 1938, Van Royen most likely discussed it with Zwart in 1929. Zwart provided Van Royen with a rough draft in 1930, and for eight years numerous ideas were sent back and forth before the publication was finally printed. Written by Zwart himself, *Het boek van PTT* was an instruction booklet for schoolchildren on how to use PTT services. Its design reflects aspects of Zwart's previous work as well as new trends of the thirties. In this single publication one encounters a combination of functionalism and Dadaism, as well as traditional and modern directions. Techniques included collage, pen and ink, black chalk, montage, colored pencil, puppets, typefaces in various sizes and weights, and handwriting. He also used photographs of actual objects, some of which were created especially for this booklet, while found objects such as a box of matches were also included. *Het boek van PTT* was printed by rotogravure wich increased the richness of the color tones.

Since *Het boek van PTT* was intended for children, Zwart felt a need to awaken their curiosity. Thus, the text is accented throughout with different typefaces and condensed and expanded letters. Dick Elffers was working for Zwart at the time and made some of the illustrations under Zwart's supervision. Most importantly, though, Elffers played a crucial role in the booklet's non-functionalist appearance. Zwart allowed his assistants to produce ideas and drawings and would then select what he considered appropriate. Two paper puppets are reminiscent of Rodchenko's paper puppets and animals made in 1926 for children's poems. Zwart could have seen photographs of Rodchenko's pieces at the FIFO Exhibition at Stuttgart in 1929.

Although Kiljan's 1931 stamps and poster design devoted to disabled children were among his strongest pieces, he was widely criticized for using photographs of the actual children themselves. In his 1932 booklet on telephone use, Kiljan used typography together with montage, symbols, and geometric forms. Cahn was another young designer who produced work for the PTT shortly before World War II. In 1932 Van Royen asked Schuitema to design a stamp series as well, and, like Zwart, he used montage. However, Schuitema found working in such a small format to be awkward, and the stamps have a cramped feeling. For this reason Schuitema did not receive another PTT commission until 1950.

The new look of the PTT was a direct result of Van Royen's efforts, and the PTT continues today to be a showcase for Dutch graphic designers. Also, through his vision, the PTT became a patron and a supporter of graphic design, and as a result progressive typography is widely accepted and appreciated in the Netherlands. Van Royen continued in his position until his arrest by the Nazi occupying forces on March 4, 1943. Three months later he died at the German concentration camp in Amersfoort.

Except when associated with other movements, Dutch poster designers remained for the most part outside the mainstream. The political instability of the thirties was an ideal environment for posters promoting causes such as the NVV (Dutch Federation of Trade Unions) and the SDAP (Social Democratic Workers' Party). A candid force aimed at specific targets always characterized these socialist posters.

Among the most prominent of the socialist designers was the unbending Meijer Bleekrode who designed many powerful posters before abandoning design for painting in 1935. Like Cohen, his family worked in the Amsterdam diamond industry, and, dying in the Sobibor concentration camp in Poland in 1943, he too was a victim of the war. Also involved in the socialist political sector as poster designers were Schuitema, Cohen, J. Walter, Albert Hahn Jr., Louis Frank, and Samuel Schwarz, the latter of whom died at Auschwitz in 1942.

Other poster designers who began in the early twenties, such as P. A. H. Hofman, continued to work into the late 1930s. Conspicuous new arrivals were Wim ten Broek, Herman Nijgh, and the illustrator E. M. ten Harmsen van Beek with his lively and colorful carnival posters for the Hotel Hamdorff in Laren. The posters of Louis Kalff, a former Philips lighting consultant, were in the Art Deco mode, and his more striking designs were posters advertising the beach at Scheveningen.

Due to the political situation in Russia and Germany after 1930, many intellectuals and artists immigrated to the Netherlands. Those from Germany included Susanne Heynemann, Helmut Salden, Hajo Rose, Otto Treumann, and Henri Friedlaender, each one bringing a new vitality and perspective and greatly enriching Dutch graphic design. Friedlaender, worked as a book designer for the printer Mouton and the publisher L. J. C. Boucher, both in The Hague.

FRANKEERING
BIJ ABONNEMENT
AMSTERDAM

NIET VOUWENI

Above: Stephan Schlesinger, envelope
for Metz & Co.'s Christmas season,
Amsterdam, 1931. Around 1930,
Schlesinger's typography became more
functionalist as he began to use sans
serif typefaces.

Opposite: Willem Sandberg, brochure for
an exhibition on advertising art, Stedelijk
Museum, Amsterdam, 1935. This was a
comprehensive exhibition where VANK
members also showed their work.

Other immigrant designers such as Stephan Schlesinger had arrived much earlier. A native of Vienna, Schlesinger first worked in the studio of the poster designer Julius Klinger. After initially studying advertising, he moved to Amsterdam in 1925. Here he first produced graphic design work for the Amsterdam furniture store Metz & Co. A master calligrapher and type designer, he designed lettering for the ink manufacturer Talens and writing paper boxes for the Van Gelder paper company. His brother-in-law, who was director of the printing firm Trio in The Hague, commissioned him to design their calligraphic logo. At the beginning of World War II he began a script typeface intended for commercial use and had only completed the lower case and a few capitals before being arrested by the Nazis. Like Bleekrode, he died in Auschwitz in 1942.

Helmut Salden, a native of Essen, left Germany in 1934, to go to Paris and Spain and then to Switzerland in 1937 after the outbreak of the Spanish Civil War. Forced by the Swiss immigration authorities to leave the country, he went to the Netherlands in 1938 where he worked for eight months as an assistant to Piet Zwart. At the end of 1938 he moved to The Hague where he began working for a number of publishers including J. M. Meulenhoff in Amsterdam and H. P. Leopold, A. A. M. Stols, and L. J. C. Boucher in The Hague. Hajo Rose arrived in Amsterdam in 1933 and taught at the Nieuwe Kunst School established by Paul Citroen to revive the recently closed Bauhaus. He taught advertising and typography, basing his course on the Bauhaus ideals of design's social responsibility and clarity of form. His influence was strongly felt after the war through students such as Treumann, Benno Premsela, and Jan Bons. Paul Guermonprez taught photography, and, together with Citroen, another former Bauhaus student, Guermonprez soon joined the faculty at the Academy of Fine Arts in The Hague.

The thirties ended with the inconclusive ideological battles among graphic designers that marked the earlier part of the century, and it would take a war to partially resolve them. Ironically, many of the designers found a common purpose and cause during the Nazi occupation.

1 Ank Leeuw-Marcar, *Willem Sandberg, Portret van een Kunstenaar*, Amsterdam:

Meulenhoff, 1981, p. 63.

2 Gerard Kiljan, 1935, quoted by Paul Hefting, *Piet Zwart, Het boek van PTT* (facsimile),

The Hague: Staatsuitgeverij, 1985.

3 D. F. Maan, *De Maniakken, Ontstaan en ontwikkeling van de grafische vormgeving

aan de Haagse academie in de jaren dertig*, The Hague: Rijksmuseum Meermanno-

Westreenianum, Museum van het boek, 1982, p. 8.

4 D. F. Maan, *De Maniakken, Ontstaan en ontwikkeling van de grafische vormgeving

aan de Haagse academie in de jaren dertig*, The Hague: Rijksmuseum Meermanno-

Westreenianum, Museum van het boek, 1982, p. 13.

5 Max Bruinsma, Lies Ros, and Rob Schrader, *Dick Elffers en de Kunsten*, Netherlands:

Het Gerrit Jan Thiemefonds, 1989, p. 6.

6 Max Bruinsma, Lies Ros, and Rob Schrader, *Dick Elffers en de Kunsten*, Netherlands:

Het Gerrit Jan Thiemefonds, 1989, p. 18.

7 Max Bruinsma, Lies Ros, and Rob Schrader, *Dick Elffers en de Kunsten*, Netherlands:

Het Gerrit Jan Thiemefonds, 1989, p. 21.

8 Egbert van Faassen, *Drukwerk voor PTT, Typografie en Vormgeving voor een

Staatsedrijf in de Jaren Twintig en Dertig*, The Hague: SDU Uitgeverij, 1988, p. 10.

9 Kees Broos, *Piet Zwart, 1985–1977*, Amsterdam: Van Gennep, 1982, p. 74.

OVERZICHT VAN UITGAVEN 1935

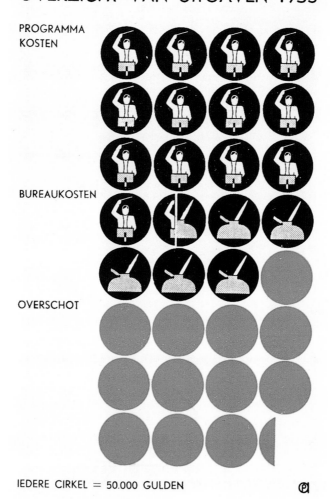

PROGRAMMA
KOSTEN

BUREAUKOSTEN

OVERSCHOT

IEDERE CIRKEL = 50.000 GULDEN

Opposite: Peter Alma, pictograms for a
survey of business expenditure in
Amsterdam. Stedelijk Museum,
Amsterdam, 1935.

Above: Dick Elffers, front and back
cover of a photobook, *The Year 1933*,
Zeist, 1934.

Above: Willem Sandberg, brochure
for Spin printers, Amsterdam, 1937.
Sandberg also designed writing
paper and photographic calendars
for the firm.

Opposite: Nicolaas P. de Koo, poster
for *AVO Zomer Feesten* (AVO
Summer Festivals), 1938.

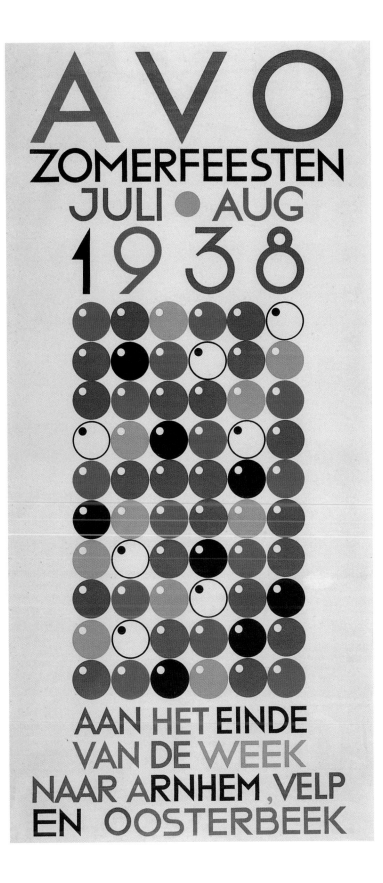

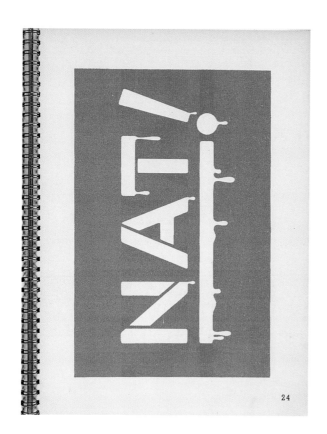

24

6

Left and below left: Stephan Schlesinger, examples of the typefaces Nat ('Wet') and Garen en Band ('Thread and Ribbon') from *Examples of Modern Lettering for Decorative Painters*, Nunspeet, 1939.

Opposite, above: Tine Baanders, calendar for Trio printers, 1939.

Opposite, below: Lotte Stam-Beese, stamped binding for the magazine *Beter Wonen 1913–1938* (Better Living 1913–1938), edited by L. van der Wal, Amsterdam: Arbeiderspers, 1939.

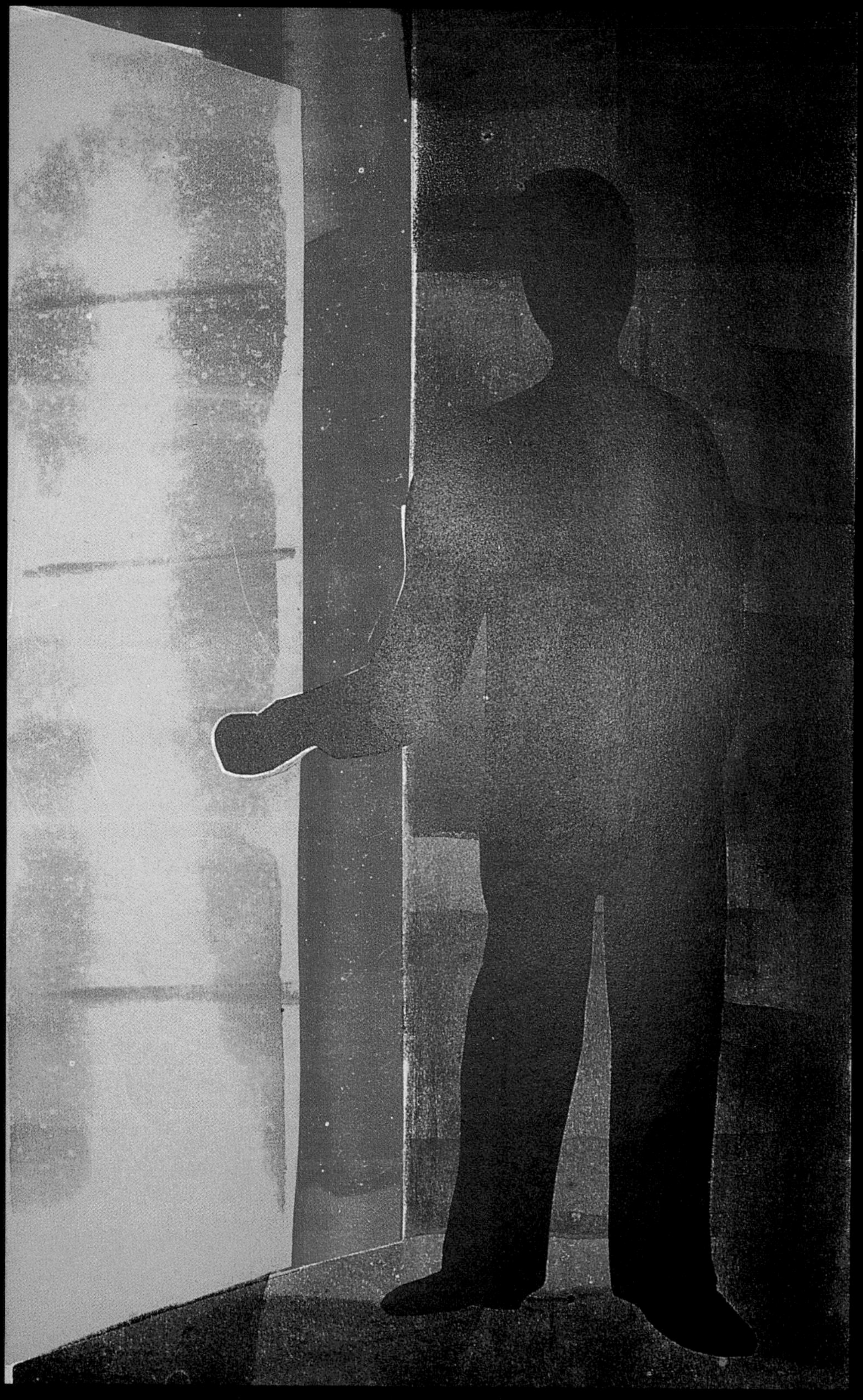

H. N. Werkman, *Chassidische Legenden* (Hassidic Legends) 2–3, *The Way Back*, 1943.

WAR, OCCUPATION, AND UNDER-GROUND PUBLICA-TIONS

On April 20, 1940, Adolf Hitler's birthday, an exhibition of German art opened at the Stedelijk Museum in Amsterdam. Organized under the auspices of the Deutsch-Niederländische Gesellschaft (German-Dutch Union) and the Kölnische Kunstverein (Cologne Art Club), its purpose was to promote a mutual awareness of Dutch and German cultures. The exhibition abruptly ended three weeks later when Germany, ignoring Dutch neutrality, invaded the Netherlands during the early morning hours of May 10. Although the Germans had expected an immediate capitulation by the Dutch, on May 14 the Dutch were still resisting. Shortly after one o'clock that afternoon, planes from the German Air Force appeared over Rotterdam, and proceeded to destroy the city's center by saturation bombing. The Netherlands surrendered the following day, beginning a five-year occupation that proved to be one of the severest of the war in Europe.

Professor H. de la Fontaine Verwey later wrote in the foreword to the book *Het Vrije Boek in Onvrije Tijd* (The Free Book in Unfree Times):

In our literary history there is perhaps no period in which literature has had such a broad and deep effect. One can say that literature was one of the forces that awakened the people and drove them to resist. Not in a direct sense: only a small portion of the books listed here could be called seditious and directly tied to the resistance.... However, never before has literature been so defiant, so national and so topical as during the years of the resistance; the power of poetry as human expression was seldom so strongly felt as in these years, not only by the youth who up until then knew little about it. Those in prison cells experienced its liberating effect, and its meaning was also revealed for countless others for whom it had previously been a closed book.[1]

Writers, artists, graphic designers, and printers were immediately faced with the task of piecing together the remains of intellectual and artistic freedoms. For most graphic designers, it was a time of spiritual regeneration where essential issues were easier to set apart from those of more minor substance. The endless ideological disputes that had separated graphic designers since the end of World War I now appeared remote and immaterial. Previous issues such as the appropriateness of sans serif or serif typefaces, symmetry or asymmetry, photography as opposed to traditional illustration, all seemed irrelevant given the situation at hand. The eventual liberation of the Netherlands and the upholding of human life and dignity quickly replaced all such issues. Any means that worked toward these ends was now considered appropriate.

At first it appeared that work at government and municipal bureaus, businesses, offices, and schools would not be severely interrupted, but each day additional constraints and petty regulations were imposed. The occupation administration was headed by Reichskommissar Authur Seyss-Inquart, an Austrian lawyer and civil servant who had collaborated with the Nazis in the annexation of his own country. One of his first moves was to give the Dutch Jewish population a non-person status, and by the fall of 1940 Jews were officially prohibited from working in the civil service. Although many groups including the legal sector, student organizations, educators, political parties, trade unions, the clergy, industrialists, artists, writers, and doctors vehemently protested, their dissent had no effect on the decree.

To present a united artistic front against the Nazi occupation, J. F. van Royen attempted to enlist all Dutch artists in a single association called the Nederlandsche Organisatie van Kunstenaars (Dutch Artists Organization) or the NOK. However, many artists were adamantly against it, fearing that it would give the Nazis yet more dominance by conveniently having everyone on a single list. Van Royen also soon realized that the NOK would be counter-productive and began to take steps to disband it. However, by the end of 1941 it was officially discontinued by the occupation administration who in turn set up their own organization, the Kultuurkamer (Culture Chamber). In order to practice their professions all artists were required to join. Many simply ignored the decree. H. N. Werkman was one of those who disregarded it, using the excuse that he was a printer and not an artist. The Kultuurkamer did not affect Jews who had already been prohibited from working anyway. A letter of protest signed by 2,700 people working in art-related professions was sent to Seyss-Inquart. Van Royen, who was wrongly blamed for being the letter's instigator, was arrested on March 4, 1942. Taken to the German concentration camp at Amersfoort, he died on June 10 after his health deteriorated.

Another prominent artist who refused to join the Kultuurkamer was Friedrich Vordemberge-Gildewart. Since he was not permitted to paint, he designed advertisements and illegal books for the Amsterdam printer Frans Duwaer. *Millimeter und geraden* was published in 1940, and, illustrated by Sophie Täuber-Arp, *Hans Arp, rire de coquille* appeared in 1944. Duwaer was executed by the Nazis on June 10, 1944, and as a tribute to him, Vordemberge-Gildewart published *FD Van Zijn Vrienden* (To Frans Duwaer from his friends) after the liberation of the Netherlands in 1945.

By the summer of 1942 Fré Cohen could no longer work in her Amsterdam studio and was forced to go underground to avoid deportation as a Jew. Constantly on the move and staying with various friends, among them Pieter Brattinga, she avoided capture until her arrest on June 12, 1943. Two days later she committed suicide.

It was soon clear that the Germans had underestimated the defiance of Dutch printers and publishers. Clandestine presses were profuse and essentially served four functions: bolstering the strength of perseverance; providing printed material for the resistance; earning funds for the resistance; and keeping the literary traditions alive through the printing of books. It was dangerous to print more than small editions, however, and distribution added to the risk. Although most of the typography was ordinary and badly printed, in the end, content was the deciding factor.

Because of endless and increasingly convoluted regulations, a shortage of supplies, and draconian censorship, normal commercial publishing soon came to a standstill. Production choices were limited, and printing anything at all became increasingly difficult. Even poor-quality paper was hard to find, and printers were forced to turn in 200 kilograms of their lead type to be used to make bullets. Permission to print anything at all had to be requested far in advance, and sometimes the process could take over a year. The few collaborator writers and publishers were, for the most part, ostracized by readers and bookstores. Duwaer was forced to print his 1942 calendar on pages salvaged from unbound books. There were also many underground newspapers such as *Het Parool* (the Password) and *Vrij Nederland* (Free Netherlands). Both survived the war and are active publications today.

Various plans were conceived by the Nazis to track down illegal printing. One such scheme was cataloging the owners of certain typefaces. For the most part, however, this proved to be ineffective, since De Roos's Hollandsche Mediaeval was used by so many printers that it became almost impossible for the authorities to use that typeface to trace the printer behind a particular clandestine publication.

Some of the more important underground presses were in The Hague, Groningen, Utrecht, Leiden, and Amsterdam. Established in Amsterdam by Geert Lubberhuizen and Charles van Blommestein, De Bezige Bij (The Busy Bee) contributed any meager earnings to a fund for those with special needs. Writers almost always used pseudonyms and donated their works. To further confuse the authorities, clandestine publishers were usually known by various names, and often the publisher's name was omitted. De doezende Dar (The Dozing Drone) and L'Abeille Laborante were both pseudonyms for The Busy Bee. Bert Bakker's Mansarde-pers (Mansarde Press) in The Hague was later named the Final Stage Press. Werkman designed some of the publications for the Groningen underground press, In Agris Occupatis.

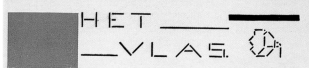

HET ___

___VLAS.

Het vlas stond in bloei. Dat heeft zulke prachtige blauwe bloemen, zoo zacht als de vleugels van een mot en nog veel fijner.

■ De zon scheen op het vlas en de regenwolken spoelden het af, en dat was niet zoo goed voor hem, als het voor kleine kinders is om gewasschen te worden en dan een kus van moeder te krijgen; ze worden daar toch veel mooier van.

■ En dat werd het vlas ook.

„De menschen zeggen dat ik er zoo bizonder goed bij sta‚"

zei het vlas, en dat ik zoo mooi lang word, er zal een prachtig stuk linnen van mij komen! Neen maar, wat ben ik gelukkig! Ik ben vast de allergelukkigste van allemaal! Ik heb het zoo goed, en ik word wat!

■ „Hoe die zonneschijn opmontert en hoe die regen smaakt en verfrischt! Ik ben onvergelijkelijk gelukkig, ik ben de allergelukkigste!"

■ „Ja, ja, ja!" zeiden de heininga: len, jij kent de wereld niet, maar dat doen wij, er zijn knoesten in ons!" En toen

Above: Bart van der Leck, page from *Het Vlas* (The Flax) by Hans Christian Andersen, Amsterdam: De Spieghel, 1941. Here Van de Leck used primary colors and an architectural approach.

Opposite: Fré Cohen, book cover, *Redder der Kinderen* (Savior of the Children) by Dr. Hellmuth Unger, Amsterdam: A. J. G. Strengholt, 1941.

Dr. Hellmuth Unger

REDDER der KINDEREN

A.J.G. Strengholt's Uitg. My. N.V. Amsterdam

There was a substantial amount of printed material by those graphic designers and printers who remain unknown. One anonymous publication printed in 1942 displays a symmetrical design for the Amsterdam Municipal Printing Company on the front and on the back a striking experimental composition constructed using the names of streets in Amsterdam. There were also collaborator designers such as Lou Manche and printers such as Mes & Bronkhorst who printed material for the occupying administration.

Through their work in serving the underground, a new generation of graphic designers received their on-the-spot training during the occupation, and some of the older ones experienced a creative rebirth during those years. Many, including Stam, Sandberg, and the German Jewish immigrant Otto Treumann, used their talents to make false identity and ration cards and stamps for passports and other official documents, and printers such as Duwaer risked and gave their lives to assist them. For the most part the designers were very successful in deceiving the authorities. Treumann's skills were especially useful. In addition to forging stamps on government documents, he actually hand-copied German banknotes, having learned the lettering style as a child. Bankers who worked for the resistance in turn laundered these counterfeit bills. Treumann later said this was the best training he ever received in graphic design.

Dick Elffers also created fake identity and ration cards, and at the same time produced some design work such as a jubilee folder for the United Shoe Dealers and book designs for Balkema. In 1944 he designed a calendar that was published illegally by Balkema's Vijf Ponden Pers and printed by Duwaer.

The Amsterdam book dealer Balkema persisted in printing bibliophile publications, and, in addition to publishing books under his own imprint, together with Van Krimpen and W. G. Hellinga, he began the Vijf Ponden Pers (Five Pounds Press). The name of the press was a reference to the maximum paper weight allowed for unofficial printing. This press produced some of the best designed and printed publications during and directly after the occupation. Two of the finest book designs from the Vijf Ponden Pers were *Huit Sonnets par Edgar Degas* (Eight Sonnets by Edgar Degas) and *Doortocht, Gedichten, 1883–1943 door H. W. J. M. Keuls* (Passage, Poems, 1883–1943 by H. W. J. M. Keuls), both designed by Elffers. One book designed for the press by Van Krimpen was *De Pendule* (The Mantelpiece Clock) by Jacobus van Looy. Using a satirical text by an unknown author smuggled out of a concentration camp, Balkema's most seditious publication was *Zehn kleine Meckerlein* (Ten Little Nuisances), handprinted by Balkema in 1943 in an edition of forty.

During the occupation Stols produced sixty books using the names of fictitious publishers, printers, places, writers, and dates. These works were typographically some of his best publications. Although the texts were not directed against the occupation per se, some were by writers considered to be decadent by the Nazis. Helmut Salden designed a number of book jackets for Stols during the occupation as well as designs for the publishers L. J. C. Boucher and H. P. Leopold in The Hague. Although the offices and warehouse of W. L. & J. Brusse survived the bombing of Rotterdam, production became so difficult that they used the war years principally to clear their back catalog. In 1944, only two new books were on their list.

Sandberg joined the resistance soon after the invasion. In October 1942, he and some compatriots came up with a plot to blow up the Amsterdam population registry.

This contained valuable records that helped the Nazis identify Jews and members of the resistance. On March 27, 1943, the plan was successfully implemented, but most of those involved were arrested and executed. Sandberg, however, managed to escape and was forced to go underground. From April 22 until the war's end he carried the identity papers of Henri Willem van den Bosch. Between December 1943 and April 1945, he produced his *experimenta typographica*, nineteen booklets containing illustrations and hand-lettered interpretations of quotations and ideas. Printed by Duwaer, the first, *lectura sub aqua*, was published in an edition of 200 by Balkema in 1944. Duwaer had set the type for another one, *gnothi se auton* (know thyself), but due to his execution in 1944, it was not printed until after the war in 1945 by the Vijf Ponden Pers. Only five *experimenta typographica* were published at all, the last one in 1968 by the Gallery Der Spiegel in Cologne.

The Nazi occupation and other corollaries of World War II had a demoralizing effect on many designers and artists, including Werkman. His predisposition for solitude increased in intensity, and he became even more detached from his business affairs. Except for some sparse commercial work often handed over to Wybren Bos, his printing company almost came to a halt.

At the end of November 1940, three people held a meeting in Winschoten, a town near Groningen. These were F. R. A. Henkels, a Dutch Reformed Minister from Winschoten, Dr. Ate Zuithoff, a member of the Chemistry Department at the University of Groningen, and Mevrouw Adri Buning, a teacher of German at the Winschoten grammar school. During the gathering they resolved to publish something to help bolster Dutch morale during the occupation. Henkels then suggested they consider using Werkman as their printer, and several days later he went to Groningen to present the project to him. Henkels and Werkman quickly agreed terms, and this first encounter was the beginning of a deep and enduring friendship. The project eventually developed into 40 publications that became the triumphant conclusion of Werkman's artistic achievement. The name of the series, *De Blauwe Schuit* (The Blue Barge), was derived from a painting by Hieronymus Bosch called *Die blau scute*, that had been displayed at the Boymans Museum in Rotterdam in 1936.

Although there were similarities, *De Blauwe Schuit* was in many ways different from *The Next Call*, which began almost two decades earlier. Werkman created *The Next Call* mainly from typographic elements, while with *De Blauwe Schuit* he followed a more illustrative approach. Although *The Next Call* contained some contributions by De Ploeg members such as Hanson, Wiegers, Alkema and Van der Zee, it was essentially Werkman's one-man show. On the other hand, *De Blauwe Schuit* was a collaborative endeavor by Werkman, Henkels, Zuithoff and Buning. Through donating some paper, Balkema was involved as well. *De Blauwe Schuit* also differed from other underground publications in that Werkman was one of the few who used artistic expression as a subtle weapon against the occupation.

The first issue of *De Blauwe Schuit* was printed shortly before Christmas 1940 and was given to friends as a New Year's memento in January 1941. It consisted of a simple design with a woodcut by Wiegers, and text was from a poem by the Dutch poet Martinus Nijhoff, *Het Jaar 1572* (The Year 1572), that commemorated the 25th birthday of Princess Juliana in 1934:

Above: A. A. Balkema, pages from *Zehn kleine Meckerlein* (Ten Little Nuisances), 1943, text smuggled out of a concentration camp.

Opposite, above: H. N. Werkman, *Chassidische Legenden* (Hassidic Legends) 2–4, *The Carriage in the Woods*, 1943.

Opposite, below: H. N. Werkman, *Chassidische Legenden* (Hassidic Legends) 2–8, *The Sabbath of the Humble*, 1943.

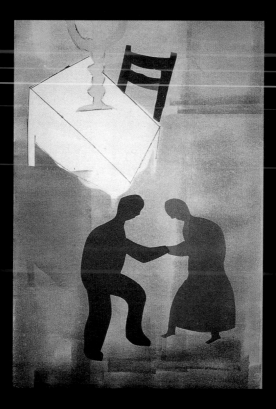

So the unusual year began
When everything turned out different from expectations.
Who had won already was vanquished.
Who conceived of sun and weather finally without thought
Created a population, when he thought of digging a grave.

258   What happened has seldom taken place.
They stood behind water and behind walls.
They held out. They were all together.

Werkman continued to produce his druksel prints at the same time that he was printing the publications for *De Blauwe Schuit*. In May 1941 he visited the Sandbergs in Amsterdam, and, together with Wiegers, was taken to the concrete vault in Castricum where art from the Stedelijk Museum was secretly stored. Seeing work by painters such as Van Gogh, Klee, Picasso, and Cézanne inspired Werkman to begin the Amsterdam-Castricum series, his first druksels after a one-year hiatus.

The second publication of *De Blauwe Schuit, Die Predigt des neuen Jahres* (The Sermon of the New Year), one of Martin Buber's Hasidic legends, was distributed in March 1941. The third and fourth issues were *Alleluia*, an Easter hymn, and *Sabbatgesänge* (Songs of the Sabbath), songs by the Jewish poet Jehudi Halevi. The next issue, *Prière, gedicht van Charles Péguy* (Prière, poem by Charles Péguy) was one of the most lyrical, and was recently used as the background for a Dutch commemorative postage stamp designed by Jan Bons. There were eight publications from *De Blauwe Schuit* in 1941, followed by fourteen in 1942, eleven in 1943, and seven in 1944.

In October 1941, Werkman started printing the thirty-two-page *Turkenkalender* (Turkish Calendar) which was distributed between Christmas and New Year's Day 1942. This piece was inspired by Gutenberg's 1454 'Turkish Calendar,' which warned of an imminent Turkish invasion of Europe. All of Werkman's amassed techniques were brought to bear, and afterwards he remarked that he hoped professional typographers would never see the calendar, as his life would be in danger for sins committed against typography standards.

In March 1942, *Het Gesprek* (The Conversation) appeared, a description by Henkels of a 1938 painting by Werkman using the same title. This was followed in April by *Bij het Graf van den Onbekenden Nederlandschen Soldaat* (By the Grave of an Unknown Dutch Soldier). *Ascensus ad inferos*, poems by S. Vestdijk and Henkels for Christmas 1942 was printed on previously used ledger paper. Although this paper was probably used out of necessity, it also served his design purposes.

Henkels gave Werkman Martin Buber's book, *Hasidic Legends*, and although Werkman was neither Jewish nor a practicing Protestant, he was quite taken with these tales. In August 1942, the first of his two *Chassidische legenden* portfolios was completed. In an edition of twenty, each portfolio contained traditionally printed texts and ten large illustrations. Each print was made separately with an ink roller and stencils. Despite its hefty price of seventy-five guilders, sixteen sets were sold within two months. One young painter sold his bicycle to buy one, a significant sacrifice considering a bicycle's value during the war. The second *Chassidische legenden* portfolio was published in December 1943.

The abortive British landing at Arnhem in September 1944 put off the liberation of the Netherlands until May 5, 1945. During the winter of 1944 the Germans took most fuel supplies from the Netherlands to use against the Allied advance through France and Belgium. This winter was known as the *hongerwinter* (the winter of hunger), and in the Netherlands over 15,000 people died from starvation and exposure. By then, there was almost no electricity in Groningen, and with no heating as well, the frozen ink was impossible to use. Other than a 1945 calendar and a few pieces for the underground presses In Agris Occupatis and De Bezige Bij, Werkman's printing came to an end by the close of 1944.

On March 13, 1945, the Sicherheitspolizei (Security Police) arrested Werkman and Henkels and took them to the SS headquarters in Groningen, the Scholtenhuis. Since books by Dostoevsky and other Russian writers were found in Werkman's house, his paintings and printed material were classified as Bolshevik art and confiscated.

Through its very openness, *De Blauwe Schuit* went largely unnoticed by the Nazis throughout the war. Although *De Blauwe Schuit* and Werkman's name were on each publication, numbers of editions were sometimes jumbled and the names of living writers were deleted or changed. Werkman declined to print obvious clandestine material during the war, because he felt that other businesses in his building would be compromised should such work ever be discovered. Most likely his arrest was a combination of several factors, one possibly being his work for De Bezige Bij and In Agris Occupatis. The main reason, though, was his identification with Jews through the *Chassidische Legenden* and other *De Blauwe Schuit* publications.

In the first week of April, an order came from the SS headquarters in The Hague to execute thirty prisoners in retaliation against the Dutch underground in Groningen. On April 8 and 9 the first two groups of ten were taken to Anlo and shot by a firing squad. When the last group was being taken on the afternoon of April 9 to the execution site, one prisoner escaped and the truck returned to Groningen. Early on the morning of April 10, Werkman was selected to replace the escapee from the previous day. Shortly afterward, Werkman and the nine others were shot near the town of Bakkeveen, two days before Canadian forces began to move into Groningen.

During the fighting to liberate Groningen, an explosion destroyed the Scholtenhuis and with it everything impounded from Werkman's house. This included documents, at least half of his paintings, and a third of his druksels. Upon his return as director of the Stedelijk Museum in 1945, one of Sandberg's first initiatives was to hold a Werkman retrospective that fall, publishing the first Werkman catalog. Also in 1945, prizes were created by the city of Amsterdam in memory of Werkman and Duwaer. The Duwaer prize went to Van Krimpen, and the first Werkman prize was posthumously awarded to Werkman himself for *De Turkenkalender*. In 1946, Balkema published Henkel's *Logboek van De Blauwe Schuit* (Logbook of the Blue Barge) designed by Elffers, another tribute to Werkman.

Many principal figures in modern Dutch graphic design died as a direct result of the war. These included Van Royen, Bleekrode, Lebeau, Cohen, Guermonprez, Werkman, and Duwaer. Designers whose careers had been put on hold by the war resumed the second phases of their careers after 1945.

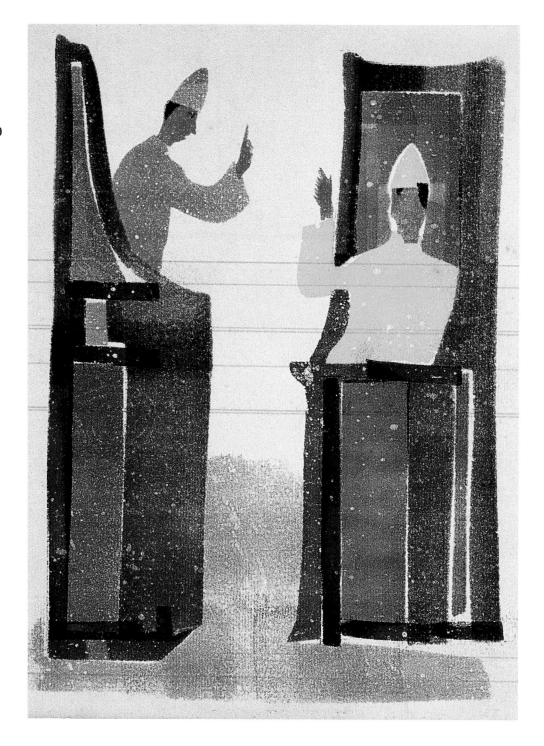

H. N. Werkman, cover (**above**) and
colophon (**opposite**) from *Ascensus
ad Inferus* (Ascent to the Pit), 1943.

Colophon

Dit kloosterlijk avontuur te Sint-Michielsgestel werd
gedrukt en verlucht door H. N. Werkman in een
oplage van 50 ex. Voor het binnenwerk werden
de archieven van het Seminarie georganiseerd, zooals dat in Brabant heden ten dage heet. In Nov.
1942 geschonken aan de vrienden van
De Blauwe Schuit.

Elffers's poster for the 1946 exhibition *Het vrije boek in onvrije tijden* (The Free Book in Unfree Times) embodies that tragic yet surprisingly productive period. Also, in the same year, his poster *Weerbare democratie* (Defensible democracy) is especially poignant. Designed for an exhibition on Dutch art produced during the war, the face on the poster simultaneously exhibits heroism, fear, grief, and shock. Elffers later said that the war years had destroyed his earlier idealism: 'During that time I arrived at the conclusion that one must not work from closed principles but instead be open, letting in doubts. I never again wanted to be caught in a net of dogmas. The naiveté of the 1930s was brought into broad daylight after the war.'[2]

The years directly following the end of World War II constituted a period of restoration, reflection, and introspection. The older vanguard was now seen as part of a rich legacy instead of a group of revolutionary leaders promoting particular doctrines. The title of the new Dutch avant-garde publication *Open Oog* (Open Eye), for which Sandberg designed the cover in 1946, suggested a fresh beginning for Dutch graphic design.

1 H. de la Fontaine Verwey, introduction in *Het Vrije Boek in Onvrije Tijd*,

ed. Dirk de Jong, Leiden: A. W. Sijthoffs, 1958.

2 Max Bruinsma, Lies Ros, and Rob Schrader, *Dick Elffers en de Kunsten*,

Netherlands: Het Gerrit Jan Thiemefonds, 1989, p. 24.

Above: H. N. Werkman, cover,
Turkenkalender (Turkish Calendar), 1942.

Opposite: H. N. Werkman, calendar pages
for July and October, *Turkenkalender*
(Turkish Calendar), 1942.

De Staten-Generael der Geunieerde
Nederlanden, allen dengenen die dese
sullen sien ofte hooren lesen, Saluyt.

Alsoo een yegelick kennelick is, dat een Prince van den Lande van Gode
ghesteldt is Hooft over sijne Ondersaten, om deselve te bewaren ende
beschermen van alle ongelijck, overlast ende geweldt, gelijck een Herder
tot bewarenisse van sijn Schapen: Ende dat d' Ondersaten niet en sijn
van Gode geschapen tot behoef van den Prince, om hem in alles wat hij
beveelt, weder het goddelick oft ongoddelick, recht ofte onrecht is, on-
derdanich te wesen ende als slaeven te dienen; maer den Prince om d'
Ondersaten wille, sonder dewelcke hij gheen Prince en is, om deselve
met recht ende redenen te regeeren, voor te staen ende te helpen
als een Vader sijne Kinderen, ende een Herder sijne Schapen, die sijn
lijf ende leven settet om deselve te bewaren. Ende soo, wanneer hij
sulcx niet en doet, maer in stede van sijne Ondersaten te beschermen,
deselve soeckt te verdrucken, t' overlasten, heure oude vrijheijt, Privilegien ende oude herkomen te benemen, ende heur gebieden ende gebruij-
cken als slaven, moet gehouden worden niet als een Prince, maer als een
Tyran ende voor sulcx nae recht ende reden mach ten minste van syne
Ondersaten, besonder bij deliberatie vande Staten vanden Lande, voor
geen Prince meer bekent, maer verlaten, ende een ander in sijn stede
tot beschermenisse van henlieden, voor over-hooft, sonder misbruycken,
gekosen werden. Te meer so wanneer d' Ondersaten met ootmoedige
verthooninge niet en hebben heuren voorz. Prince konnen vermorwen,
noch van sijn tyrannigh opset gekeeren, ende alsoo geen ander middel en
hebben om heure eygenen, heurer Huysvrouwen, Kinderen ende Nakome-
lingen aengheboren vrijheijt (daer sij nae de Wet der Natueren goet ende
bloedt schuldigh sijn voor op te setten) ende te beschermen . . .
't Welck principalick in dese voorsz. Landen behoort plaetse te hebben
in stant te grijpen, die van allen tijden sijn geregeert geweest, ende hebben oock moeten geregeert worden, naevolgende den Eedt bij heure Prin-
cen 't heuren aenkomen gedaen, na uytwijsen heurer Privilegien, Cos-
tuymen ende oude herkomen: hebbende oock meest alle de voorsz. Landen
haren Prince ontfangen op Conditie, Contracten ende Accoorden, de welcke
brekende, oock naer recht den Prince vande heerschappije vanden Landen
is vervallen. . . .

Uit het Plakkaat van verlating
van 26 Juli 1581.

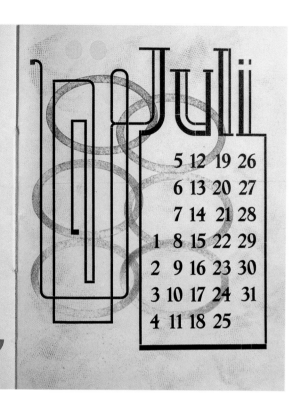

Juli

5 12 19 26
6 13 20 27
7 14 21 28
1 8 15 22 29
2 9 16 23 30
3 10 17 24 31
4 11 18 25

	4	11	18	25
	5	12	19	26
	6	13	20	27
	7	14	21	28
1	8	15	22	29
2	9	16	23	30
3	10	17	24	31

OCTOBER

Gentsch Vader-onze.

Helsche duvel, die tot Brussel sijt,
Uwen naem ende faem sij vermaledijt;
U rijck vergae sonder respijt
Want heeft geduurt te langen tijt;
Uwen wille sal niet gewerden,
Noch in hemel noch op erden;

Ghij beneempt ons huijden ons dagelicx broot,
Wijff ende kynderen hebbent groote noot;
Ghij en vergeeft niemant sijn schult,
Want ghij met haet ende nijt sijt vervult;
Ghij en laet niemant ongetempteert,
Alle die landen ghij perturbeert.

O, Hemelsche Vader, die in den Hemel sijt,
Maekt ons desen helschen duvel quijt,
Met sijnen bloedigen, valschen raet,
Daer hij mede handelt alle quaet,
Ende sijn Spaensch krijchsvolk allegaer,
't Welck leeft of sij des duvels waer.

Amen.

arp

arp

taeuber

taeuber arp *taeuber*

taeuber

arp

arp

Left: Friedrich Vordemberge-Gildewart, cover and typography from *Hans Arp, Rire de Coquille*, Amsterdam, 1944. Illustrated by Sophie Taeuber-Arp and printed by Frans Duwaer.

Below: Anonymous, *c*. 1944.

Opposite, above: Suzanne Heynemann, cover of *Ten Poems by Emily Dickinson*. Amsterdam: A. A. Balkema, Vijf Ponden Pers, 1944. Printed in a limited edition of 55 with a German translation by Rosey E. Pool, the text was hand-drawn by Heynemann.

Opposite, below: Dick Elffers, calendar, illegally printed by Frans Duwaer, 1944.

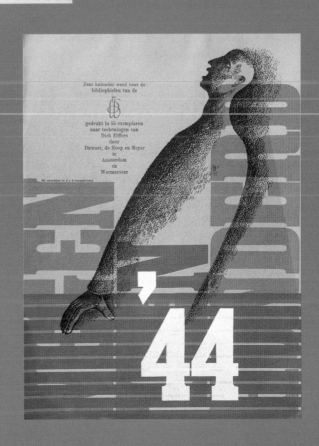

Above: Friedrich Vordemberge-Gildewart, page from *FD Van Zijn Vrienden* (To FD from his Friends), in memory of the clandestine printer Frans Duwaer, 1945.

Opposite: Dick Elffers, poster for the exhibition *Het vrije boek in onvrije tijd* (The Free Book in Unfree Times), 1946.

het vrije boek

in onvrije tijd

tentoonstelling
Stedelijk Museum Amsterdam
van 27 Juni tot 23 Juli

ontwerp W. Brusse.

druk Senefelder Amsterdam

avantgardecahier 1

open oog

CHAPTER

60

POST-WAR RATIONALISM AND EXPRES-SIONISM

As the thirties drew to a close, graphic designers in the Netherlands began to be thought of more as serious professionals rather than mere advertising draftsmen. This change in attitude was due in many respects to the unbending efforts of designers such as Zwart and Schuitema. Also, before World War II, publishers rarely employed full-time designers, but after the war, book designers became an essential part of a publisher's staff. Now the graphic designer was no longer considered an extravagance but instead a necessity.

Dutch society was completely disrupted by World War II and the German occupation, and the period immediately following liberation was a time of rebuilding cultural, social, and economic institutions. During this time two currents emerged as Dutch graphic design underwent a transformation. The first was a practical manifestation of Constructivism influenced by what became known as the Swiss-inspired International Style as exemplified by firms such as Total Design. The second was rise of nonconformist designers, some of whom were involved with Fluxus and Provo, movements that rebelled against the social and artistic values of the times. This engendered a new expressionism in Dutch graphic design that increased significantly during the seventies and eighties. Late twentieth-century designers and studios such as Anthon Beeke, Studio Dumbar, Hard Werken, and Wild Plakken overrode traditional values as they sought personal interpretations and subjectivity.

272

M. VASALIS

DE VOGEL PHŒNIX

Opposite: Otto Treumann, poster,
*Federatie, The New Dutch Federation of
Artists' Trade Unions*, Amsterdam, 1946.

Above: Helmut Salden, cover of the
poetry anthology *De vogel Phoenix*
(The Phoenix Bird) by M. Vasalis,
The Hague: A. A. M. Stols, 1948.
This publication was selected as one
of the 50 Best-Designed Books.

After Sandberg's return to the Stedelijk Museum in September 1945, the institution became a leading advocate for the avant-garde and under his enlightened leadership built one of the finest collections of modern art in Europe. Sandberg was not afraid to take chances with unknown artists, many of whom at least partially owe their success to him. Sandberg designed over three hundred Stedelijk Museum catalogs that were in many ways carry-overs from the *experimenta typographica* produced during the war. Lower-case bold type and vivid colors predominated, and the negative inner forms of letters were often utilized in the designs. These museum publications helped to establish a new criterion for similar institutions throughout the world. Sandberg never hesitated to delegate, and staff members carried out the designs for a number of the museum catalogs and posters according to Sandberg's concepts. Sandberg would then add further suggestions during the design process. In his post-war graphic design, Sandberg provided a connection between earlier designers such as Zwart and Werkman and later designers such as Wim Crouwel, Jan Bons, and Otto Treumann.

In addition to his responsibilities as director of the Stedelijk Museum, Sandberg was involved with the revitalization of Dutch art in general. He was elected to chair the Gebonden Kunsten Federatie, the GKF (the Aligned Arts Federation), a position he held until 1948. This new association satisfied another of Van Royen's ambitions and was a successor to the VANK However, the GKF encompassed even more than the VANK and included additional professions such as film, dance, photography, and theater. At first, however, it was tainted somewhat by politics, and its philosophy was determined to some extent by some of the more left-leaning members. Those who worked for advertising agencies were not considered admissible because it was felt they were too closely tied to the capitalist sector. Thus, they formed their own group in 1948, the VRI (Association of Advertising Designers and Illustrators).

Although Elffers used photography in his post-war graphic design, his work became less decorative and more reflective of his painting and drawing background. Elffers was a devotee of Henri Matisse who greatly influenced his work. More intense colors and hand-drawn typography became part of his expanded visual vocabulary, and his drawing became more simplified. Letters became objects in themselves, and influences of German Expressionism and the French Fauves became increasingly evident. In his posters Elffers experimented with printing errors and layers of transparent colors, often working directly on the actual printing plates. As with Werkman, Elffer's solutions were often derived from the printing process itself, with the unexpected playing an active role.

Otto Treumann was born into a Bavarian Jewish family and immigrated to the Netherlands in 1935 to avoid the Nazis who had then seized power in Germany. He first took design courses at the Amsterdam School for Graphic Art, and in 1936 he enrolled at the New Art School that had been started by Paul Citroen to continue the traditions of the then closed Bauhaus. As part of the Dutch resistance during World War II, Treumann falsified official documents such passports, identification cards and ration tickets.

In 1945 Treumann began working as a freelance designer with assignments such as posters, magazines, book jackets, and corporate design. His stamps for the PTT included *Telefoonnet* (Telephone Network) in 1962, *Verzetsmonumenten* (Resistance Monuments) in 1965, *Kinderzegels* (Children's Stamps) in 1966, *Benelux* in 1969, *Bevrijding* (Liberation) in 1970, *Natuur en Milieu* (Nature and Environment) in 1974), *Energie* (Energy) in 1977;

Europees Parlement (European Parliament) in 1979, *H.M. Juliana 70 jaar* (Her Majesty Juliana's 70th Birthday) in 1979, *Universiteit Amsterdam* (University of Amsterdam) in 1982, and *Vincent van Gogh* in 1990.

Employing photography, asymmetrical typography, abstract elements, and illustration, Treumann was particularly adept at combining texts and images. Many of his posters displayed a unique use of spatial layering and a poetic sensibility, and, like his contemporary Elffers, his work often evolved while he was at the printer 'on press.' He also deigned distinctive logos for El Al airlines, the Anne Frank Foundation, De Nederlandse Gasunie (The Dutch Gas Union), and the publisher Wolters Kluwer.

The movement in the Netherlands toward functional design was evident by the early 1960s. In January 1963 a group that included Wim Crouwel, Benno Wissing, Friso Kramer, and the brothers Dick and Paul Schwartz (who handled the managerial and business side), started a large, multimedia design studio in Amsterdam called Total Design (TD). At that time there was no firm capable of handling large comprehensive design commissions in the Netherlands, and for this reason such projects were given to designers in other countries. Using a multidisciplinary approach, Total Design soon produced extensive design programs for business, industry, and government. As implied by the firm's name, its objective was to conceive and produce design solutions for all areas and to achieve a unified result.

Many young designers gained valuable experience at Total Design and then moved on to establish firms of their own. Total Design, now Total Identity, remains a major force in European design, with offices in six cities and employing over one hundred and fifty design professionals including Aad van Dommelen and Rob Vermeulen.

Crouwel had a vital function in formulating Total Design's philosophy and focus. During the early fifties he had been in close touch with Swiss designers who were working in the international typographic style. Crouwel's own approach, however, was less dogmatic regarding universal form and homogeneous design. For him, the role of the graphic designer was to solve problems objectively through research and analysis, distilling the message and the way it was presented. Like Jan Tschichold almost forty years earlier, he was convinced that the inundation of typographic communication in modern society could be best conveyed through unambiguous and minimal methods. Using this approach, Crouwel attained an extraordinary simplicity instilled with an aesthetic strength.

From 1947 until 1949 Crouwel studied at the Minerva academy in Groningen and afterwards at the Institute of Arts and Crafts in Amsterdam. In 1952 he began his own graphic design bureau, and from 1957 until 1961 he worked with the interior designer Kho Liang Ie in exhibition design. During the latter half of the 1950s Crouwel designed posters and catalogues for the Van Abbemuseum in Eindhoven. After the director of the Van Abbemuseum, E. I. I. de Wilde succeeded Sandberg as director of the Stedelijk Museum in 1961, he brought in Crouwel to design a new image for the museum. Using a systematic approach, Crouwel insisted upon standardized methods to provide visual harmony for the museum's publications. In addition, he designed a number of typefaces and his first postage stamp for the PTT in 1976.

Above: Helmut Salden, binding for
Verzamelde Gedichten (Collected Verse)
by J. Slauerhoff, The Hague:
A. A. M. Stols, 1948.

Opposite: Otto Treumann, poster for
Utrecht's 50th Industrial Fair, 1948.

Crouwel has taught at various art academies and institutions including the Royal Academy of Arts and Crafts at s-Hertogenbosch, the Institute for Arts and Crafts in Amsterdam, Delft University, the Royal College of Art in London, and Erasmus University in Rotterdam. Crouwel also served as Director of the Boymans van Beuningen Museum in Rotterdam and is the recipient of numerous awards for his commitment and excellence in graphic design and typography.

One of Crouwel's earlier protégés was Gerard Unger. After graduating from the Rietveld Academy in 1967, Unger became an assistant to Crouwel at Total Design. His work in graphic design education includes teaching at the University of Reading in the United Kingdom, the Rietveld Academy, Rhode Island School of Design, and Stanford University. Since 1975 he has worked as a freelance designer, and in 1976 his first digital typefaces Demos and Praxis were marketed by Dr. Rudolf Hell in Kiel, Germany. His work in graphic design has included stamps, coins, magazines, newspapers, books, corporate identity, and type design. He has been the recipient of numerous awards for his work in typography including the H. N. Werkman Prize in 1984. His numerous type designs include Markeur in 1972, Demos and Praxis in 1976, Flora, his best-known face, in 1980, in 1985 Hollander and Swift, the latter designed using a digital format for newspapers, Amerigo in 1987, Cyrano in 1989, Argo in 1991, Oranda in 1992, Decoder and Gulliver in 1993, Swift 2.0 in 1995, Coranto in 1999, and Vesta in 2001. Among his other typographic achievements were Dutch road signs and the signage system for the Amsterdam Metro.

In 1986 Unger was an early devotee of the Macintosh computer. Enthusiastic about the possibilities that the Macintosh held for type design, he was quick to take advantage of what it offered and soon began to design directly on the monitor. After distributing his first PostScript font Argo through URW and the Dutch Type Library, Unger soon began to publish his fonts independently. Unger has even gone so far as to participate in the creation of several computer design programs. In spite of his enthusiastic utilization of computer technology, Unger remains essentially focused on historical and fundamental design principles. His typeface Hollander, for example, is based on seventeenth-century type with a high contrast between the thick and thin strokes.

Another designer who can be called a protégé of Crouwel is Rudy Vanderlans (Ruud van der Lans before moving to the United States) who studied at the Royal Academy of Fine Arts in The Hague from 1974 to 1979. Initially intending to become an illustrator, he spent his first year at the academy in the evening program where he was one of my drawing students. In the same year the graphic design department headed by the preeminent book designer and teacher Jacques Janssen accepted him. After graduation, he had a brief apprenticeship at Total Design followed by work doing corporate identity for Vorm Vijf and Tel Design. He then moved to California to study at the University of California at Berkeley. In 1984 Vanderlans decided to publish a magazine called *Emigre* for which he was also the designer and editor. Joining him were two Dutch friends whom he had known at the Royal Academy of Fine Arts and who were also living in San Francisco. They originally intended to present their unpublished works along with creative works by others. The journal's name was selected because its founders believed exposure to various cultures, and living in different cultural environments, had a significant impact on creative work. Vanderlans used typewriter type and copier images in the first issue, then used low-resolution Macintosh type for early subsequent issues. A magazine with a print run of seven thousand copies, *Emigre* became a beacon for experimentation in typography, outraging many design professionals while captivating others who embraced the potential of computer technology to redefine graphic design. *Emigre*'s experimental approach helped define and demonstrate the capabilities of the new technology, both in its editorials and by presenting work and interviews with designers from around the world whose work was too experimental for other design publications.

In 1987 Vanderlans began a partnership with his wife Zuzana Licko which they called Emigre Graphics. Licko's background included computer programming courses, and dissatisfied with the limited fonts available for the early Macintosh, Licko used a public-domain character-generation software application called FontEditor to create digital typefaces. Her first fonts were designed for low-resolution technology, and were then converted to high-resolution versions.

After initially working with Tel Design in The Hague, Gert Dumbar founded Studio Dumbar in 1977. First located in The Hague and now in Rotterdam, this studio encompasses a wide-ranging spectrum that includes experimental work for cultural clients, corporate identities, government agencies, and literature. Dumbar discards what he considers to be the dehumanization of graphic design and advocates a stylistic permanence that is intended to endure longer than a fleeting moment in time. Dumbar originally studied painting at The Hague Academy, and, while pursuing his graphic design studies at Royal College of Art in London during the early 1960s, he began using a method that he labeled *staged photography*. This incorporated environments made from found material, papier-mâché figures, and other objects produced specifically for the project. These were then photographed, often by Lex van Pieterson, in front of collage backdrops. With complex multi-layered typography, often elaborate to the point of disorder, many of Dumbar's designs initially shocked more conservative graphic designers. As in Piet Zwart's booklet *Het boek van PTT*, Dumbar used illustrations, photography, typography, and sculpture in single design statements. After many designers throughout the world began to imitate these approaches in the late 1980s, Dumbar placed their use on hold.

Humor, innovation, and playfulness characterize Studio Dumbar. The designers make a consistent effort to produce provocative graphics using diverse techniques generally homologous with fine arts. Teamwork and a lively exchange of ideas play an important role at Studio Dumbar. Gert Dumbar never hesitates to acknowledge the achievements of his staff while he invites and almost demands personal initiative. In the studio there is a surprising absence of bureaucracy which allows designers liberty to follow their own paths of discovery. There are few Dutch studios more sought-after for internships. Needless to say, enlightened clients play a major role as well.

As Crouwel remarked during a symposium on Studio Dumbar at the Rietveld Academy, Dumbar has always managed to charm and irritate at the same time: 'Gert's views and image language are different from mine,' Crouwel said, 'I can get very wound up over his sardonic posters for the Piet Zwart and Mondrian exhibitions. I don't understand the placing of ideals in perspective. Studio Dumbar is an exponent of the pure emotional movement of the 1970s and 1980s that attacked rational modernism.' However, perhaps this is one of the very reasons why Dumbar has been an inspiration to many young designers. In the Netherlands, Dumbar, Stolk, Beeke, and others were among those who lashed out at the International Style, yet it would be incorrect to simply label Studio Dumbar as avant-garde. How could we, taking into account their clients such as the NS, ANWB, KPN, the Rijksmuseum, the Dutch Defense Department, and the Dutch police.

Left: Otto Treumann, poster, *Atoomenergie en zijn gevolgen* (Atomic Energy and its Results), Amsterdam, 1950.

Below: Alexander Verberne and Ton Raateland, cover of the quarterly in-house journal *Range*, Eindhoven: Philips Communication Division, 1950.

Opposite: Dick Elffers, cover for *Honderd jaar lettergieterij in Amsterdam* (A Hundred Years of Typefounding in Amsterdam), 1951.

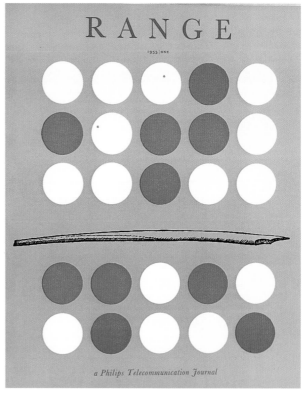

HONDERD
JAREN
LETTER-
GIETERIJ
IN
AMSTERDAM

DOOR Dr G. W. OVINK

N.V. LETTERGIETERIJ «AMSTERDAM» V/H N. TETTERODE

Gert Dumbar seems to enjoy this conflict and rightfully so. Studio Dumbar has always been controversial, and the recent identity system for the Dutch police was strongly criticized before being eventually accepted.

Jurriaan Schrofer, son of the painter Willem Schrofer, was one of the singular Dutch graphic designers after World War II. First a student of law, he moved to Amsterdam with the ambition of becoming a film director. There he met figures such as Cas Oorthuys and Piet Zwart and soon became an assistant to Elffers. Afterwards he moved on to Meijer Printers in Wormerveer where he learned monotype typesetting. Throughout his graphic design career, his work included logos, book jackets, brochures, advertisements, and photography books for various businesses, publishers, and institutions. Schrofer used words as images and designed many of his display faces himself. Using photography, he distorted letters to create striking visual effects through skillfully manipulating light and depth in his compositions. Also, he was intrigued by minimalist alphabets constructed from geometric elements.

Schrofer was highly active in the graphic design organization GVN, and in 1972 he was asked to become a co-director of Total Design. His work gradually became more poetic and simplified as he used letters cut from paper and cardboard in his designs. Devoted to design education, he taught at the Rietveld Academy and at the Rotterdam Academy until he was appointed director of the Arnhem Academy.

Although not a partner, Ben Bos was a senior designer and part of Total Design's management team. He remained associated with Total Design longer than any of the founding members. Bos and those working closely with him were instrumental in bringing in much of the company's revenue and in so doing, helped to give the partners latitude to produce their more experimental work. Although Bos greatly admired Crouwel, he became disillusioned when many at Total Design felt they had to compete with subjectively-based firms like Studio Dumbar. This was one of the reasons that Bos severed his ties with Total Design in 1991.

Pieter Brattinga, another major force in Dutch graphic design, received his training in printing through working at his father's Hilversum-based printing company, De Jong & Co. During the 1950s Brattinga served as an intermediary between graphic designers and printers. From 1954 until 1973, he organized exhibitions for a small gallery at De Jong & Co, which made progressive art and graphic design available to a larger number of viewers. He designed posters for these exhibitions based on a grid of fifteen square components; with one or more of these elements always used as a part the design itself. Brattinga was the editor of a square-format magazine called *Kwadraatblad* (Square Journal). This De Jong & Co. publication was mailed to clients to illustrate their printing resources while at the same time giving important artists and graphic designers a forum to experiment with new frontiers in printing. Although at times the subject of controversy, this magazine demonstrated a wide scope of possibilities for both clients and designers. Each of the twenty-three issues was devoted to themes such as music, design, literature, typography, architecture, and the fine arts. In 1957 the topic of the first issue was Marc Chagall's 'Clocks,' and other issues concerned topics such as Buckminster Fuller, Jan Bons's mural in Mexico, Rietveld's Schröder House, a recent alphabet by Crouwel, and Anthon Beeke's alphabet constructed from female nudes. Brattinga served as the editor, and a new designer was used for every issue. Sandberg designed and provided the texts for the two themed *NU* ('Now') issues.

Jan Bons has many influences including The Hague Academy, the New Art School in Amsterdam, Sandberg, Treumann, and Duwaer. He began working in graphic design before the war and during the occupation managed to continue his profession in spite of the severe limitations. In addition to forging official documents, he designed and helped to publish the first Dutch translation of *Ein Landarzt* (A Country Doctor) by Franz Kafka. After the war his work included murals, exhibition designs, interiors, posters, calendars, signage, catalogues, magazines, brochures, logos, trade shows, and postage stamps for the PTT. His posters for De Brakke Grond and De Appel theater group in Amsterdam rate among his notable achievements. Bons has always been selective in accepting clients who have always given him the latitude he needs to pursue his own direction.

In addition to the corporate sector, Dutch cultural organizations and government bureaus were early graphic design patrons. Every government bureau now maintains a visual identity system and makes a concerted effort to communicate with its customers. Also, cities and major public projects have commissioned extensive visualidentity programs. Van Royen's goal to improve government design was institutionalized in 1945 when an aesthetic advisor was appointed to head a new government branch called the Dienst Esthetische Vormgeving (Aesthetic Design Department). When one of Van Royen's former colleagues, W. F. Gouwe, assumed this post in 1946, it was clear that his earlier efforts would be continued. With dedication and insight, Gouwe maintained Van Royen's practice of providing commissions for gifted graphic designers. He directed his attention toward all areas of the PTT, including furniture, industrial, and interior design.

The Aesthetic Design Department served as a liaison between the PTT, the public, and the artists and graphic designers who were given assignments. During the twenty years following the war, ornamental and illustrative approaches were still prevalent, but after 1966 the department began to assume a more modern and bold direction. In 1976, R. D. E. Oxenaar assumed the post of aesthetic advisor, and under his guidance, design at the PTT advanced to a new level of excellence. Oxenaar supported a belief in independent expression balanced by practical considerations. This allowed the PTT to attain visual inventiveness while fulfilling its own needs and those of the public. Dutch postage stamp design has been particularly innovative and embraces a variety of styles including classical modernism and expressionism. Many young designers have received stamp design assignments when beginning their careers, and today the design of postage stamps continues to give Dutch graphic designers a venue to explore new visual frontiers.

The PTT adopted a new visual identity program in 1981. Total Design and Studio Dumbar were commissioned to work together on this wide-ranging venture. Exacting design standards were adopted, but many products including stamps continued to be created by diverse graphic designers. Also, some publications such as annual reports and the interiors of post offices located in historic buildings were not obliged to adhere to the new system.

On January 1, 1989, the PTT was officially privatized and was immediately confronted by avid competition in many fields. The Aesthetic Design Department was renamed the Corporate Policy Unit for Art and Design and continues to commission product and graphic design assignments. Although the PTT considered the existing identity system to be adequate, changes were needed to accommodate the change from government agency to private entity. To this end, Studio Dumbar was commissioned to revise the identity system. The sans serif PTT initials were continued, and bright colors and geometric elements were introduced to strengthen and invigorate PTT graphic design, products, and

Left and below: Dick Elffers, cover and double-page spread for the Christmas issue of *Drukkersweekblad* (Printers' Weekly), Amsterdam, 1952.

Opposite: Henk Krijger, Raffia Initials typeface, Type Foundry Amsterdam, 1952.

manuaren

environments. Specific colors were used to identify the various PTT sectors; red represented the postal service and green the telephone service. The bright green color of the telephone booths was chosen to make them easily recognizable in city environments.

Oxenaar first studied fine art at The Hague Academy under, among others, Paul Citroen, and then changed his focus to graphic design. For him, movements such as German Expressionism, Dada, Constructivism, and De Stijl remain important sources for his work in graphic design. In 1965 the Nederlandse Bank commissioned Oxenaar to re-design the Dutch paper currency. He was disappointed with his first attempt, a green five-guilder note (on which his nickname 'Ootje' is included in tiny letters), and agreed to continue with the commission only if he could fully participate in future design and production procedures. These involved issues such as production methods, anti-counterfeiting measures, and ease of recognition. In 1978, Oxenaar was allowed to select his own subject for a new hundred-guilder note. Rejecting traditional motifs such as engravings of historical figures and national symbols, he chose a snipe, a long-billed marsh bird, as the central design element. This was so well received by the public that the Nederlandse Bank allowed Oxenaar to select additional banknote subjects. He chose a sunflower for the fifty-guilder note and a well-known lighthouse for the two-hundred-and-fifty-guilder note. Each banknote had its own color theme, and large sans serif numbers denoted the value. Both in composition and color these were unparalleled in currency design. Oxenaar managed to satisfy his own aesthetic needs while at the same time designing a successful currency.

A native of Amsterdam, Anthon Beeke had no formal graphic design training except for a few months of evening classes at School of Applied Arts. After being an apprentice for various design firms, he worked for a year as an assistant to Jan van Toorn. In 1963, Beeke began his own design studio, and his first clients were mainly publishers, museums, cultural journals, and the theater. From 1976 until 1982, he was an assistant director at Total Design. Between 1982 until founding Studio Anthon Beeke in 1987 he worked intermittently with Swip Stolk. Beeke's designs have always been controversials beginning with his 1969 alphabet constructed from photographs of female nudes. Beeke's clients have included the Stedelijk Museum, Toneelgroep Amsterdam, Zuidelijk Toneel/Globe, the newspaper publisher Perscombinatie, and the book publisher Prometheus. He is currently the publisher of the international magazine *View on Colour* and is chief lecturer at the Design Academy in Eindhoven.

Beeke is a maverick for whom design is not a matter of beauty but instead a search for fundamental truth. Deciphering his posters can often be a demanding task, as they defy definition through normal means. Beeke aims to create interactions between his posters and their viewers.

During the 1960s Beeke was involved with Fluxus, a neo-Dada group concerned with artistic manifestations such as happenings, performance art, and experimental poetry. This association greatly influenced his approach to designing theater posters. Even though some of his posters have the aura of a pagan pageant, this veils a more sinister aspect. When humor does emerge it is ironic and esoteric; his posters are never intended as jokes. Beeke's succinct messages are never embellished with superfluous decoration. Backgrounds are flat planes of color, increasing legibility and helping one to focus on the content. The typography in his pictorial posters has a supportive role and never competes with the image in conveying the underlying message. Beeke's posters are intuitive creations, with symbolic images deliberately selected to express a particular theme:

Beeke probes beneath the surface to almost primordial depths and makes a radical inquiry into the substance of the drama. He designs like a circling hawk that never quite alights and leaves questions rather than answers. As with a fairytale, his creations baffle, mystify, bemuse, and bewitch in a world of fantasy and illusion. With his command of irony and innate capacity to jolt reactions and challenge rationality, he openly confronts our sensibilities. Paradox invariably astounds, challenges, agitates, perplexes, and places demands upon the viewer. Part of his genius lies in his ability to elicit, simplify, and articulate the essence of a subject and to subtly and tersely distil its intrinsic meaning through a masterful mixture of unorthodox components.[1]

Conversely, tradition, simplicity, and basic techniques and materials distinguish the graphic design of Karel Martens. After graduating from the Arnhem School of Art in 1961, Martens worked for the publisher Van Loghum Slaterus where design quality took precedence over commercial considerations. Kluwer, a much larger firm, for whom profit was the major objective, eventually absorbed Van Loghum Slaterus, and it was soon evident that designers such as Martens did not fit in with their business format. From 1975 until 1981 he worked for SUN, a publisher concerned with social issues, who later brought him back to be responsible for the visual aspects of their entire book sector. As a typographer, Martens consistently attempts to subtly imply the content of any publication assignment, and his work is always characterized by a pervasive elegance. In addition to his work for publishing houses, Martens has continued on a freelance basis as a designer of books, posters, catalogues, magazines, postage stamps for the PTT, telephone cards, signage, and typographic building façades. Since 1977 Martens has been involved with educating new generations of graphic designers as a teacher at the Arnhem School of Art. In 1994 he joined the faculty at the Jan van Eyck Academy in Maastricht, and since 1997 he has been a visiting lecturer in the graphic design department at the School of Art at Yale University.

Walter Nikkels approaches typography like a conceptual artist. Having studied at art academies in Rotterdam, Munich and Milan, his roots are more international than purely Dutch. Much of his work has been for museums. He designed the new image for the Dordrechts Museum and has designed numerous exhibitions in Germany. His typography embraces both traditional and modern concepts and depends to a large extent upon intuition. Encouraged by Rudi Fuchs, former director of the Stedelijk Museum, Nikkels brilliantly redefined the museum's public image. He received both the prestigious H. N. Werkman and the Charles Nypels Prizes for his work in typography. He has been active in exhibition design and since 1985 has taught at the Kunstacademie in Düsseldorf.

For many years Swip Stolk has been active in every sector of graphic design including posters, logos, books, stamps, exhibitions, institutions, magazines, and museums. By nature a bold designer, he unceasingly seeks the confrontational edge. The 1970s in the Netherlands was a period of radical movements and a pervading sardonic humor in the media. This approach was exemplified by the left-wing radio and television network VPRO, for which Stolk designed a house style in 1978 using the socialist hen as a symbolic element. Oddly, after being in use for only a few months it was discarded by the network whose visual tastes apparently did not measure up to their political ideology.

Stolk's yearly calendars for the offset printer De Boer and Vink used unusual themes such as 'visual irritation' and highly unusual packaging methods. Stolk provides the principal design direction for the Groninger Museum, and his posters, catalogues, and other printed material exhibit the museum's progressive philosophy. When the new Groninger Museum

CÔTE d'AZUR

fortissimo

Opposite: Otto Treumann, poster
for the sculpture exhibition
Sonsbeek '52, Arnhem, 1952.

Above: Dick Elffers,
double-page spread from *Facetten*
van boekdruk (Aspects of
Letterpress) by Cor Pels,
Amsterdam: Van Gelder Zonen,
1952. Jurriaan Schrofer assisted
in producing the book, and
Cas Oorthuys, Carel Blazer,
and Emmy Andriesse took
the photographs.

opened in 1995, Stolk designed the corporate identity. Stolk has a preference for both harsh metallic and muted pastel colors and an expressionist approach to typography. Through his teaching at the AKI in Enschede and at the Rietveld Academy, the message that he conveys to his students is more about feelings and thoughts than formal graphic design training.

The Amsterdam graphic designer Jan van Toorn received his training at the Institute for Industrial Arts in Amsterdam, later renamed the Gerrit Rietveld Academy, and has been active as a designer since 1957. Van Toorn's work in graphic design is closely tied to his belief in exploring the purpose and social significance of graphic design in addition to pragmatic and artistic needs. Through the influence of Mart Stam, Bauhaus social ideals were stressed which reinforced Van Toorn's inherent idealism. For Van Toorn the delivery of the message is the essential factor. He stated: 'An ostensibly large diversity of styles, such as you now see, in my opinion only draw attention to themselves. They serve as a mask over a situation in which almost nothing is actually raised. The designer can enjoyably indulge in the most fantastic discoveries of form, yet this luxury veils a deficiency of real discussion. Bear in mind that printed matter is made to function within a situation. Thus, its value should first be determined in this manner.'

Van Toorn designs mainly for cultural and educational institutions. His clients include museums, printing firms, and the PTT. From 1965 until 1974 he worked as a designer for the Stedelijk Van Abbemuseum in Eindhoven, where the architect Jean Leering was then director. For both Leering and Van Toorn, art could not be separated from society as a whole, and they were firmly against the idea of art for art's sake. Photography is a vital design tool for Van Toorns and an essential tool for presenting reality. For him, the designer's mission is to address the essential message with form serving this end.

Through his role in design education Van Toorn has inspired a generation of young designers. He has taught at numerous academies and universities including the Rietveld Academy, the Technical University in Eindhoven, and the Rijksacademie in Amsterdam. From 1991 to 1998 he held the post of director at the Jan van Eyck Academy in Maastricht, and was largely instrumental in making it an international postgraduate school of fine art and design. He continues as a visiting professor in the graduate graphic design program at the Rhode Island School of Design in the USA. His influence on design education also manifests itself in his advisory role for the publications *Design Issues* and *Visible Language*. In 1985 Van Toorn was the first recipient of the Piet Zwart Prize, and his work is included in important collections such as the Stedelijk Museum, the Museum of Modern Art in New York, the Centre Georges Pompidou in Paris, and the Bibliotheque Nationale de France.

Ghislain (Gielijn) Dapnis Escher is another Dutch designer who is impossible to categorize. Through their direct simplicity and flat areas of color, his posters contrast with the urban surroundings where they are usually seen and draw attention on crowded streets through a restrained dignity. In his posters the colors of the type and images are often enhanced by dark backgrounds. He rarely uses photography and always produces his own images. Superlative artistic accomplishments, Escher's posters are unbending aesthetic affirmations, far detached from the modern graphic design mainstream, and with a subjective allure they subtly attain the essence of the subject they represent.

Irma Boom studied the AKI School of Fine Arts in Enschede and afterward worked for five years as a designer in the Dutch government publishing office in The Hague. In 1991 she founded the Irma Boom Office in Amsterdam. In 1992 she began teaching at the Yale School of Art in the USA and beginning in 1998 she taught for two years at the Van Eyck Academy at Maastricht. One of her major undertakings was the book commemorating the Dutch corporation SHV. This monumental project took five years to complete and contained 2,136 pages without page numbers or an index.

In 1978 a group of Rotterdam designers founded the monthly magazine *Hard Werken* (Hard Working) and two years later founded Hard Werken Design. More a relaxed association than a formal company, the group eventually included Henk Elenga, Gerard Hadders, Tom van der Haspel, Helen Howard, Rick Vermeulen, Willem Kars, and Jan Willem de Kok. As a response to functional design and modernism, Hard Werken used a laid-back approach with no restrictions whatsoever. They had no communal design approach or dogma other than a reaction against functionalism and the International Style. Shunning all modes and systems, they arrived at solutions through subjective readings of the challenges at hand with all established graphic design guidelines placed on hold Their willingness to embrace any imaginable typographic or image option produced unexpected and sometimes perplexing solutions. Hard Werken not only stressed the content of the message but also the process and materials as well. In contrast to the collaborative environment at Studio Dumbar, Hard Werken was essentially a cooperative group of independent graphic designers.

Hard Werken associates considered themselves a part of contemporary art and disallowed any refinement in graphic design. Although its work was often seen as crude and even offensive, Hard Werken had no rigid political or aesthetic stance and instead adopted a form of artistic rebellion. Denying limitations of any sort, they created audiovisual productions, exhibitions, furniture, interior design, lamps, and theater scenery. Alas, by 1990, Hard Werken developed into a more structured entity, and in 1994 it combined with the Ten Cate Bergmans design studio to become Inízio, a larger and more conservative communications firm.

Unlike Hard Werken, Wild Plakken, a more collaborative association, had a distinct cultural and social agenda. Founded in 1977 by three Rietveld graduates, Frank Beekers, Lies Ros, and Rob Schröder, they only accepted clients involved with what they considered to be important social or political issues. Idealists such as El Lissitzky, John Heartfield, Schuitema, Rietveld and some of their teachers such as Van Toorn motivated them. Wild Plakken is roughly translated as 'Wild Pasting' or 'Unauthorized Bill-Posting.' This became the studio's name in the early 1980s when they illegally hung posters in Amsterdam for which Schröder was gleefully arrested several occasions. The 1970s was a period of political turbulence, and the Vietnam War, South African apartheid, inadequate housing, women's and gay rights, abortion, and nuclear arms were all Wild Plakken topics. They accepted assignments based on a client's philosophical perspective; approved clients included trade unions, the Dutch Communist Party, museums, and theater, but never capitalist industry.

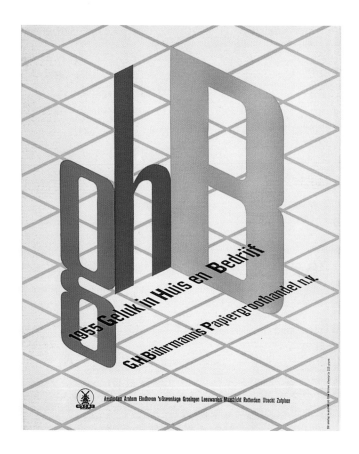

Jurriaan Schrofer, back cover and
title page spread of the Christmas
issue of *Drukkersweekblad*
(Printers' Weekly), Amsterdam,
1954. The back-cover ad is for the
paper merchant G. H. Bührmann.

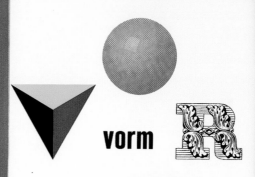

idee en vorm

In the beginning, Wild Plakken used lucid, uncomplicated images known as closed texts because they could only be interpreted in one restricted manner. Later, Wild Plakken gave viewers more latitude for their own interpretations through using surrealist imagery, photomontage, and brilliantly colored forms. Their work displayed a crude strength when compared to conventional print advertising. Wild Plakken designers supplied most of their photography since this gave the designers the freedom to cut, tear, and combine images without having to respect the work of someone else. They believed that graphic design should be founded on the character and content of a particular theme and that designers would inevitably become stale imitators if not involved with the complete design process.

After eleven years, Beekers left Wild Plakken to begin his own design studio, and eventually the studio dissolved. Their ingenuity and energy and that of Studio Dumbar and Hard Werken motivated the next generation of designers to both challenge and respect previous rules and move on to new graphic design frontiers.

1 Alston W. Purvis, *Een bespreking van de theateraffiches van Anton Beeke*

in Aanplakken toegestaan, 50 jaar werk Anton Beeke, Amsterdam, 2004.

VoRmentaal

uitgave van Van Gelder Zonen n.v. Amsterdam

SPECTRUM

ABCDEFGHIJK
LMNOPQRST
UVWXYZ
1234567890
&

abcdefghijklmn
opqrstuvwxyzij
1234567890

.,:;!?‘’-(*[—

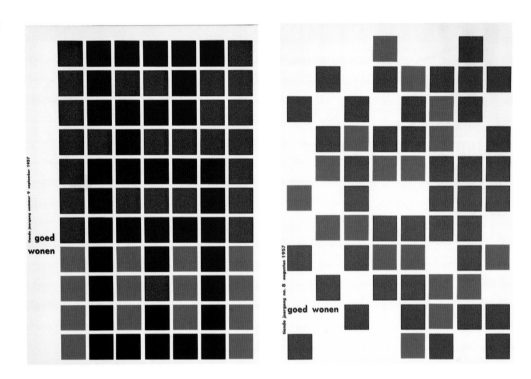

Above: Charles Jongejans, covers for the monthly magazine *Goed Wonen* (Good Living), vol. 10, Amsterdam: Goed Wonen Foundation, 1957.

Opposite: Jan Bons, *Opdracht* (Assignment), poster for an exhibition by the Association of Practitioners of Monumental Art, Stedelijk Museum, Amsterdam, 1956.

Above: Willem Sandberg, cover
of the Stedelijk Museum's library
catalog, Amsterdam, 1957.

Opposite: Willem Sandberg,
143 International Posters,
exhibition poster, Museum Fodor,
Amsterdam, 1958.

302

Joodse
rituele kunst
uit Parijs

Joods Historisch Museum

Waaggebouw Amsterdam

Otto Treumann   Offsetdruk: Steendrukkerij de Jong & Co, Hilversum 1955

Within the image:
De bestverzorgde vijftig boeken
van het jaar 1957

Juryrapport en catalogus

Vereniging ter bevordering van
de belangen des Boekhandels

Commissie voor de Collectieve
Propaganda van het Nederlandse Boek

Opposite: Otto Treumann, *Jewish Ritual Art from Paris*, exhibition poster, Jewish Historical Museum, Amsterdam, 1958.

Above: Wim Crouwel, cover of a jury report and catalog for the 50 Best-Designed Books of 1957, Amsterdam: VBBB and CPNB, 1958.

Wim Crouwel and Kho Liang Ie,
Gesel van de Oorlog (The Scourge of War),
poster for a touring exhibition organized by
the Nederlandse Kunststichting, 1958–59.

Below: Jan Bons, *Atomium, Visitez Bruxelles* (Atomium, Visit Brussels), poster, Brussels, 1958.

Overleaf: Jan Bons, *Rietveld*, exhibition poster, Stedelijk Museum, Amsterdam, 1959.

Offsetdruk: Steendrukkerij de Jong & Co. Hilversum 1959

6 maart - 6 april

RIET

stedelijk museum amsterdam

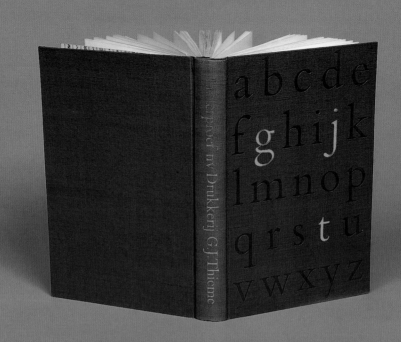

Thomas Dekker

the guls hornbooke

first published at
London, 1609
reprinted in 1960
for the members of
de Roos, Utrecht

Opposite, above: Jan Vermeulen, cover of a type reference book for G. J. Thieme Printers, Nijmegen: Thieme, 1959.

Opposite, below: Jan Bons, title page for *The Guls Hornbooke* by Thomas Dekker, Utrecht: De Roos Foundation, 1960. Bons's design and illustrations are quite unusual for this largely traditionally designed series of books.

Left and below: Willem Sandberg, cover and spread from the themed issue *NU: in het midden van de twintigste eeuw* (NOW: In the Middle of the Twentieth Century) from *Kwadraatblad* (Square Journal), Hilversum: Steendrukkerij de Jong, 1959. Sandberg also contributed an article to this issue on the subject of contemporary museums.

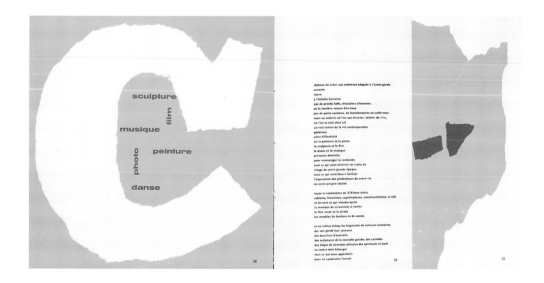

Below: Pieter Brattinga, *Carel Visser*, exhibition
poster, Stedelijk Museum, Amsterdam, 1960.

Opposite: Willem Sandberg, *Henry Moore*, exhibition
poster, Stedelijk Museum, Amsterdam, 1950.

carel visser

van 20 mei tot 20 juni   stedelijk museum a'dam

stedelijk muse um

amsterdam

tot 25 feb.

henry

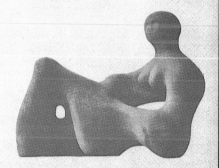

moore

stadsdrukkerij van amsterdam

GERRIT JAN THIEMEFONDS

Above: Hans Barvelink, cover of a
jury report for a competition for
well-designed calendars and office
diaries, Amsterdam: Gerrit Jan Thieme
Fund, 1962.

Opposite: Jurriaan Schrofer, exhibition
poster for *i10, Internationale Avantgarde
1927–1929*, Stedelijk Museum,
Amsterdam, 1963. The letters are
constructed from two basic elements:
a rectangle and a quarter circle.

i10

internationale
avantgarde
1927-1929

stedelijk museum
amsterdam
18-10–18-11 '63

Above: Willem Sandberg, cover for the
Christmas issue of *Drukkersweekblad*
(Printers' Weekly), Amsterdam, 1963.

Opposite: Jurriaan Schrofer, pages from
the company diary, The Hague: PTT, 1965.

Raadpleeg eerst de telefoongids
voordat u zich voor inlichtingen wendt
tot de telefonistes van PTT. In de
gids zult u meestal de gewenste
inlichtingen vinden.

vragen staat vrij . . . .

zaterdag	24	israelitisch pasen

zondag	25

Raadpleeg voor inlichtingen
eerst de telefoongids

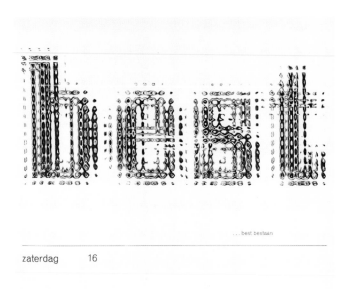

. . . best bestaan

zaterdag	16

zondag	17

Neem een beleggingsrekening
bij de Rijkspostspaarbank

tentoonstelling

kunsteten

27 februari tot 16 maart

tien uur tot half twaalf en twee tot vijf uur

zaterdags tien uur tot half twaalf

zondags gesloten

kantine

steendrukkerij de Jong & Co

's-gravelandseweg 19 bij de kei hilversum

Opposite: Pieter Brattinga, *Kunsteten*
(Eating Art), exhibition poster, Hilversum:
Steendrukkerij de Jong, 1965.

Above: Wim Crouwel, *Vormen van de kleur*
(Color Forms), exhibition poster, Stedelijk
Museum, Amsterdam, 1966.

318

Above: Otto Treumann, three
commemorative stamps for the
PTT, The Hague, 1965. The series
depicted Dutch war memorials.

Opposite: Anthon Beeke, themed
issue of *Kwadraatblad* entitled
Anthon Beeke Alphabet, Hilversum:
Steendrukkerij de Jong, 1970.
Photographed by Geert Kooiman
and produced by Anna Beeke.

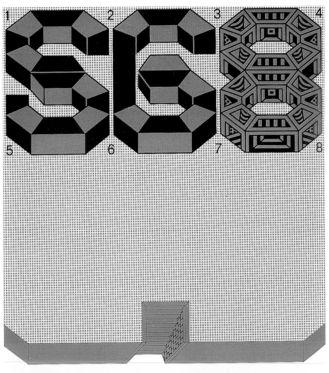

Opposite: Swip Stolk, *Upperground*,
poster for De Bijenkorf department
store, Amsterdam, 1966.

Above: Swip Stolk, *S68*, poster, Studium
Generale Rijksuniversiteit, Utrecht, 1968.

Above: Studio Dumbar, house style
manual for the PTT, The Hague, 1989.

Opposite: Jan Bons, poster for *Tuin der
Lusten* (Garden of Desire) by Fernando
Arrabal, Studio Theater Group,
Amsterdam, 1969.

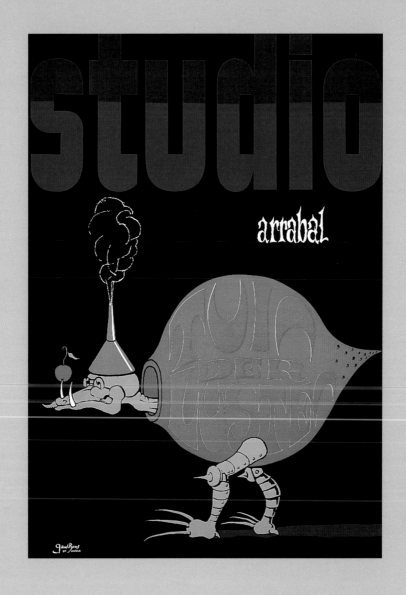

Above: Jan van Toorn, cover of exhibition
catalog for *Three Blind Mice*,
Van Abbemuseum, Eindhoven, 1968.

Opposite: Wim Crouwel and Daphne
Duijvelshoff (Total Design), catalog
cover, Jan Bons, Affiches (The Posters of
Jan Bons). One of a series produced for
Museum Fodor, Amsterdam, 1969–77.

fodor 28

Jan Bons,
affiches

Above: Jan Bons, poster for *De nonnen*
(The Nuns) by Eduardo Manet, Studio
Theater Group, Amsterdam, 1969.

Opposite: Otto Treumann, poster for
Musement, a joint museum display,
Utrecht Industrial Fair, 1969.

Eerste gezamenlijke presentatie van de Nederlandse musea
19 juni tm 13 juli 1969
Irenehal Jaarbeurs Utrecht

Above: Ben Bos (Total Design), poster for
Randstad employment agency, *c*. 1970.

Opposite, above: Anthon Beeke, *Toeval*
(Coincidence), poster, Studium Generale
Rijksuniversiteit, Utrecht, 1972.

Opposite, below: Anthon Beeke, cover for
Hollands diep magazine, Amsterdam, 1976.

330

Left: Jan van Toorn, cover of the PTT
Annual Report 1972, The Hague, 1973.

Below: Jan van Toorn, catalog cover
for *Museum in Motion* exhibition,
The Hague: Staatsuitgeverij, 1979.

Opposite: Jurriaan Schrofer, cover of
*Cognition: International Journal of
Cognitive Psychology*, The Hague
and Paris: Mouton, 1972.
The design is created through three
dimensional, geometric letterforms.

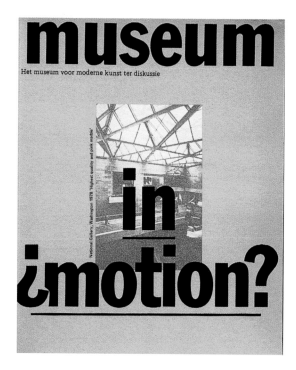

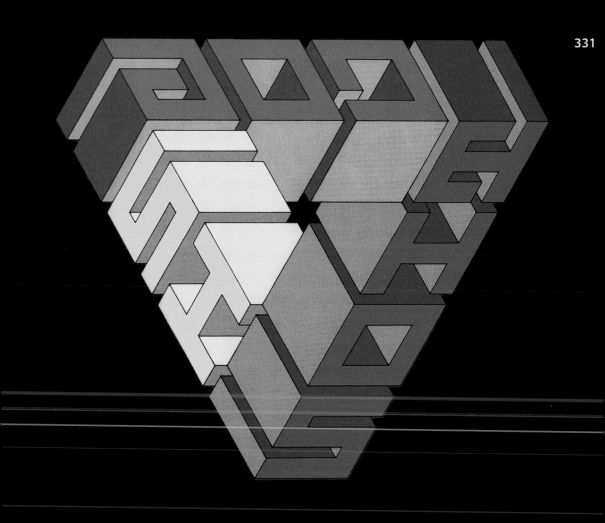

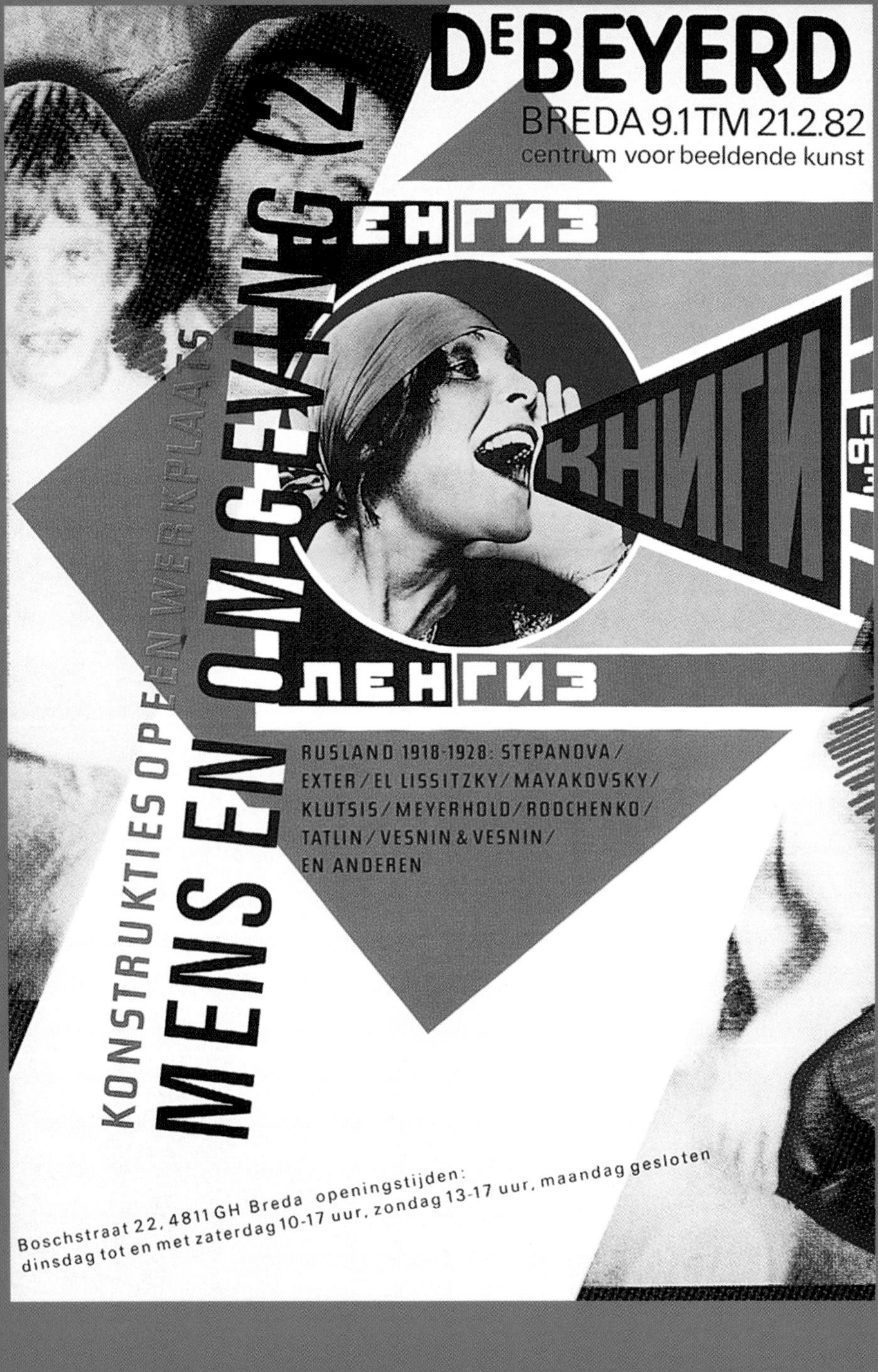

De**BEYERD**

BREDA 9.1 TM 21.2.82

centrum voor beeldende kunst

ЛЕНГИЗ

КНИГИ

ЛЕНГИЗ

RUSLAND 1918-1928: STEPANOVA /
EXTER / EL LISSITZKY / MAYAKOVSKY /
KLUTSIS / MEYERHOLD / RODCHENKO /
TATLIN / VESNIN & VESNIN /
EN ANDEREN

KONSTRUKTIES OPEN WERKPLAATS

MENS EN OMGEVING (2

Boschstraat 22, 4811 GH Breda openingstijden:
dinsdag tot en met zaterdag 10-17 uur, zondag 13-17 uur, maandag gesloten

Opposite: Jan van Toorn, poster for an exhibition series, *Mens en omgeving* (Mankind and the Environment), De Beyard Center for the Visual Arts, Breda, 1982.

Right: Wim Crouwel, two calendar pages for the printer Ervin E. van de Geer, Amsterdam, 1975 and 1976.

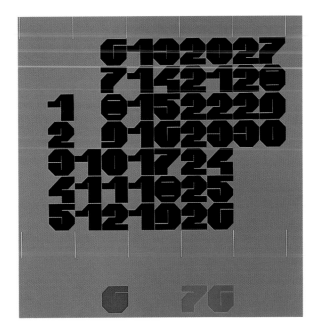

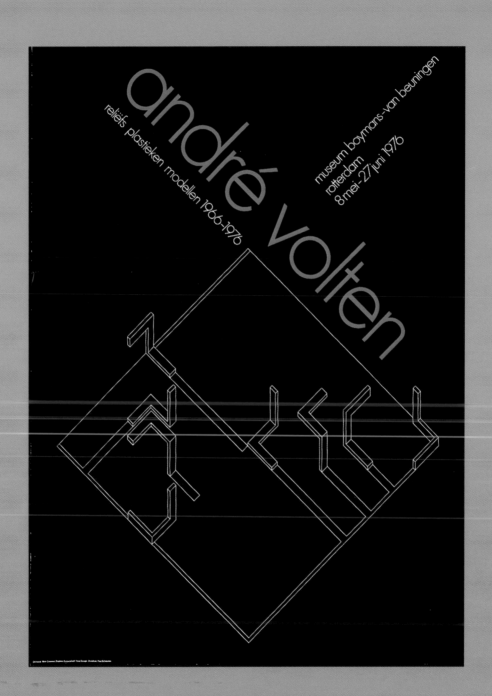

336

Above: Swip Stolk, calendar, *zakken vol ongeloof* (Sacks of Unbelief), Zaandijk, 1974.

Opposite: Wild Plakken, poster for a national charity campaign for Vietnam, Amsterdam, 1975.

338

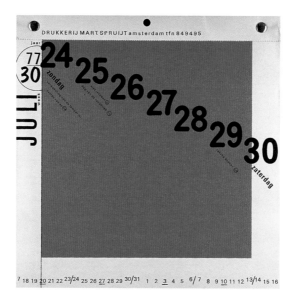

Above: Jan van Toorn, page from a
1977–78 calendar for Mart. Spruyt
Printers, Amsterdam, 1977.

Opposite: Jan van Toorn, covers for
the magazine *DA+AT: Dutch Art and
Architecture Today*, Rijksdienst
Beeldende Kunst, The Hague.

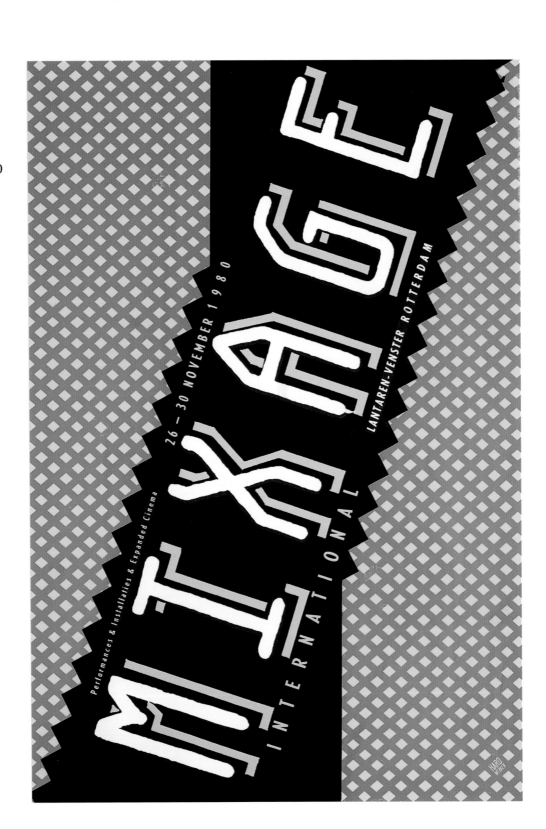

MIRAGE INTERNATIONAL

26 – 30 NOVEMBER 1980

LANTAREN-VENSTER ROTTERDAM

Performances & Installaties & Expanded Cinema

HARD WERKEN

Opposite: Hard Werken (Gerard Hadders),
Mixage International, poster for a
multimedia show. De Lantaren,
Rotterdam, 1980.

Above: Hard Werken (Gerard Hadders),
poster for the dance production *Even*,
Kunst Stichting, Rotterdam, 1981.

Opposite: Gielijn Escher, poster for the Festival of Fools, Amsterdam, 1980.

Above: Anthon Beeke, poster for *Leonce and Lena* by Georg Büchner, Globe Theater, 1979.

VICTOR OF DE KINDEREN AAN DE
MACHT VAN ROGER VITRAC GESPEELD
DOOR DE APPEL VANAF

DE APEL

Victor
of
de kinderen
aan de
Macht

13 OKTOBER
TOT EIND
JANUARI

Opposite: Jan Bons, poster for
Victor of de kinderen aan de macht
(Victor or the Children in Power),
De Appel, The Hague, 1982.

Above: Paul Mijksenaar, calendar,
Mart. Spruyt, Amsterdam, 1980.

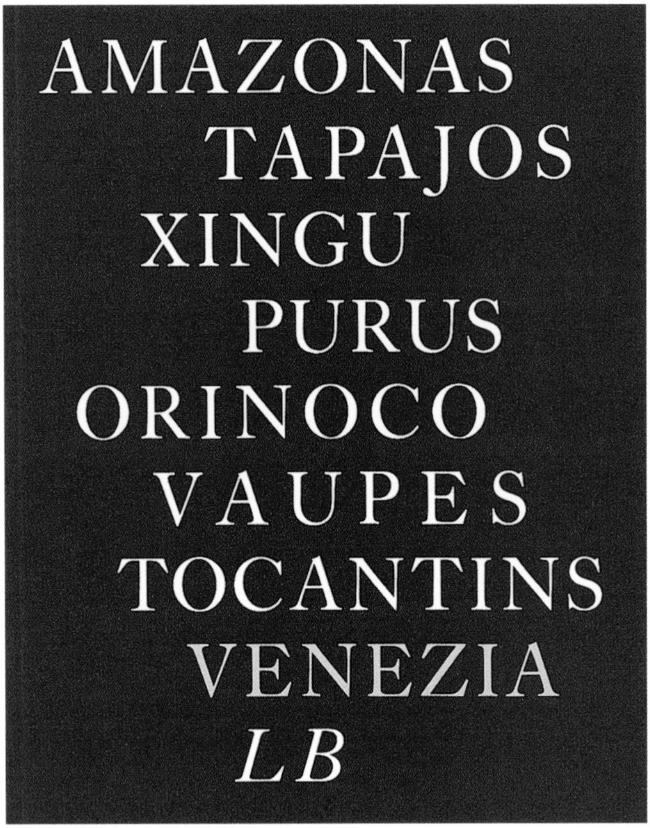

AMAZONAS
TAPAJOS
XINGU
PURUS
ORINOCO
VAUPES
TOCANTINS
VENEZIA
LB

Above: Walter Nikkels, cover of
catalog for the exhibition *Lothar
Baumgarten*, German Pavilion,
Venice, 1984.

Opposite: Wild Plakken, poster,
Pasgeboren kunst (Newborn Art),
Amsterdam, 1984. The text is by
Willem Sandberg: 'Newborn art,
uneducated and demanding,
does not speak but shouts.'

pasgeboren kunst
onopgevoed en veeleisend
spreekt niet maar schreeuwt

willem sandberg

een uitgave van D E B A L I E , centrum voor theater, politiek en literatuur - Amsterdam 1984

MOORDDADIG!

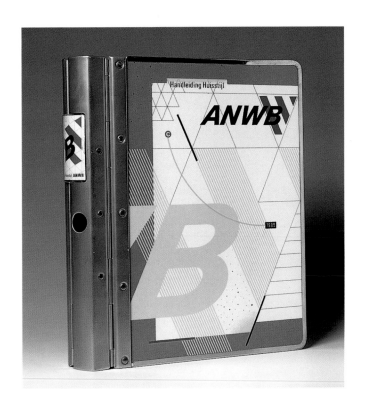

Opposite: Gielijn Escher, *Moorddadig*
(Murderous), poster opposing the
deployment of cruise missiles in
the Netherlands, Amsterdam, 1985.

Above: Studio Dumbar, house style
handbook for ANWB, The Hague, 1985.

Right: Walter Nikkels, catalog cover for *Antoni Tàpies*, Stedelijk van Abbemuseum, Eindhoven, 1986.

Below right: Walter Nikkels, exhibition invitation for *Ooghoogte* (Eye Level), Stedelijk van Abbemuseum, Eindhoven, 1986.

Opposite: Walter Nikkels, exhibition poster for *Rundgang* (Round Trip), Kunstakademie, Düsseldorf, 1986.

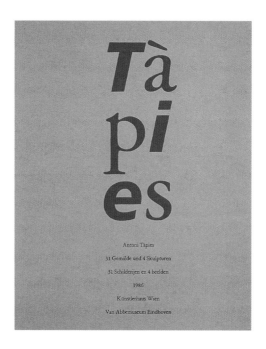

Antoni Tàpies

31 Gemälde und 4 Skulpturen

31 Schilderijen en 4 beelden

1986

Künstlerhaus Wien

Van Abbemuseum Eindhoven

ǀ/ə/ʌ/ə/ǀ /ə/ʎ/e/ǀ

e/y/e/ /l/e/v/e/l

o/o/g/h/o/o/g/t/e

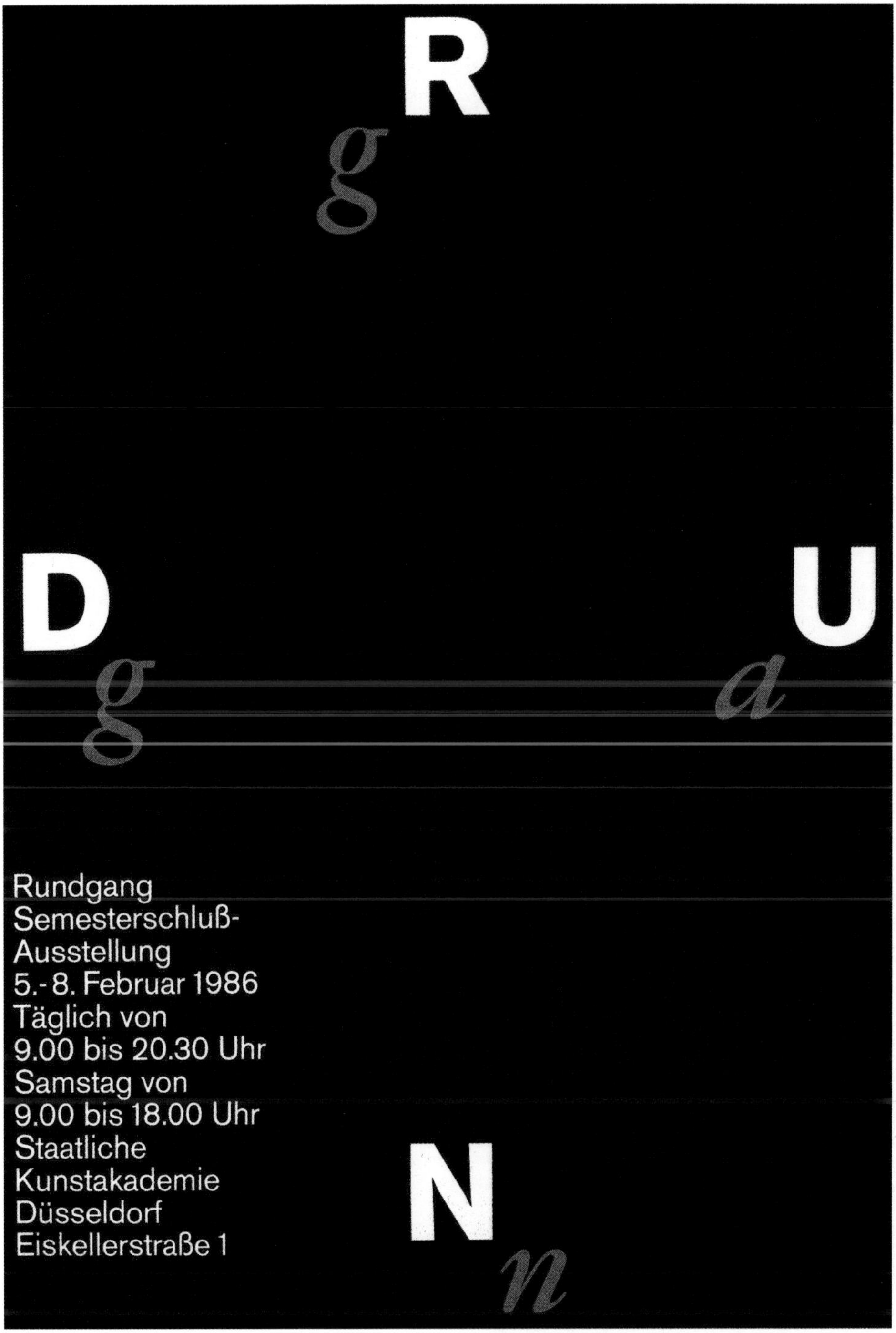

R

g

D

g

U

a

Rundgang
Semesterschluß-
Ausstellung
5.- 8. Februar 1986
Täglich von
9.00 bis 20.30 Uhr
Samstag von
9.00 bis 18.00 Uhr
Staatliche
Kunstakademie
Düsseldorf
Eiskellerstraße 1

N

n

Gielijn Escher, *Wat Amsterdam Betreft*
(What Amsterdam Means), exhibition
poster, Stedelijk Museum, Amsterdam, 1985.

Gielijn Escher, poster for *Nummer
Achtenveertig* (Number 48),
a performance by the Krisztina de
Chatel Dance Group, Amsterdam, 1986.

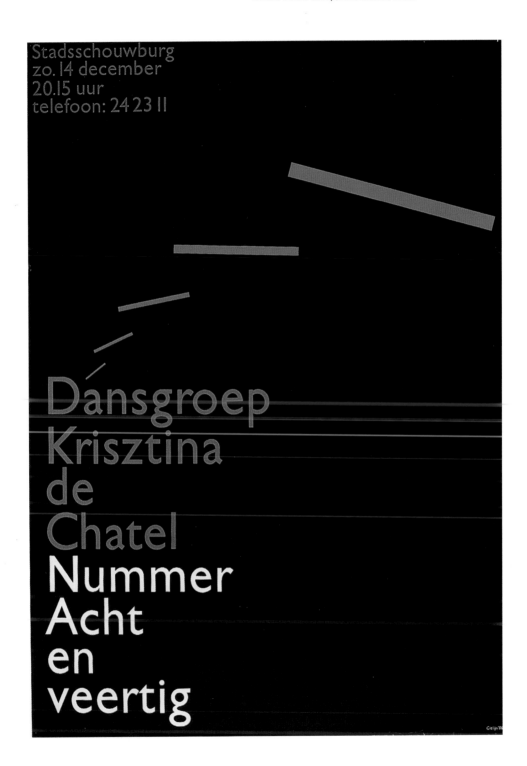

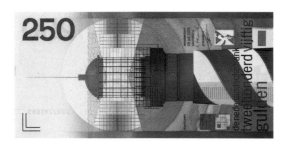

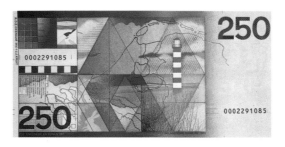

Above: R. D. E. Oxenaar and Hans Kruit,
250-guilder banknote, Haarlem:
Johan Enschedé, 1986.

Opposite: Studio Dumbar, poster for
Zeebelt Theater, The Hague, 1986.

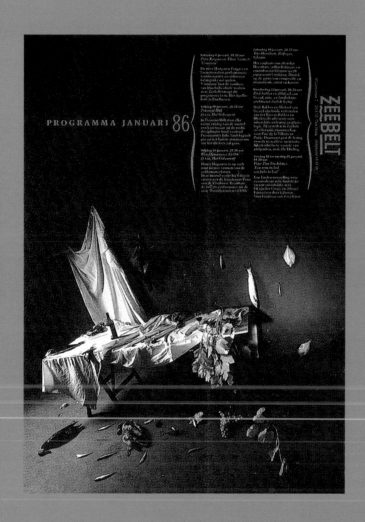

Above: Max Kisman, poster for the
Tegentonen music festival, Paradiso,
Amsterdam, 1986.

Opposite: Max Kisman, cover of *TYP/*
Typografisch Papier magazine, *De Letter*
leeft (The Letter Lives), Stichting Typ,
Amsterdam, 1986.

TyP

TYPOGRAFISCH PAPIER

DE LETTER LEEFT

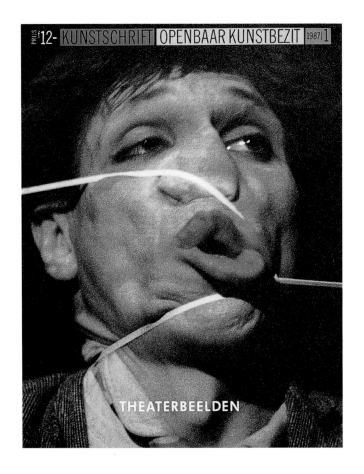

Above: Anthon Beeke, cover for *Kunstschrift*
(Art Magazine), Amsterdam, 1987.

Opposite: Lex Reitsma, *Hollands Landschap*
(Dutch Landscape), exhibition poster,
Museum Overholland, Amsterdam, 1987.

museum
museumplein 4 amsterdam

dit affiche is aangeboden door de NMB bank

Overholland

hollands
landschap

1

09/5 tm
di t m za 11.00 - 17.00 uur   zo 13.00 - 17.00 uur
28/6 '87

Ben Akkerman

Frank van den Broeck

René Daniels

Marlene Dumas

Ger van Elk

Hans van Hoek

Rob van Koningsbruggen

Jan Schoonhoven

Marien Schouten

Kees Smits

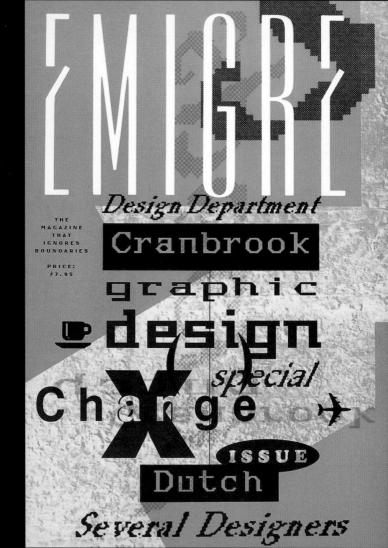

EMIGRE

THE
MAGAZINE
THAT
IGNORES
BOUNDARIES

PRICE:
$7.95

Design Department

Cranbrook

graphic

design

special

Change

ISSUE

Dutch

Several Designers

Opposite: Rudy Vanderlans and
Zuzana Licko, cover of *Emigre*, 1988.

Left: Rudy Vanderlans and Zuzana Licko,
Emigre, pages showing a selection of
previous cover designs, 1993.

Above: Arlette Brouwers, cover of the
Christmas issue of *Grafisch Nederland*,
Amsterdam, 1987. This issue was devoted
to the history of recording techniques.

Opposite: Jurriaan Schrofer, cover for
Onvolmaakt Geheugen (Incomplete
Memories), Bührmann-Ubbens Paper
Prize, Amsterdam, 1988.

ONVOLMAAKT GEHEUGEN

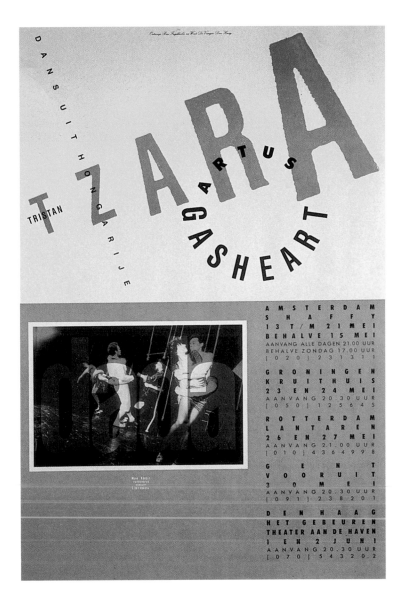

Opposite, above: Ben Faydherbe and Wout de Vringer, *Kunst en technologie* (Art and Technology), poster, 1987.

Opposite, below: Ben Faydherbe and Wout de Vringer, *Image + Sound*, poster, 1987.

Above: Ben Faydherbe and Wout de Vringer, *Tzara*, poster, 1990.

Cees W. de Jong, cover and pages
for the Christmas issue of *Grafisch
Nederland*, 1989.

PANAMARENKO een overzicht ¹⁹65 ¹⁹85

MUSEUM VAN HEDENDAAGSE KUNST
ANTWERPEN

MUHKA LEUVENSTRAAT 32
B-2000 ANTWERPEN 03.2385960
dagelijks van 10.-17.00 uur,
maandag gesloten

17'6 tm 23'7'1989

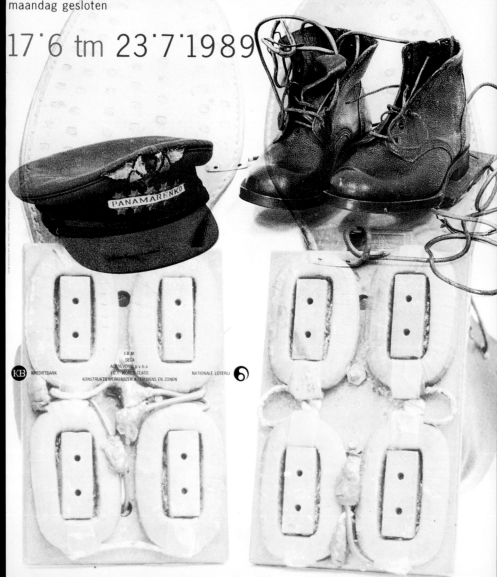

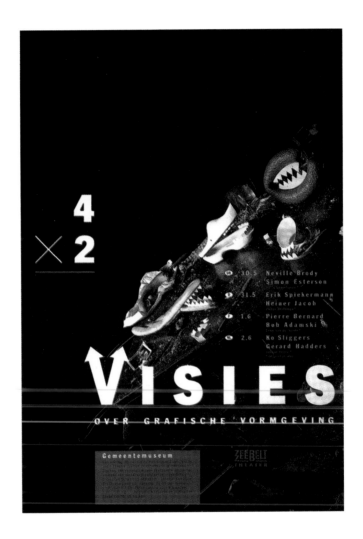

Opposite: Karel Kruysen, poster for a retrospective exhibition on the Belgian artist Panamarenko, Museum of Contemporary Art, Antwerp, 1989.

Above: Studio Dumbar, poster for *4 x 2: Visies over grafische vormgeving* (4 x 2: Views on Graphic Design), The Hague, 1989.

Irma Boom, two posters for the Holland
Festival, Amsterdam, 1990.

Above: Jelle van den Toorn Vrijthoff, *Dutch Passport.*
The history of the Netherlands is visualized in some 120 moments. Each page contains a collage of these moments.

Below: Jelle van den Toorn Vrijthoff, *Dutch Passport.*
Detail of microtext.

Opposite: Karel Martens, two covers for *Oase*, an architectural magazine, SUN Publishers, Nijmegen, 1991.

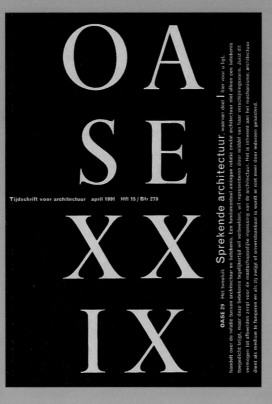

OA SE XX IX

Tijdschrift voor architectuur   april 1991   Hfl 15 / Bfr 270

OASE 29 Het tweejulijk **Sprekende architectuur**, waarvan deel I hier voor u ligt, handelt over de relatie tussen architectuur en betekenis. Een fundamenteel ambigue relatie omdat architectuur niet alleen een betekenis toegedicht krijgt, maar deze betekenis tegelijkertijd wil verbeelden, wil representeren door middel van haar verschijningsvorm. Juist dit vermogen tot afbeelden zorgt voor de maatschappelijke inpassing van de architectuur. Het is inherent aan het mechanisme; architectuur dient als medium te fungeren en als zij zwijgt of onverstaanbaar is wordt er niet meer door iedereen geluisterd.

Redactioneel De moderne architectuur heeft het vraagstuk van de vorm altijd trachten te omzeilen. Idealiter zou de vorm als vanzelf moeten voortkomen uit een of ander proces, als het zuiver logistieke resultaat van een aantal factoren, of als een wat duistere intuïtie van een autonome voortgang die zich uitkristalliseert in een soort momentopname. In de plattegrond levert dit niet direct problemen op; de scheidingen en verbindingen binnen dit horizontale vlak laten zich veelal gemakkelijk lezen als een directe uitdrukking van een aantal interne relaties. Anders ligt het in het verticale vlak, met name aan de buitenzijde. Zoals Joost Meuwissen stelt in zijn in deze OASE afgedrukte artikel: 'Van boven ziet het er allemaal nog wel aardig uit, in de plattegrond. Maar van voren beginnen de problemen.' Een proces heeft geen buitenkant. Aan een proces kun je niet vragen welke positie het inneemt binnen een (historisch gegroeide) maatschappelijke constellatie; je kunt niet vragen waar het proces voor 'staat', je kunt alleen maar vragen of het 'werkt'. Het is vermoedelijk vooral hierdoor dat de moderne architectuur neigt naar een transparantie, die de motoriek van het proces min of meer volgens het model van het aquarium poogt te veraanschouwelijken of, wanneer we het begrip 'modern' niet al te nauw definiëren, naar een gebruik van het gevelvlak als 'bill-board', als een soort reclamepaneel waarop los van het eigenlijke gebouw tekens worden aangebracht. De door het gebouw opgeroepen beelden zouden, in dit laatste geval, als tekens mee moeten rouleren in de stedelijke communicatie, maar krijgen juist doordat ze worden bevrijd van elke consequentie, van elke binding aan een structuur, nooit een werkelijke (maatschappelijke, algemene) betekenis.

In de moderne architectonische handboeken en voorbeeldenboeken gaat de aandacht dan ook vrijwel volledig uit naar de plattegrond. Anders dan in de leerboeken uit de renaissance en het classicisme ontbreekt een uiteenzetting van de tektonische middelen waarmee de opstand van het gevelvlak als architectonisch ontwerp zou kunnen worden opgebouwd vrijwel volledig. Toch moet, natuurlijk, elk architectonisch ontwerp uiteindelijk een precieze vorm krijgen, ook aan de buitenzijde. Le Corbusier is een van de weinige moderne architecten die zich welbewust en expliciet hebben beziggehouden met de vorm van de opstand; eerst

Oase N° 31 over de tektoniek van de opstand & Aldo Rossi's plan voor het Bonnefantenmuseum   Tijdschrift voor architectuur   december 1991   Hfl 15 / Bfr 270

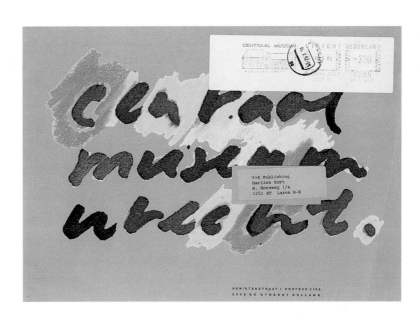

Opposite, above: Martijn Swart, letter
paper, Centraal Museum, Utrecht, 1991.

Opposite, below: Mireille Geijsen, letter
paper, Centraal Museum, Utrecht, 1991.

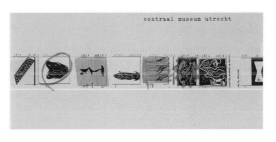

Left, above: E. Gruson and E. Traast,
A4 envelope, Centraal Museum,
Utrecht, 1991.

Left, center: Mart Warmerdam,
information booklet, Centraal Museum,
Utrecht, 1991.

Left, below: Gea Grevink, *Doolhof* (Maze)
A5 envelope, Centraal Museum,
Utrecht, 1991.

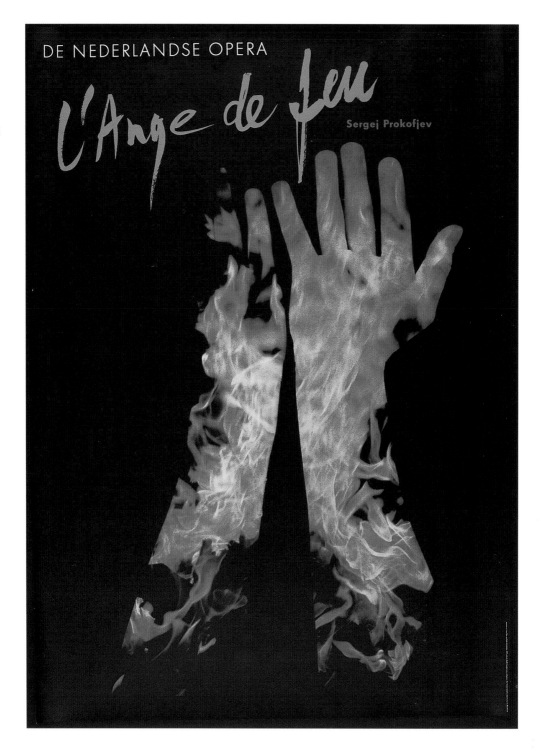

Wild Plakken, poster for *L'Ange de Feu*
(The Fiery Angel) by Sergei Prokofiev,
De Nederlandse Opera, Amsterdam, 1990.

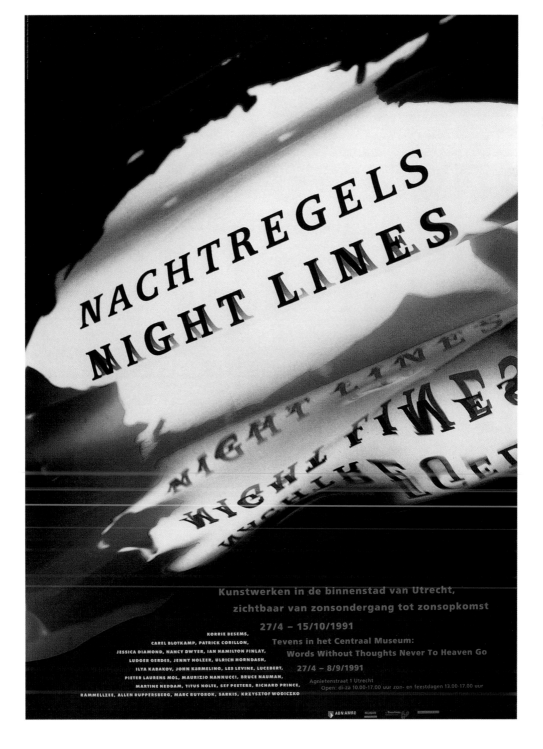

Wild Plakken, exhibition poster for
Nachtregels (Night Lines), Centraal
Museum, Utrecht, 1991.

Left: R. D. E. Oxenaar, book cover for *PTT: Tien jaar kunst + vormgeving* (PTT: Ten years of Art and Design), The Hague, 1992.

Below: Stephan Saaltink, cover of *De schok van het nieuwe* (The Shock of the New) by Robert Hughes, Amsterdam: Veen, 1991.

Opposite: Jacques Koeweiden and Paul Postma, *No Kidding*, poster, Oilily Store, Amsterdam, 1993.

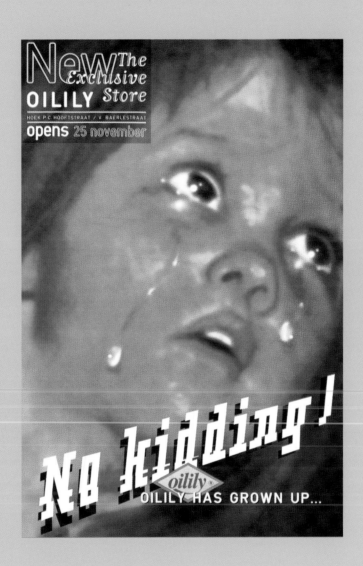

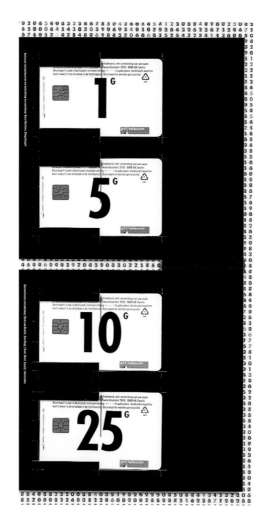

Above: Karel Martens, phone cards, PTT
Telecom, The Hague, 1994.

Opposite: Marten Jongema, *North Sea
Jazz Festival*, poster, The Hague, 1994.

Programmvorschau für den Sender VPRO von Max Kisman

Wenn die Ansagerin auf dem Bildschirm erscheint, um ein neues Programm anzukündigen, wird es meist Zeit, umzuschalten, oder etwas zu trinken zu holen. Doch diese Programmansagen sind manchmal schöner, als die Programme, die sie ankündigen. Die collageartigen Computeranimationen haben eine eigenwillige Formensprache, sie sind klar, charakterisch und oft sehr geistreich. Der Entwerfer macht nicht nur diese Animationen, sondern sucht auch die passenden Musikfragmente aus. Das ganze passt vorzüglich zu den lakonischen VPRO-Ansagerstimmen. Der Druck auf die Produktion ist gross, da jede Woche neue Kurzfilme gezeigt werden, doch die Lösungen zeugen immer wieder von grosser Kreativität und behalten ihren ungezwungenen Charakter.

Bumpers and leaders for VPRO Television by Max Kisman

When the presenter appears on screen to announce a new programme, it is usually a cue to zap or fetch a drink. But these bumpers and leaders are as engaging as the programmes they introduce, if not more so. The collage-like computer animations have a highly original formal language. They are clear, highly recognizable and often witty. Not only does the designer create the animations, he also selects the accompanying music fragments. They form a perfect complement to the VPRO's curt voice-overs. New trails are needed every week, placing production under considerable pressure, but the films consistently display a high level of creativity and maintain their artless quality.

Above: Niki Gonnissen and Thomas Widdershoven, catalog, *Mentalitäten* (Mentalities), Design Institute Amsterdam and Rotterdam Art Foundation, 1995–96.

Opposite: Mevis & van Deursen, *Another & Another & Another Act of Seeing (Urban Space)*, poster, De Singel International Art Center, Antwerp, 1997.

ANOTHER & ANOTHER & ANOTHER ACT OF SEEING (URBAN SPACE)

Left, below and opposite, above:
Series of posters for FontShop
International's *FontFont Fifteen*
exhibition. These generated posters
show a random cross section of all
typefaces of the FontFont type
library. The texts were picked
randomly from various sources and
assembled by a Python program.
Digital prints, 2004.

Opposite below: Erik van Blokland,
series of posters for an exhibition,
2005. During its 430 years, Leiden
University library collected over
2 million titles. The 11 posters show
every single title, the year of
acquisition, the country of origin
and in some cases the size of the
spine. This mass of information
displayed on the posters record the
exponential growth of titles in the
last century and the increasing
exchange of information, first
within Europe, then the entire
world. Here the posters are shown
in the old 'index room' of the
library, providing an overview of
the collection once more. Designed
with Jan Willem Stas, produced in
cooperation with the Leiden
University Library and the students
of the TypeMedia department of
the Royal Academy, The Hague.

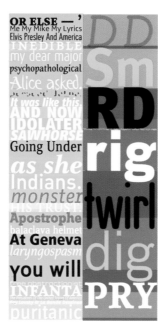

Left and below: Erik van Blokland, colorfields generated by 'superpolation', a method of interpolating complex systems. Though initially intended to produce intermediate typefaces, the process can also be applied to other parametric designs. The colorfields were used to test the algorithm during development. Python code, 2004.

Opposite, above: Erik van Blokland, superpolation applied to nine different variations of a letter. The background colors indicate the extent of the influence of each variation. Intermediates can now be calculated. Python code, 2004.

Opposite, below: Just van Rossum and Erik van Blokland, Twin typeface for Minneapolis-St. Paul, commissioned by the Design Institute, Minneapolis, 2003. Twin is a complex typeface which offers a wide range of variations. An online version reacted to the weather in the twin cities: cold weather would cause a more formal typeface, while warm weather made it look round, loopy, and quirky. The specimen poster maps the variations of the typeface to an imaginary streetplan.

Mon Jun 7 16:12:15 2004

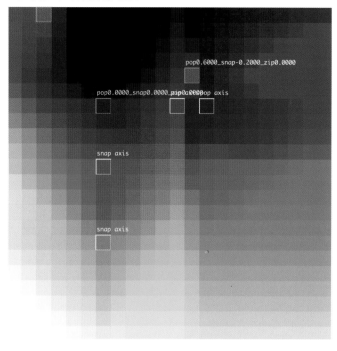

Mon Jun 7 16:30:35 2004

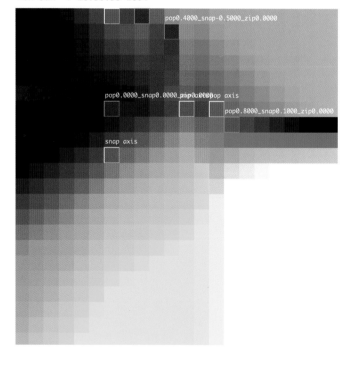

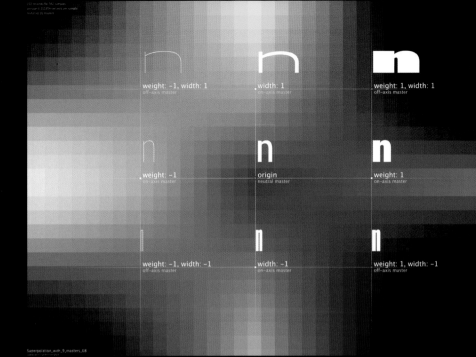

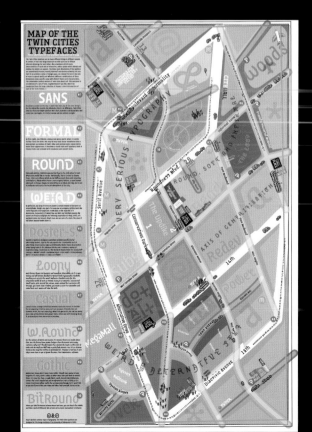

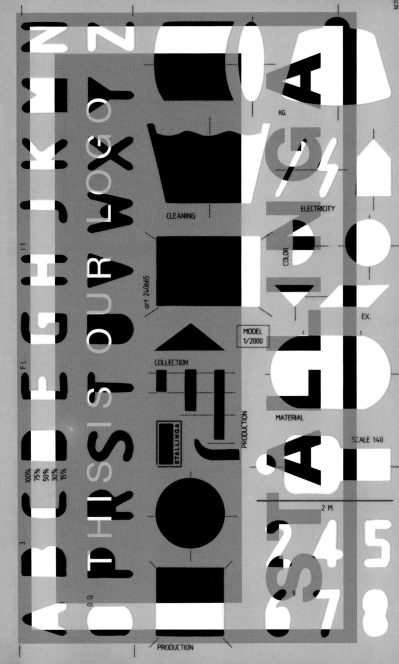

THE CENTURY'S CLOSE AND BEYOND

Describing a period while in its midst is laden with complexity. Giving a definitive account of contemporary Dutch graphic design will always be a precarious undertaking, as this will ultimately be a chapter that has no end. Referring to this kind of question, the modern historical and art philosopher R. G. Collingwood wrote in 1924: 'Contemporary history embarrasses a writer not only because he knows too much, but also because what he knows is too undigested, too unconnected, too atomic. It is only after close and prolonged reflection that we begin to see what was essential and what was important, to see why things happened as they did, and to write history instead of newspapers.'[1]

During the last quarter of the twentieth century, electronic and computer technology advanced at an incredible pace, altering many sectors of our lives. Graphic design in the Netherlands and throughout the world has been irrevocably transformed though digital computer hardware and software as well as the extraordinary expansion of the Internet. During the industrial revolution the procedures of graphic design and printing had been separated into various tasks, each requiring a specific expertise. By the time phototype entered the scene during the 1960s, the design and production process involved trained professionals at each stage. First were the graphic designers. Then came the typesetters, production specialists, camera operators, strippers (who put the negatives together), platemakers, and finally the press workers. However, by the beginning of the 1990s new digital advances allowed a single individual to control most (sometimes all) of these functions using a desktop computer.

At first this change was strongly opposed by some graphic designers, notably those of the older generation, but as the technology became more sophisticated this initial hostility began to disappear. It became obvious that graphic designers now had the increasing ability to control both the design and production procedures. Computer technology and new software also permitted graphic designers to manipulate spatial effects, color, forms, and images in unparalleled ways. In addition the design process was far faster than in the past, and assignments that would have taken weeks or even months were now handled in a matter of days.

The rapid expansion of cable and satellite television at the end of the past century inspired creative and technical advances in broadcast and animation graphics. The extraordinary growth of the Internet and the World Wide Web during the 1990s forever altered the way we communicate and obtain data, creating an upheaval that has equaled or even surpassed that generated by Gutenberg in the fifteenth century. Today many people rely on the Internet for information and entertainment, a change that has touched all aspects of cultural life, while creating boundless possibilities for graphic designers. We have only just begun to fully sense the impact of this revolution.

Especially in the Netherlands, the use of computer-generated design has helped to engender an era of pluralism and variety, two words that aptly characterize the current graphic design field. Clearly, global economics and instantaneous communication demarcate the end of the past century and the beginning of the current century. Economic, industrial, and technological growth has engendered many changes in the way graphic design is perceived both by its practitioners and clients. The new technology and international exchanges have made many Dutch graphic designers re-evaluate the purpose, necessity, and responsibilities of their field in a rapidly changing world.

Many Dutch graphic designers are at the vanguard of their profession, and deciding which of them to include in this chapter was a difficult if not impossible task. Contemporary Dutch graphic design is so rich and diverse that it would require a separate volume to do justice to what is taking place today. Many designers mentioned in the previous chapter are as active today as in previous years and have boldly entered new stages in their careers. The graphic design produced by Studio Dumbar today is very different from that of its earlier years in many ways. Design from Studio Anthon Beeke remains vibrant, surprising, and increasingly intellectually and visually rich as Anthon Beeke continues to reinvent himself. Irma Boom now takes book design into another, almost sculptural, realm. Gielijn Escher continues to refine and expand upon his aesthetic poster statements.

A relatively new design studio that stands out among many is Koeweiden-Postma, founded by Jacques Koeweiden and Paul Postma in Amsterdam. As with Dutch graphic design in general, the work of Koeweiden-Postma is so extensive that one only scratches the surface of their accomplishments when selecting a particular project to mention.

In 2000, after having lived and worked together as graphic designers for seven years, Nikki Gonnissen and Thomas Widdershoven founded the Amsterdam design firm Thonik in 2000, a combination of their first names. From the beginning, Thonik has been at the vanguard of a new generation of Dutch graphic designers. Working concurrently as designers, art directors, and conceptual and media artists, their work covers an extensive spectrum. For the past five years, Thonik has undertaken a steady turnover of largely unrelated assignments, and none of their solutions have been in any way predictable. Similar to many contemporary Dutch graphic design studios, Thonik is mainly involved with ideas, and its uncompromising and sometimes provocative designs are often challenging for both the client and viewer. As stated in the 2001 monograph on their studio, 'Thonik's approach is a breath of fresh air. Intellectual but not intellectualized.'

Max Kisman opened his own graphic design studio soon after graduating from the Gerrit Rietveld Academy in 1977. During the mid-1980s he utilized digital technology in his designs for *Vinyl* and *Language Technology* magazines, posters for the Paradiso theater in Amsterdam, and *Red Cross* stamps for the Dutch Postal Service. In 1986 he co-founded *TYP/Typografisch Papier*, a magazine on typography and the arts. From 1989 until 1992 Kisman lived in Barcelona where he created digital versions of many of his earlier typefaces for FontShop International in Berlin. From 1992 until 1996 he worked as a graphic designer and animator for VPRO Television in the Netherlands. In 1994 he became more involved in graphic design for interactive media for VPRO-Digital and HotWired in San Francisco and in 1997 began working for Wired Television and then as art director for Wired Digital, also in San Francisco. Kisman's studio MKDSGN is now in Mill Valley, California where he founded Holland Fonts to publish his own typeface designs in 2002. As in his poster celebrating a century of Toulouse-Lautrec, Kisman approaches his work with openness and wit. Between 1984 and 1988, he taught graphic design and typography at the Gerrit Rietveld Academy, the College of Arts and Crafts in Utrecht, and the postgraduate Jan van Eyck Academy in Maastricht. In 1996 he received the prestigious H. M. Werkman Award for Graphic Design from the Amsterdam Foundation of the Arts, for his television graphics in 1996 for VPRO TV network. He works for various clients in the Netherlands and the United States where he teaches graphic design, motion graphics, and animation at the College of Arts and Crafts in San Francisco and typeface design at the UC Berkeley Extension in San Francisco.

In Amsterdam, Linda van Deursen and Armand Mevis maintain their graphic design studio Mevis & van Deursen, which they began after graduating from the Gerrit Rietveld Academy in 1986. From the very outset, they have been an influential force in contemporary Dutch graphic design. They are widely known and admired for their discerning and inventive work for a wide range of cultural graphic design projects, including the exceptional new identity of the Stedelijk Museum. In addition to many books about architecture and design, they have also designed Dutch cultural publications and were the winners of a contest to design the identity for Rotterdam as a Cultural Capital of Europe. Their work has been exhibited in museums and educational institutions throughout the United States. They are both devoted to design education with Van Deursen acting as head of the Graphic Design Department at the Gerrit Rietveld Academy and Mevis as a design critic at the Werkplaats Typografie in Arnhem. Both have been visiting critics at the School of Art at Yale University in the United States.

Based in The Hague, over the past years the graphic design firm of Ben Faydherbe and Wout de Vringer has produced many ground-breaking designs for cultural institutions, government agencies, and the business sector. Their design commissions range from corporate identities, annual reports, and posters. Especially for these two graphic designers, an active and penetrating dialogue between designer and client is an essential part of the design process. In the graphic design of Faydherbe/De Vringer one sees traces of previous

Ben, Poster campaign
The launch of a new mobile telephone network, Ben, is the result of KesselsKramer creating the name, look and brand and taking on the total branding approach that made Ben into one of the most famous brands in the Netherlands. Launch posters feature new users of Ben and serve to blur the line between consumer and company into one brand.
ナスホカボホモドびらはイもやヤへォォケラみっかとてどっべぐずぶっちぉぉ
ササンっラべスナドキャっめオボボォモドォもモトボォもモドサウチポォモドナコ
はイもやヤへォォケラみっかとてどっべぐずぶっちぉぉまむむナスポっボぉ。

Ben, Poster campaign
Ben always speaks in the first person, 'Ik ben Ben.' ('I am Ben) and focuses more on personal communications than on mobile phone rates and technologies. Ben makes everything simple, with one flat rate and easy-to-understand contracts that are made for human beings rather than consumers.
ナスホカボホモドびらはイもやヤへォォケラみっかとてどっべぐずぶっちぉぉ
ササンっラべスナドキャっめオボボォモドォもモトボォもモドサウチポォモドナコ
はイもやヤへォォケラみっかとてどっべぐずぶっちぉぉまむむナスポっボぉ。

1.17422 kilo   9   9   1.17649 kilo

Above: KesselsKramer, poster, 2005.

Opposite: *2 Kilo of KesselsKramer*, cover and page from an overview of the last nine years of the agency's work, 2005.

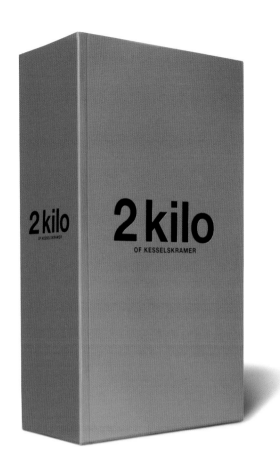

design movements combined with their own personal vision and visual language. Their posters are included in the permanent collections of the Museum of Modern Art in New York and the Museum für Kunst und Gewerbe in Hamburg.

Co-founded by Erik Kessels and John Kramer in 1996, the highly controversial advertising firm KesselsKramer has lifted graphic design out of any familiar realm and has to a large extent redefined the advertising field in the Netherlands. In the monograph on their work they pose questions such as 'what is graphic design?' If their word is reality, graphic design as we know it is now dead, destroyed by super-computers. In their 'no-holds-barred world,' the idea itself is the governing factor, totally unrestrained by any rules or limitations.

In choosing those Dutch designers who are now making significant contributions to the profession there will inevitably be many who will be overlooked and deserve a place in this chapter. Other designers and firms that deserve far more than a mention include, among others, Lust Design in The Hague, and Vandejong, De Design Politie, Martijn Oostra, and Lava in Amsterdam.

In the 1950s, the Canadian Marshall McLuhan predicted that typesetting as begun by Gutenberg would in due course be replaced by electronic progress. Of course, the accuracy of his prediction is nothing less than astounding. Yet the poster and the book will remain as art forms in the new age of electronic technology, and graphic designers will help to define new future developments in electronic media.

As the graphic design field expands and develops, a redefinition of the very makeup of graphic communications has already begun. At this moment in time we are witnessing a phenomenon similar in many ways to the industrial revolution of the nineteenth century. Computer technology and webpage design are radically changing the way we use and view images, and the graphic design field, like many other spheres of activity, is undergoing significant transformations. Yet even though the tools with which graphic designers work are changing, the very essence of graphic design remains the same. Graphic design will always have the task of providing structure for information and giving form to ideas and feelings. As graphic design in the Netherlands and throughout the world enters a time of technological innovation, traditional modes of expression and aesthetic values will retain their significance. United by an innate desire for discovery, we are all connected to the past.

1 R. G. Collingwood, *Speculum Mentis, or The Book of Knowledge*.

Clarendon Press, Oxford 1924, p. 236.

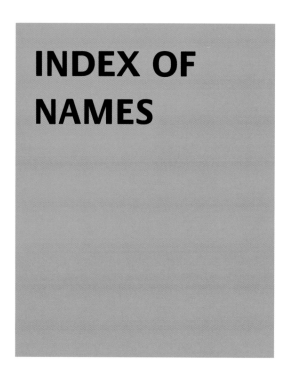

INDEX OF NAMES

Design Cees W. de Jong VK Projects, Laren
© 2006 VK Projects, Laren

Every care has been taken in properly crediting
the reproductions in this publication.

The reproductions in this book are from the works of
individual designers and from the collections of
Martijn F. Le Coultre, Laren; Alston W. Purvis, Lincoln; Cees W. de Jong, Laren.

First published in the United Kingdom in 2006 by
Thames & Hudson Ltd, 181A High Holborn, London WC1V 7QX

www.thamesandhudson.com

British Library Cataloguing-in-Publication Data
A catalogue record for this book is available from the British Library

ISBN-13:   978-0-500-51285-2
ISBN-10:   0-500-51285-X

Printed and bound in Slovenia